Series 2 Books

Learn'n More About
Track & Field

Handbook/Guide
for Kids, Parents, and Coaches

By Bob Swope

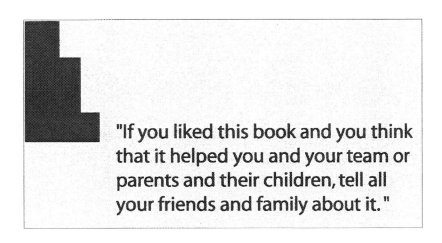

"If you liked this book and you think that it helped you and your team or parents and their children, tell all your friends and family about it."

Jacobob Press L.L.C.

D1604637

Our Basic Platform

"Our mission statement is we want this book to become the "Bible" for learning more about youth Track & Field basic fundamental skills. We will continue to help kids or anyone learn as much as possible about this sport."

Cover Photo of Alyssa Beavers Competing in the
High Jump at the 2007 AAU National Junior Olympics

Published and distributed by:
Jacobob Press LLC
St. Louis, Mo.
Tel: (314) 843-4829
E-Mail: jacobobsw@sbcglobal.net

Check our Web site at: www.jacobobpress.com

ISBN 10- 0-9820960-1-1
ISBN 13- 978-0-9820960-1-7
San 257-1862
Copyright 2008

Printed and Bound by:
No Waste Publishing
Fenton, MO. 63026

Series 2. Book 4
First Edition 2008

This book is the fourth book of the "Learn'n More About" series 2 of Jacobob's books. This is volume (edition) one. Every three or four years, or when possible, we will update this book with a new updated and expanded volume (version) two.

DEDICATION

This book is dedicated to my son Mark who, along with his team mates, had one of his best days ever on the track when he helped his team win the Nevada State track and field championship by 1/2 point in his sophomore year in high school.

AUTHORS ACKNOWLEDGMENTS

My thanks to the following St. Louis elementary schools, high schools, club, colleges, and university, track team kids and all their coaches in St. Louis, Mo. for all of their help.

St. Catherine Laboure School, Lindbergh High School, Oakville High School, Fox High School, Washington University, and St. Louis Blazers track club. Also thanks to the Olympiad Gymnastic Training Center, Festus, Mo. and the Shell Oil Company for all their help. The pictures will really help illustrate what I am trying to get across to everyone using this book, help children learn more about and improve on their basic track & field plus cross country skills.

ST. CATHERINE LABOURE TRACK TEAM (2006)

ABOUT THE AUTHOR

Bob Swope is a long time youth sports coach and teacher. Over the past 39 years of experience working with kids he has spent 21 years coaching, managing, and teaching younger kids (6-14 Yr. olds), both boys and girls in five different sports. His teams are known for their knowledge and use of the fundamentals. He has written fourteen youth sports fundamentals books, covering twelve different sports or activities, over the past seven years. His philosophy is kids will have more fun out there when they know the basic fundamentals, and how to apply them to what they are doing. He has taken a team of left over kids, after a draft had been performed, and taken them to a championship and playoffs in just three years. This was basically accomplished by teaching them the fundamentals, and getting good knowledgeable, friendly coaches to work on them at practices with the kids. He uses lots of training and teaching techniques from one sport and will use them in another. He is a former member of the "Youth Football Coaches Association of America," and is currently a member of the "National Youth Sports Coaches Association." He is certified in football, and is working with the NYSCA to get certification in several other sports. He is a member of the USA Fencing Association (USFA), USA Boxing and USA Track & Field.

* * * * * * * * * * * **W A R N I N G** * * * * * * * * * * * * * *

If your child or the participant has any physically limiting condition, bleeding disorder, high blood pressure, pregnancy or any other condition that may limit them physically, you should check with your doctor before participating in these drills and exercises.

Be sure participants, making hard contact, are of the same weight and size to avoid injury.

All drills and exercises should be supervised by an adult. **AUTHOR ASSUMES NO LIABILITY FOR ANY ACCIDENTAL INJURY OR EVEN DEATH THAT MAY RESULT.**

EXTRA CARE AND CAUTION SHOULD BE TAKEN WITH ANY OF THE VARIOUS FIELD EVENT DRILLS, SUCH AS SHOT PUTTING, DISCUS THROWING, HAMMER THROWING, JAVELIN THROWING, POLE VAULTING, AND ALSO SOME OF THE HURDLING AND STEEPLE CHASE DRILLS AS THEY ARE THE MORE DANGEROUS ONES.

TABLE OF CONTENTS

Introduction

My Interest

I have been thinking about doing a more complete track & field, with cross country, reference book for young boys and girls for some time now. The reason I am doing this type of book is to speak right to the reader. Also because I am very involved as a coach in teaching track & field. If you can learn the basic fundamentals at a young age, think of how good you could become by the time you reach high school. Not as many kids get into this sport compared to other sports until they get to high school. This sport has a certain appeal for me because when I was at the age of five to twelve years my friends and I used to go up to the park and practice high jumping and pole vaulting. We went out and cut down our own bamboo poles and high jump bars. When I was growing up there were not any books out there, like this one, to show you how to perform track events. My dad could not teach me because he was not into athletics. Since he came from an era when men started to work at a young age, I guess he never thought about sports.

Family Participation

I really never did do much with the sport then until I had two young boys that were interested in high jumping. I was interested in track & field while I was growing up, this is when I started to try and learn what I could about high jumping. The two boys and I made up a home made high jump stand and started practicing. When I was little we only knew about two styles of high jumping. The "scissors" style and the "western roll". We started with the scissors style, then when we got better at jumping we moved to the western roll (1950s).

If you really think about and analyize it there is probably some niche or event in track & field where you can find success. If you are strong, it could be one of the throwing events. Or if you are fast, it could be the running or cross country events. I might point out here that not only boys can be successful in track & field. Many girls participate in track & field these days, and they have the athleticism to be successfull. I know because I coach many of them. These same fundamentals can help you girls as well as the boys. On evenings and weekends the boys and I used to go out to the backyard and practice high jumping for hours. My boys seemed to like it, so we tried to work on their skills every chance we had. My oldest son went on to high jump in high school.

His high school coach taught him how to do the "fosbury flop" as they called it then. In the state championship meet, he was one of several boys to tie the state record for high jump. The problem was the boy that held the record was also in the meet later. He went on to raise the record up another six inches, to win the event. What is amazing, he did this using the old western roll style while all the other boys were using the "flop". Ask your parents to come out and help you. Believe it or not, you can have fun with them while you learn. They can read the book with you then you cn both learn. I have included "cross country" in the book because it's really another running event. It is running very long distances over rough terrain as compared to running on a smooth track, then using endurance to get a faster time over the course.

My History

A little history about me. I have coached in five different sports over a 21 year period. I have managed and coached mostly the younger boys and girls, seven to ten years old, because my thinking is if I can start you out with good fundamentals and techniques, those fundamentals will develop into long term habits for you (muscle memory). Most of you kids have been very good at listening to what I had to say. Those that listened carefully were very successful in their events.

Some Advice

Some things I would like to mention. Before you do any of these drills and exercises, make sure you are healthy and in good shape. Also make sure your eyesight is good. Get checked, then get glasses or contact lenses if you need to. There are a number of reasons for this. When you are working on the hurdles and some of the field events, such as the shot put or hammer throw, they are very hard to learn at first. You can get hurt if your sight is not too good. Especially if you get hit in the head area. Another area to be concerned about is tripping while going over a hurdle. Depending on how you fall, you could do more damage than a skinned knee or arm. Also throwing a javelin could hurt a by-stander if it accidentally hits them. Another thing I want to mention is make sure you are falling onto a special cushioned landing pad when practicing high jumping or pole vaulting.

I have tried to keep all the drills and exercises simple, so they can be accomplished without using expensive equipment. There are things you have around the house that you can use as training aids. As you go through the book you will find these items pointed out to you. However, you will at some point in training, need to go out to a high school track. This is to get the proper feel of the running events, and even the field events. They have the equipment available as long as you ask permission first.

Those Who Want to Learn

This book is for all you kids who think you might want to learn how to compete in one or more of the track & field, or cross country events. If you just sit around at home all the time, then mom and dad would probably like to see you get outside more and get involved in sports. But they probably don't know what sport to get you into. Well if it's track & field, or cross country, this book is for you. Track is not just running. If you are strong, but slow and not too fast at running, then you might want to try shot putting or discus throwing. You could learn to be very successful at those events. I have found that some of you have a mom or dad that would like to get out there and do something with you. But they don't know how to go about it. All of you that are in this situation, tell your mom or dad that with this book they can get out there with you and actually help you learn more about how to compete in track & field or cross country. For all of you kids, here is a book you can use as a guide, or reference manual, for the fundamentals and techniques with pictures. Take it with you out to the backyard, park, or high school track, and use it as you go about learning and having some fun. When you stop and think about it, you and your mom or dad working together, this could become a turning point and a bonding in both of your lives.

Attitude & Behavior Development

Parents Influence

Most of you boys and girls, from the age of *five through eight,* are very impressionable and you are influenced a lot by your mom or dad. Also by older brothers and sisters or bigger kids at school. Don't let anyone influence you to do something that you know is wrong, just because they do it. There is a lot of camaraderie in track and field. Get your best friend to join and come out with you to participate in youth track & field. But also make new friends. Their is a lot of teamwork going on. Individuals can win events, but their is team points being awarded for placing in events. Learn to work together in events such as the "relays." It can be very rewarding. A good team mate can be a good influenceIt is also important that you learn that these events are really only a game, and what is most important for you to realize is you need to develop good sportsmanship. You don't need to hate your competitors. Learn to always try your best, and if you don't do well every time, there is always another day.

Kids Improving

One of the things I have learned is that if something is worth all this work and training then try to be the best you can be at it. I realize this is very hard for some of you kids to learn. What I always told the kids on my teams was, have someone watch you to see what it is you might be doing wrong. Then that person (coach or parent) should work with you, over and over, to correct these fundamental problem areas and techniques. I explained to them that if they worked hard they would begin to see that they were getting better and better. If you have a good attitude, this will usually be reflected to the rest of the kids on the team. In other words it can be contagious to everyone else on the team, and everything will be more fun than agony.

Kids Attitude

Your attitude towards other teammates on the team, coaches, managers, and officials, will depend a lot on how your mom and dad normally act. You will often reflect their attitude towards these people. So, be very aware of what people say when you are present or nearby. Many times I have seen parents screaming from the sidelines at referee's, officials, or another kid on the team when they make a mistake. Then, following that example during practice, their son or daughter will belittle one of their team mates or the coach. This is really just learned behavior from your mom, dad or coach. Don't do it just because your mom, dad or coach was doing it. It's wrong.

Here is a concept for all of us, we are not perfect so why should we expect everyone else to be perfect. Think about it if you need to rely on a official to make a perfect call, or a team mate being perfect to win the event, then maybe you didn't deserve to win. So, please try to get along with your team mates, coaches and officials. If you are a better competitor than your team mates are, you can help the whole team more by being a leader and encouraging team mates rather than by belittling them. A little teasing when you are practicing with them is OK as long as it does not bother them. Make sure your team mates know you are only teasing and you are not serious (a common courtesy). You attitude will also help show your friends how they can become a better competitor like you are.

On my Nevada football team I had a boy that was so good at this, he had the full respect of all the other boys on the team. I could even let him run the drills if I had to go over and talk to a parent or one of my coaches. He was like an extra coach on the team. He was that good. Do you know what he is doing now? He coaches and works with young kids in his area on different sports. He is also very well respected in the community there.

Kids Showing Respect

Learn to have respect for the event judges, coaches and instructors. If you are on a club, only your head coach, instructor, or trainer should ever question an official on a call or a rules intrepretation. Also ask your mom or dad not to question them either. And consider this, maybe the official was just out of position to see what happened. Many times, at the youth sports level if your coach is reasonable with a official, and ask them to consult with the other officials, they may even on occasion reverse their opinion or ruling. Another official may have had a better view of the event. What usually happens when the competitors, coaches, and parents, start screaming and complaining about the ruling, the official will favor their original ruling on anything that is questionable or even close.

In the long run it is better to just let the official make their call. Then, after the meet is over or the next day, go to your "head coach" and tell them why you think the officiating was poor. Your head coach should then go to the head of officials, and explain the complaint. Maybe the official is inexperienced, new, or just doesn't understand the rules. But they will never improve if the head of officials does not know that they had a problem, then helps them correct the problem. Believe me, they probably never will change or learn by someone yelling and screaming at them.If you think you have a valid complaint then go to your head coach with your complaint and explain it to them. When you grow up and get out into the work force, you will find that respecting the boss will make life a lot easier for you. If the boss is not fair, then get a job somewhere else. When you learn respect for the rules, then you learn respect for law and order later in your life. Remember the example you set by your actions at practice or out on the track may also influence lots of friends around you.

General Health

Good Health Habits

It is generally a good idea for you to start out in life with good health habits. What we are talking about is plenty of sleep, a good nutritious balanced diet, and timely exercise and conditioning. By timely we mean don't over exercise a few hours before time for the track meet. Not being tired, or sick, will improve your mental outlook, abilities, endurance and attitude during the meet.

A few words about dietary supplements. **DO NOT** take anything containing *"Ephedra"*. It is illegal to use in high school now, and has some very serious side effects. Death being one. So why take a chance. Also stay away from *"Anabolic Steroids"*. They also can have bad side effects such as increased irritability, and possible liver or kidney trauma. You kids are not going to be hitting home runs or blocking and tackling in track & field, so you don't have to be strong in that way to be good in track & field. Let yourself develop naturally for the long term. Also see the section on "Equipment" for some additional health concerns.

One more thing to point out, a recent study of teenage girls found that those who drink *Coca Cola* were three to five times more likely to experience bone fractures, than girls who do not drink it. Taking the punishment your body is normally going to get while competing in track is enough without having to worry about bone fractures. So you girls out there drink water instead, and don't take the chance. The Caffeine and high level of phosphoric acid alters calcium metabolism and, in effect, may cause or aid in bone loss.

Fitness

I have had boys come to a summer afternoon or early evening baseball game, really dragging their feet, so to speak. And after talking to them, I found out mom let them go over to a friends house all morning at their swimming pool. Swimming is a good workout, but not the day or day before a track meet. They need at least one days rest from any heavy exercise before a meet. As training for a sport these days becomes more complex, the trainers, and strength coaches, have found that some exercises actually can be dangerous. So what I have tried to do is find out the latest techniques, and tailor the exercises to fit kids competing, and practicing, for track & field events

In track & field it takes lots of stamina, and endurance, to stay at the same level all the way until the end of the meet which may last half or two thirds of the day. This means you kids need to have "***cardiorespiratory fitness***" and "***muscular fitness***". In simple terms cardiorespiratory fitness has to do with your bodies aerobic and anaerobic capacity. Muscular fitness has to do with your strength, power, speed, muscle endurance, and flexibility. In the later stages of a meet you need a physical and mental advantage going for you, so you can stay focused on your technique, and have plenty of endurance. To be able to do this you kids need to work on your aerobic, anaerobic, and muscle conditioning constantly. When young kids have good muscular fitness they tend to have less injuries. And when they are hurt they tend to heal more quickly. Do not over do it though, but keep at it every day, for at least a few repetitions.

Competing in track & field events takes lots of stamina, to compete at a high level all the way through to the end of the meet. Towards the end of the meet you especially need a physical advantage going for you. To be able to acomplish this, you need to work on your conditioning, and endurance, constantly. Not over do it, but keep at it every day for at least a few repetitions.

Strength Levels

When I was coaching Football in the 60s and 70s we tried all kinds of techniques to help the kids keep their strength level at or near it's peak. Most participants in a sport will go through some type of a warm up or exercise routine, just before an event starts, to get themselves loosened up. So don't worry about exercising before you leave for a practice or a track & field meet because the coach or trainer will tell you what they want you to do. We had some boys, that appeared to loose stamina during football games, eat a banana the day before a game to let the vitamins get into their systems by game time. The idea was to make sure these vitamins did not get all sweated out of their system during the game. Now days they have "*Gatoraid*," and "*Powerade*," and "Pedialyte" power drinks for that.

Plenty of Water

I suggest you bring some water with you to a practice or a track & field meet. Then after about every **15 OR 20** minutes of continuous working, take a water break if you are out working on a hot or warm day. After about an **HOURS** work, when you have been really sweating a lot, get out your "*power drinks*" to replace the lost minerals. You kids will sweat a lot, especially when you are doing a lot of sprint running. You overheat quicker than adults even when you are inside of a gym or building with air conditioning. I suggest taking a hand towel with you, to use in wiping off from time to time because you will sweat.

A suggestion is have mom or dad get you some "*Power drinks (GatorAid) and water,*" to take with you to a practice or a track meet. Take a bottle of each with you when you are out working on the track. Especially if it's warm where you are practicing or competiting. We had one coach that had one of the parents cut up oranges, and hand them out to suck on during the half time break at our football game. Both of these ideas helped, but then when they came out with "*Power Drinks*" that worked out much better when they were heavily sweating during practice or events.

Infectious Disease Control Safety

Here are some rules for you to follow, with respect to infectious diseases being spread through contact with blood. This would be when you, a competitor, or even a official is bleeding. If the official notices that anyone on the track, or in the field, is bleeding they should stop the event immediately. Or if your mom or dad is in the stands watching the meet, and notice someone on the track, or in the field bleeding, tell them to let an official know right away. The person bleeding should be removed from the meet, or practice, for evaluation and treatment. The competitor should not be allowed to return until cleared by an official. If the player returns, the injury must be covered with a bandage, or cover of some kind that won't come off and expose the blood.

Hepatitus-B is a serious illness easily transmitted through blood contact. It can be prevented by vaccination, and you are strongly advised to see your doctor about getting vaccinated if you are going to be in any contact type sport. HIV is also a blood borne disease to be careful of, but far less likely to be transmitted in sporting contacts like track & field. If your uniform, or track suit, has blood on it then it should be changed to a clean uniform. If the track or field surface, the shot, the discus, the hammer, the javelin, the baton, or any other piece of equipment gets blood on it, then the event should be stopped. And the area along with the equipment, should all be cleaned. All of these precautions should be taken to protect everyone, from coming into direct contact with blood that could be infectious. For safety purposes, these general rules also apply when you are working with your son or daughter, or friends, out in the yard. Even though they are young kids it's better to be safe than sorry.

Nutrition and Diets

Overweight

If you are even slightly on the overweight side, be extra careful not to over work, or push yourself too hard. Especially when you begin to exercise. Don't worry your body will tell you. If there is any question, have mom or dad take you to your doctor and talk to them about it. And, by the way, you very big heavy large bone structured kids can become very good at the shot put, hammer throw, and discus events. Many of your class mates and friends are not as big and strong as you are. So take advantage of that! You only increase repetitions when you see that you are getting into shape, and can handle it. If you are even just a little overweight, it's probably a good idea to have a doctor check you out before starting any track and field training. Your doctor will give you a better idea of what you can or can't do. You have to be in excellent shape for track & field running. As you will find out when you try to run around the track for two laps without stopping. It will drain you, especially when you are not expecting it.

Is Overweight a Problem

Overweight can be a big problem with young kids reaching puberty (around 12-13 yrs. old), especially girls. I was just talking to a coach last year at a track-meet about my "Track and Field" book. I was trying to sell him on getting a copy of the book. He said, "Can I take a look at it," and I said, "Yes." He thumbed through the pages for several minutes. Then he said, "This is a great book for kids to learn about track." Then he looked through it some more. Then said, "I don't see anything in here about diets." He then asked me if I had any information about "nutrition" and "diets" in my books. And I told him, "Very little."

Then he told me that I should put information in my books about the subject because it's very important to young kids, especially when you are going into *puberty*. He said, "At that point they start to eat way too much fast food, and then their weight balloons up. This makes it very difficult for them to compete in sports." The more I thought about it, the more I thought he was right. Many of you kids do not watch your nutrition. You are always in a big hurry to get somewhere, or do something. So mom or dad pulls into the fast food restaurant and gets burgers to go. What you get there is not the most nutritious food. Probably has a high fat content. Then you put on weight!

Advice

What advice can I give you? Here is what I have come up with. After researching the subject, I have decided to basically follow some of the suggestions and recommendations of Nancy Clark, MS, RD. She has a book out called, "Sports Nutrition Guidebook." (See the reference section) But also you need to get mom and dad to help you out at home by following through on what you need to do in order for it to work. Actually I guess I should not say "diet," What I really mean is kids getting the proper nutrition.

Nancy Clark offers tips to help you fuel yourself for optimal growth and performance. I will try to explain some of her tips to help you with your nutritional needs, but I have to stress that I am not an expert at this. From what I read the critical time is when you reach *puberty*. Your body is going through a change. This is also when your nutritional needs start to change. Adults usually talk about dieting to lose weight. You kids do not need to diet in this way. You just need a variety of healthy foods to keep your bodies growing properly.

Your Weight

Some of you kids are overweight, but even you can improve your health by just eating nutritious foods and being more active. However, you kids can damage your health by doing something drastic, like deciding to eat only lettuce or skipping meals. I'm sure some of you kids feel you weigh too much or too little. But remember some kids have large frames and some kids have small frames. Take that into consideration. If you are worried about your weight, have your doctor check your body mass index (BMI). This is a way to estimate how much body fat you have. If your doctor is concerned about your weight they can recommend some goals. They may want you to lose some weight or gain weight at a slow pace. To do this right, it really should be done with your doctor's help. If you need to lose weight, and mom or dad can afford the cost, you can also work with a dietitian who can show you how to reduce calories safely while still getting the necessary nutrients.

What Can Kids do?

The best general thing you can do is eat a balanced diet, and get plenty of physical activity. Physical activities can be things like playing on a sports team (track & field), riding your bikes, shooting baskets above the garage door, running out at the track, swimming, dancing, helping you rake the leaves, or even helping you clean the house. What you want to limit is your nonactive things, like watching TV for long periods, or playing computer games. You can try to eat a variety of healthy foods. A balanced diet means you should not eat the same thing every day. Have mom help you eat a mix of foods from different food groups. These would be things like:

     a. Fruit and vegetables

     b. Meats, nuts, and other protein rich foods

     c. Milk and dairy products

d. Grains. Especially whole grain foods, like whole grain cereal and breads.

The protein helps build your muscles and other body structures. The calcium helps your growing bones. Vitamins and other nutrients in the fruit and vegetables keep your bodies working as they should. The Fiber helps prevent constipation. The carbohydrates give you energy.

Tips-Here is some of Nancy's tips:

Fluids

Kids need to have fluids at training sessions and at competitions, and your mom or dad needs to make sure you have these fluids when you are at these practices or track meets. Don't depend entirely on yourself to bring them, have mom or dad remind you. The fluids needed are cold water, diluted juice, or a sports drink. Any *non stop* physical activity that lasts 30 to 40 minutes will cause you kids to get overheated when compared to an adult doing the same activity. At a given running speed, you kids will produce more body heat, sweat less, and gain more heat from the environment than an adult would doing the same activity. I always like to send kids on a water break between every 30 minutes and an hour, depending on what we are doing and how hard you are working. Coaches, I know it's hard to remember when you are in the middle of a drill, so try not to forget.

Protein

An adequate amount of protein is very important for you kids in sports. It helps you grow and it builds strong muscles. Athletic kids may need .5 to 1.0 grams of protein per pound of body weight per day. As an example, a nine year old who weighs 75 pounds would need about 37 to 75 grams of protein. You kids can easily get this in three glasses of milk (about 30 grams each) plus a small serving of a protein rich food at lunch and dinner. If you do not drink very much milk, and eat meatless pasta dinners often, you are at risk for a protein deficient diet. Although you kids need an adequate amount of protein, any extra (too much) protein will NOT build bigger muscles. Even strength training, using a light-to-moderate resistance technique that reduces stress on the joints and ligaments, won't bulk up your muscles. At *puberty* it's the hormones that kick in that causes or creates the muscular bulk.

Junk Food

You active kids (on track teams) can meet your nutrient needs with a variety of wholesome foods that are within 1200 to 1500 calories per day. So believe it or not, you actually have SOME room for fatty junk food. Your parents should not restrict all the fat you kids might eat. Generally you need a diet where about 30 per cent of the calories are from fat (see the reference section for sample menus). You may not get enough energy if you eat significantly less fat. The danger is too much junk food snacks might kill your appetite for nutritious meals. This is especially important if you eat too little lunch at school, then devour too many afternoon junk food treats. The ideal thing is for you to eat a second lunch after school instead, to meet your fueling needs.

Calorie Intake

Active kids (on the track team) may need as many calories as your mom or dad do, in fact maybe more. As an example, a six year old boy or girl who weighs about 45 pounds requires about 1800 calories per day. That would be about 40 calories per pound of your weight. Plus you will need about 100-300 more calories if you are involved in sports (like on the track team). An average nine year old at 78 pounds needs about 2500 calories per day. This is 32 calories per pound of your weight, plus the extra calories for sports. A normal growth sign that you are eating enough is that you notice that your training does not stunt your growth when your energy needs are met. If you notice that you seem to be overly fatigued, irritable and lethargic, it's probably because you are not taking in enough calories.

Weight and Pressures

Many of you young kids are under a lot of pressure to be thin, especially girls. Even in the third grade, dieting is common now. A California study showed that 30-45 per cent of nine year old girls, and 40-86 per cent of ten year old girls had, or were showing signs that they had, an eating disorder. Athletes in sports that emphasize leanness such as ballet, gymnastics, figure skating, and running (track), have you kids dieting. This is standard. Pressure to be thin and have the "perfect body" means trouble ahead for you kids. Dieting, after all, is a health risk for you kids to develop a full blown eating disorder. You need to have your mom or dad recognize that dieting is not just about eating, it's about feeling not "good enough", having a poor self image, and low self esteem. Make sure you down play people teasing you about your body size as an important part of your worth, and instead tell them they need to learn to value and accept there are individual differences in kids.

Don't you comment about the size of large children to your friends either because that large person might hear you, and conclude from your comment that they should be thin to be valued and loved. Next thing you know they are dieting. This is very important with young girls who are coping with body changes during *puberty*. Their efforts to control their weight may lead to a sense of frustration, guilt, despair, and failure. And it can lead to a pattern of unhealthy eating, and an eating disorder. They need to be watched closely by their parents.

Childhood Obesity

These days, child obesity is an epidemic. Competitive sports, that are directed at only winning games with the best athletes, offers only humiliation to overweight kids who long to be fit and be adopted by their peers. Appropriately prescribed and competently supervised strength training is good for these obese children because it gives them a chance to shine and be noticed. They are probably one of the strongest kids in their class. So if you are that person then use that to your advantage. It may work for you, try it.

Planning

Many of you kids often eat poorly because both you and your parents have failed to plan for better choices. As an example when you are rushing off to after-school sports practice, do you think ahead and bring bagels and bananas to be eaten in the car. Or do you just take the easy way out and succumb to mom or dad getting you a candy bar or chips from the snack shack?

What about fluids? Does your mom or dad make you bring your own water bottle? Before evening games or practices, have you prepared to eat an early pasta dinner, or do fast food burgers and tacos fill your empty stomach on the way to the game or event.? Proper post game refueling with carbohydrates and fluids is very important. Does your mom or dad have juice boxes ready for you? Think about it, your mom or dad can really help you if you just let them know what you need so that they can do a little planning.

Menus

We have reprinted several of Nancy Clark's sample menus in the back of the book in the reference section. These are just to give you and your parents some ideas. They are not etched in stone. If you are having some eating or weight problems, these menus may be helpful. The best thing though is to get Nancy's book. You will be glad you did (See the reference section). It is the best book on "nutrition" I have ever seen for kids in sports.

In Summation

You kids take care of yourself. Don't get caught up in the "I don't have time mode." Take the time to plan ahead, with or without mom or dads help. There is an old saying that says, "Sometimes the best pace to find a helping hand is at the end of your own arm." You have to understand that you are going into *puberty*, and there is going to be a change in your body. However, if you can't help yourself, then at least have mom or dad plan things out for you and point you in the right direction. Trust me it will pay off later in your life.

Track & Field History

The Beginning

Here is a short chronological history of track and field for you. Track & field basically started in ancient Greece. Possibly going back as far as the ninth and tenth century BC where bronze tripods have been found at Olympia (Greece). Some suggest these may in fact be a prise for some of the early events at Olympia. The first ancient "**Olympic Games**" begin in the year 776 BC at Olympia, Greece. They were held there every four years for almost 12 centuries (1200 years). Additional events were gradually added until, by the 5th century BC, the religious festival consisted of a five day program of events.

Divided Groups

Track and field is divided into two groups, "amateur" and "professional." Basically the professionals get paid for performing in events, and amateurs don't. Although, modern track and field athletes do get paid money for promoting various types of equipment. As track & field developed as a modern sport, one of the major issues for all athletes was their status as amateurs. For many years track & field was considered a purely amateur sport. And the athletes could not accept training money or cash prises for competing in events. If an athlete was charged with professionalism, they could be banned from competition for life. Even if they were paid money for playing in another sport such as baseball.

Amateur or Professional

Now amateur track athletes can openly get paid. They can have their housing, meals, equipment and travel paid for. For competition and training purposes only though. A company, organization, or person can NOT directly give them money to keep and spend as they wish. To keep this all fair, they have to fill out forms for what their assistance is, and where it came from.

During the 70s world track & field enjoyed a boom in popularity. During this time the United States based "International Track Association" (ITA) organized a professional track circuit. It was popular among fans, but went bankrupt after several years. Probably because many world class athletes did not participate because they were afraid it would disqualify them from participating in future Olympic Games. International professional running, which was initiated in the 70s, has only had limited success. The legitimate athletes that did participate were paid. However, many athletes were receiving larger illegal payments for just appearing at amateur meets.

Following is a short chronological history of track & field in the USA:

1860s: Track & field in the USA has it's beginnings.

1873: The Intercollegiate Association of Amateur Athletes of America becomes the first national athletic group, and holds the first collegiate races.

1878: William B. Curtis founded what later becomes the "Amateur Athletics Union (AAU).

1887: The name "The Amateur Athletic Union" (AAU) is formally adopted.

1888: The Amateur Athletic Union (which governed the sport for nearly a century) held it's first championships.

1913: Jim Thorpe was stripped of his 1912 Olympic victories in the decathlon and pentathlon and banned from further competition after it was learned he had played semiprofessional baseball.

1921: The first NCAA national championship is held for men.

1928: Women's track and field becomes part of the Olympic Games.

1970s: Women's track finally gets acceptance. The International Track Association (ITA) organizes a professional track circuit.

1979: The Amateur Athletic Union (AAU) relinquished it's role as the American governing body for track & field long distance running and race walking. It was replaced by The Athletics Congress (TAC). Alvin Chriss is named special assistant to the new director. To keep road runners from being disqualified for accepting prise money, Mr. Chriss devised "The TAC Trust".

1982: The International Olympic Committee (IOC) posthumously restores both of Jim Thorpe's Olympic medals.

1992: The TAC name is changed to USA Track & Field (USATF) to increase recognition.

1999: The USATF establishes the "Golden Spike Tour", now called the Visa Championship Series (VCS), to showcase track & field in America.

The Fundamentals

What are they

     Fundamentals are the basic skills needed to successfully compete in track, field, or cross country events. The Basics are walking, sprinting, running, hurdling, hopping, jumping, vaulting, pushing and throwing. Even though it would be good to learn all of these basic skills, I am going to break them down into the different events for you. The reason being that most of you boys and girls will not be able to master all of these basic skills or compete in every event. If you can't, figure out in your mind what event you might be good at, then start out by learning strength, speed, endurance and coordination. You can always use these skills no matter which event you are in. As an example if you are very tall for your age, with a long legs on a thin frame, and come from a tall thin family, then you might be good at high jumping, distance running, or cross country. Have mom or dad go over thes events with you, then to make a decision on what it appears your size and stature will become when you grow older. Try and imagine what event you might naturally fit into when you get to high school age, then match them up with the possible event examples we will give you.

     Look at your own parents and see what kind of body structure they have. Boys, many times you will inherit a similar structure to your mom and her side of the family. Girls, most of the time you will inherit a similar structure to your dad and his side of the family. Tell your dad, that please whatever they do don't try to make you into a competitor at an event they were in or always wanted to be in. Boys if your dad is big and tall, but your mom is smaller in size, you will probably be smaller than you dad. And girls your mom may be big and tall, but if your dad is small, you will probably be small also. Although these days there are always exceptions. Take this into account when you decide what event to start training for. As an example if you are very small and fast, don't try and turn yourself into a high jumper or a shot putter. Maybe working on sprinting or relays would be better. The trick is learn an event you can succeed at.

     After a few years if it appears you are changing into a different size, skill level, or stature than you imagined, you can always go back and learn the additional skills you will need for another event. Don't spend a lot of time trying to learn how to be a high jumper if you are going to end up a sprinter. Spend it more wisely on improving your strength, speed, coordination, and endurance at a young age. These skills will help you in track and field, or any other sport you might get into.

Sprinters

     The fundamental skills you need are leg strength, quickness, agility, and anaerobic endurance. A sprinter also needs to have good mental focus, and be a good athlete. In the sections on ***"Drills and Exercises,"*** you will find out how to learn these skills. Make sure you have good sprinters track shoes. They come with a variety of spikes on the bottom. Some have fixed plate spikes, others have removable spikes. Probably the fundamental you need to concentrate first on is your foot push off strength, then quickness, then mental focus, then anaerobic endurance, and last agility. You need foot push off strength to get out of the starting blocks fast, low and hard. You need reaction quickness to explode out low on the first few steps. You need to have good mental focus to drive out off the starting blocks exactly when the starting gun goes off. You need to build up your anaerobic endurance to make sure the oxygen demand on your muscles is met. You need agility to react and be in control if you should accidentally get tripped or fall down. When you first start to sprint or run, take note of your speed and quickness. How do you compare with the other runners? If you are naturally fast and quick compared to the competition, and have strong legs, then you could become a good sprinter.

Relay Runner

The fundamental skills that you need are the same as a "sprinter." This is because the shorter distance races are really a series of sprints. In addition though you need to learn baton passing skills. You also need to learn about "lanes." You should know when to run on the inside of a lane, and when to run on the outside of a lane. In the sections on *"Drills and Exercises,"* you will find out how to learn these skills. The fundamental skills you need to concentrate on first are the same as a "sprinter". Except work on your baton passing skills, and about lanes before working on your agility. When you first start to run, take note of your speed and quickness. If you are naturally fast and quick compared to the competition, and have strong legs, then you could become a good relay runner. Also have someone watch your body positioning and leg turnover, to determine if you are a good curve runner compared to a straight lane type of runner.

Hurdler

The fundamental skills you need are also the same as a "sprinter." This is because hurdling is basically a controlled paced sprint between the hurdles. The fundamental skills you need to concentrate on first are the same as a "sprinter." In addition, a hurdler needs to be very flexible and know how to jump over the hurdles, which is a special kind of jumping skill called "hurdling." You also need to learn about pacing, tempo, rhythm, stride length, and stride count. Another basic skill you must learn is which leg will always be your lead leg over the hurdle. In the sections on *"Drills and Exercises,"* you will find out how to learn all of these skills. Work on your flexibility, hurdling, and pacing skills before agility. The more flexible you are, the easier it is to get over the hurdle. Stride length and count are very important between hurdles because if they are not correctly adjusted for each competitor, you could hit the hurdle stumble and fall down. When you first start to run, take note of your speed and quickness. How do you compare with the other runners? If you are naturally fast and quick compared to the competition, flexible, have long strong legs and good jumping skills, then you could become a good hurdler.

Distance Runner

The fundamental skills you need are strength, speed, aerobic endurance, and agility. However, you still have to work on your anaerobic endurance to sprint to the finish line. In long distance races there can be a lot of jockeying for position going on. This is why you need to have some agility, to keep from being tripped or bumped into falling down. In the sections on *"Drills and Exercises,"* you will find out how to learn these skills. The fundamental skill you need to concentrate on first is speed, then leg strength, then aerobic endurance, then anaerobic endurance, and last agility. When you first start to run longer distances, take note of your speed and endurance, for running long periods of time without getting too tired. If you are naturally fast compared to the other runners, have strong legs, and like to run around all the time, then you could become a good distance runner. I might also point out that if you are on the thin side, and kind of wirey in build, then with good training you could still become a good distance runner. Some of the worlds best marathon runners, men and women, don't look big and strong. They are quite lanky, and wirey, and sometimes short in build.

Cross Country Runner

The fundamental skills you need are very similar to, and in some skills the same as a distance runner. You need to learn skills in speed, strength, aerobic endurance, anaerobic endurance, and agility. In addition you need to learn how to run on all kinds of different surfaces such as concrete, emulsion fortified with rubber (on the track), hard dirt, soft dirt, mud, gravel and grass. You also need to learn how to run uphill and downhill (not as easy as you think). Learning agility skills is more important in cross country running than in distance running. This is because distance running is on a flat course where cross country running is on all kinds of surfaces. Much more chance of falling in cross country. In the sections on *"Drills and Exercises,"* you will find out how to learn these skills.

The fundamental skill you need to concentrate on first is speed, then aerobic endurance, then strength, then agility and last anaerobic endurance. When you first start to run longer distances, take note of your speed and endurance as compared to the other runners, for running long periods of time without appearing to get too tired. If you are naturally fast, in comparison, have strong legs, and like to run around all the time, then you could become a good cross country runner. I might also point out that if you are on the thin side, and kind of wirey in build, then with good training you could still become a good cross country runner. Some of the worlds best cross country runners, men and women, don't have big muscles and look strong. They are more lanky, wirey and weaker looking in build.

Steeplechase Runner

The fundamental skills you need are the same as a distance runner, a hurdler and a cross country runner all combined. In addition you need to learn how to jump up on then off a water barrier. In particular you need to have good agility skills because of the jumping. On the other side of the water barrier is a pool of water which you need to learn to deal with. In the sections on *"Drills and Exercises,"* you will find out how to learn these skills. The fundamental skill you need to concentrate on first is technique, then leg power and strength, then speed, then hurdling, then jumping on and off a barrier (agility), then aerobic endurance, and last anaerobic endurance. When you first go out to run the longer distances, take note of your speed and endurance as compared to the other runners, running long periods of time without appearing to get too tired and last your jumping abilities. If you are naturally fast in comparison, have strong legs, like to run around all the time, are always jumping around, then with training you could become a good steeplechase runner. Some coaches and trainers think being tall, long legged, and lanky in build could be a slight advantage for you in this event.

Race Walker

The fundamental skills you need are very special. It's like a special form of power walking with all the swinging arm movements. This is a technique I'm not sure will be easy for you kids to learn. This technique is what I would describe as walking stiff legged and kind of waddling along where the feet don't leave the ground. Once learning the technique, you need to learn how to build up speed and aerobic endurance. There are three phases a race walker must learn. They are the "double support" phase, the "traction " phase and the "drive" or "thrust" phase. In the sections on *"Drills and Exercises,"* you will find out how to learn these skills. The fundamental skill you need to concentrate on first is learning the "technique," then learning the three walking phases. Speed will not help you until you learn how to do the walk technique correctly. Last work on your aerobic endurance. I don't think many of you kids will have a natural talent for this technique, but you can try race walking and see. It's different, and because of that some of you kids might want to try it.

High Jumper

The fundamental skills you need are speed, jumping, quickness, agility, and controlled falling. Even though it looks hard, this technique can be easily learned. The quickness relates to the explosive type take off that is needed to raise your center of gravity. In the sections on *"Drills and Exercises,"* you will see how to learn these skills. The fundamental skill you need to concentrate on first is learning how to do the backward jump technique. You must have good flexibility, and be able to arch your back and flip onto the high jump mat. Next work on leg strength, then agility, then controlled falling, then quickness, and last speed. When you first go out and try jumping, take note of how you do in comparison to the other jumpers. If you are tall for your age, have long legs, and have good strength in your legs, then with training you could become a good high jumper. If you have ever been in gymnastics or cheerleading you may be good at high jumping because of what you learned (muscle memory) in those activities.

Long Jumper

The fundamental skills you need are basically the same as a high jumper. The basic difference is the long jumper explodes from the take off line and goes outward instead of upward. Speed and sprinting are very important in order to get the momentum to take you farther outward. This is why good sprinters often make good long jumpers. They have the speed and the strong legs for jumping. Long jumpers also need to learn the technique of how to control your body while in the air. In the sections on *"Drills and Exercises,"* you will find out how to learn these skills. The fundamental skill you need to concentrate on first is speed, then leg strength, then jumping technique, and last body control. When you first try jumping, take note of your speed and natural jumping abilities when compared to the other jumpers. If you are naturally fast, have strong legs, and like to jump, then with training you could become a good long jumper.

Triple Jumper

The fundamental skills you need are basically the same as a long jumper. In addition the skill of hopping and skipping, or stepping, while at a full run are needed. Leg strength is very important to be able to rebound from the hop to the step to the jump. A good long jumper could learn to be a good triple jumper. In the sections on *"Drills and Exercises,"* you will find out how to learn these skills. The fundamental skill you need to concentrate on first is your leg strength and power, then speed, then agility, then hopping, stepping, jumping and last body control. When you first start jumping take note of your speed and natural jumping abilities when compared to the other jumpers. Some coaches and trainers say being tall is an advantage because you have longer strides, longer bounds, which makes it easier to go way out into the pit. This is an energy draining event, so you also need to have a lot of stamina and endurance, and have very strong legs in order to become a good triple jumper.

Pole Vaulter

The fundamental skills you need are speed, strength, and acrobatic body control in the air. You need to be fearless. Otherwise you might not be able to handle the height, and the falling. You will need to learn some gymnastic skills also to help you learn the technique. In the sections on *"Drills and Exercises,"* you will find out how to learn these skills. The fundamental skill you need to concentrate on first is speed, then strength, then agility, then body control in the air, and last the gymnastic skills. When you first go out and try vaulting, take note of your speed, natural jumping and tumbling abilities when compared to the other vaulters. If you are naturally fast, can tumble around on the ground or floor, then with training you could become a good pole vaulter. You will need to be very strong in the arms in order to pull yourself up in the air while hanging on a pole.

Shot Putter

The fundamental skills you need are arm and shoulder strength, strong legs, agility, quickness, flexibility, and torque. You will need to learn the "spin rotational" move as well as the "glide" move. Since shot balls are potentially dangerous and could accidentally hurt someone, competitors need to learn the proper safety techniques. In the sections on *"Drills and Exercises,"* you will find out how to learn these skills. The fundamental skill you need to concentrate on first is arm strength, then throwing technique, then leg strength, then agility and last quickness. When you first go out and put the shot, take note of your strength, and natural throwing abilities when compared to the other shot putters. If you are big for your age, and strong, then with training you could become a good shot putter. Many of you kids are big and a little clumsey, and don't really fit in soccer, basketball, or baseball. If that is the case, then maybe this is something you could become sucessful at.

Discus Thrower

The fundamental skills you need are basically the same as a shot putter. In addition you will need to learn how to hold and throw the discus in order to get the proper lift to your throw. Since a discus is potentially dangerous and could accidentally hurt someone, you need to learn the proper safety techniques. In the sections on *"Drills and Exercises,"* you will find out how to learn these skills. The fundamental skill you need to concentrate on first is arm strength, then throwing technique, then agility, and last quickness. When you first go out and try throwing, take note of your strength and natural throwing abilities when compared to the other throwers. If you are big for your age, and strong, then with training you could become a good discus thrower. Also being wirey and loose in the arms and shoulders make it easier to throw the disk. Many of you young kids are big and clumsey and don't really fit in soccer, basketball, or baseball. If that is the case, then maybe this is something you could become sucessful at.

Javelin Thrower

The fundamental skills you need are basically the same as a shot putter and discus thrower. In addition you will need to learn how to hold and throw the javelin, and leg strength for run-up. They have a "mini-jav" now that is used in AAU and USATF youth track & field meets. Since a javelin is potentially dangerous and could accidentally hurt someone, you need to also learn the proper safety techniques. The "mini-jav" has a blunted end for safety purposes. In the sections on *"Drills and Exercises,"* you will find out how to learn these skills. The fundamental skill you need to concentrate on first is arm strength, then throwing technique, then agility, then leg strength and last quickness. When you first go out and try throwing, take note of your strength and natural throwing abilities when compared to the other throwers. You will need upper body strength like that of a baseball/softball outfielder that has a good rhythm to their long throws. If you are big for your age, and strong, then with training you could become a good javelin thrower. Many of you young kids are big and clumsey, but strong, and don't really fit in soccer, or basketball. If that is the case with you, then maybe this is something you could become sucessful at.

Hammer Thrower

The fundamental skills you need are basically the same as a shot putter and discus thrower. In addition you will need to learn how to hold and throw the hammer. The hammer throw is the most complex of the throwing events to learn. It is even difficult for good throwers to let go of the hammer so it goes in the right direction. Since a hammer is potentially dangerous and could accidentally hurt someone, you need to learn the proper safety techniques. In the sections on *"Drills and Exercises,"* you will find out how to learn these skills. The fundamental skill you need to concentrate on first is strength, then the hammer throwing technique, then agility, and last quickness. When you first go out and try throwing, take note of your strength and natural throwing abilities when compared to the other throwers. If you are big for your age, and strong, then with training you could become a good hammer thrower. It won't be easy though. But not many kids know how to throw, which may be an advantage for you. Many of you young kids are big and clumsey, but strong, and don't really fit in soccer, basketball, or baseball. If that is the case, then maybe this is something you could become sucessful at. You need to be really smart and focused to throw the hammer, or you could accidentally injure yourself in this event.

Combined Events Competitor

Some of you young kids are just naturally good athletes. And because you may be good at several events, you might make a good combined events competitor. If this is the case, you could become good at "Triathlon's," "Pentathlon's," "Heptathlon's," and "Decathlon's." Multiple events take lots of stamina and endurance, both anaerobic and aerobic. These events are very prestigeous in track & field if you are able to compete in them. If you want to get into this type of event, then you will need to work hard on your endurance and strength.

Games Training

According to the "American Sport Education Program" (ASEP), the games approach to training may be better than endless hours of drills on fundamental skills. But too many hours of training only for your event is not the answer either. By games, I mean playing some kind of game that is directly related to your event. And knowing today's youth sports programs they may be on to something. However I think the answer is a little of both may be the best way. There are a lot of clever ways to play competitive fun games with your friends out in the backyard, and still learn some skills without even knowing it. Our suggested approach is play the game(s) with your friends, then maybe on alternate days or sessions, go over with mom or dad the related fundamentals that you were using and how they relate. Let mom or dad watch, keep score or whatever is needed. Then have mom or dad discuss with you how you could improve on your techniques and skills. You can't do it all by yourself. This will help you to learn quicker.

Every week or so try to get some of your friends to come over and play one of these games with you. Some of you kids do have a very short attention span. You get bored very easily. So when you look at the "practice" times we have for a particular fundamental, you will see the times are fairly short. The trick is mixing up your training so that it repeats every other week or so. Also games will keep you busy with different types of things to do (not so boring). This is why I suggest that you have mom or dad help you develop a learning plan. Scattered throughout the book we have added backyard type games to play for this purpose, that relate to the specific skill activities we are discussing in the activity. This makes it more fun for you.

Organize your Training

To organize your training, have a plan. My suggestion is sit down, read the section in the book where I talk about how to determine what event you might be good at. Then go through the rest of the book, and read the sections where I show the exercises, drills, and skills, needed for that event. At this point I think it is a good idea to get mom or dad to help you with this. As you go through the book, start a list of what you need to practice. Next to that drill or exercise, put down approximately how much time will be needed to accomplish the learning and practicing. This way you can plan your sessions. I am sure that when you get done, you and your parents will both see that it takes a lot of hours to go over fundamentals. And with the few hours your coach has with you, time runs out and the coach has to start working on something else. So learning at home using this book as a guide, you kids from five years old on up working even a little each year, will really help you improve on your track & field skills and make it more fun.

Youth Track in General

Youth track in general is basically the "AAU" (Amateur Athletic Union), and the "USATF" (USA Track & Field) organizations. In St. Louis we also have the "CYC" (Catholic Youth Council) as a governing body for youth track & field. In other parts of the country, different areas have their own spinoff organizations. Each one of these groups set the standards they want to follow. There is is not a whole lot of difference between all of them, except in the rules. Most of the spinoff groups relax and bend some of the rules a little so that it makes it easier for kids to compete. Some of these groups start as young as 3 years old. Then in addition to the organizations you have "Indoor" and "Outdoor" track & field. They are slightly different because of running on different types of surfaces, and track sizes which are smaller for indoor meets. Indoor track & field offers training during the winter months if you can find an indoor track in your area. USATF has indoor track championships. In this book we will refer to "outdoor" track and Field.

Where Events take place on the Track

There are probably slightly different layouts for almost every outdoor track. The one we will show is a typical full events layout (not the most common). This layout has been added, to give you at least some idea of where the events are being conducted when you go to a meet *(SEE DIAGRAM 1)*. With everything going on, it's nice to know generally where to look for the location of your event. You will need a program of events though to see the time and place your event is scheduled. Your track coach may give you one ahead of time. Track meets can last most of the day, and sometimes on saturday and sunday. It helps to know what day, and when your events are going to be run .

Some high schools and colleges will let the public use their outdoor track. The tracks in my area have posted rules on a big sign near their entrance, telling you what you can and can't do. Basically if you want to go there and work out, try to follow their rules. Make sure you leave the area in the same condition you found it when you are finished. No trash left laying around, that sort of thing. They usually do not have a bathroom there that is open for you to use. So make sure you go before you come. Less problems that way!

Drills and Exercises

How do they help

Modern track and field training, and conditioning, is advancing all the time. In this book we will follow the latest recommended exercises, and tailor them for you younger kids. Over the past several years researchers and physicians have identified exercises that are commonly used that can, in some cases, be potentially harmful to your body. These exercises can be modified, to eliminate the undesirable characteristics. This book will now use the safer alternatives.

I will break them down into the fundamental categories, and how they relate to what you want to learn. We will use picture figures, and diagrams as much as possible, to eliminate some of the confusion for you. So bear with us those of you that are older and have already been through all this. This book was written as a "reference" book for kids to use when competing in track and field or cross country. You can take the book right out in the yard, park, or track, along with you to look at for reference purposes.

I suggest that if you are not very interested in exercising, then try to make a game out of them. Get mom or dad to come out and do these exercises with you. For instance say something to them like, "I bet I can do this better than you," or "I bet you can't beat me down to the fence." Then try to do the exercise faster or better than your mom or dad. This will keep you interested. If mom or dad can't come out to help, then get one or two of your friends to come over and do the exercise with you. Get into exercising at home. It can be fun, and it is good for your overall health. I still do many of these exercises all the time. And I am really old compared to you! You will need to be well conditioned to compete in track and field, or cross country. And it will condition you for doing exercises even as you grow older in life.

Warm up and Stretching

You need to warm up before doing any flexibility, stretching, strengthening, or other exercises. Before starting, you can *slowly* "jog" around the yard or do "jumping jacks," for about one to three minutes to get your muscles warmed up. Warming up raises your body temperature

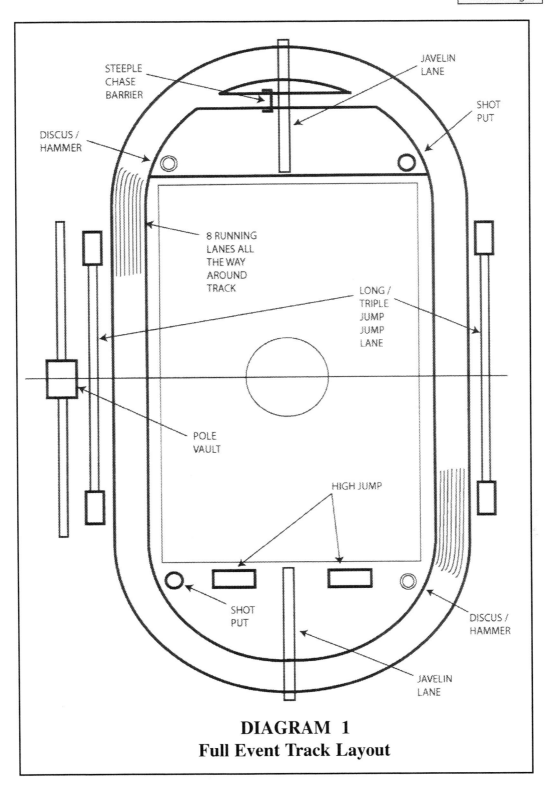

DIAGRAM 1
Full Event Track Layout

several degrees while rushing blood deep into your muscles and connective tissues. It also reduces the chance of ligament strains, muscle tears, and general soreness. A warm up is required before you start any of these flexibility, strength, or stretching exercises. The shorter time is for you five to seven year olds. The longer time is for you 12 year olds and up. Adjust the time accordingly with all the ages in between.

Start stretching with the upper part of your body first, and end up with the lower part of your body last. When doing the stretches you need to inhale and exhale deeply and slowly two or three times (Breaths) while your body is in the stretching position. This is a yoga technique. By breathing deeply in and out, it lets you stretch out farther. After vigorously stretching and exercising unless you are going to the strengthening or other exercises next, be sure to do a "*COOL DOWN*"

DIAGRAM 2

routine, instead of just stopping cold. Or do your cool down after the strengthening or other exercises have been completed.

Warm-Up No.1 - Jumping Jacks

From the standing position put both feet together and both hands down at your sides. The first move is jump up slightly kicking both feet out to the side while raising both arms up together over your head. For the next move you jump up slightly and bring both of your arms back down to your sides while bringing both feet together. Then you repeat this over and over with a constant jumping motion for one to two minutes. You can increase how long you do them each week as you get stronger if you like *(SEE DIAGRAM 2)*.

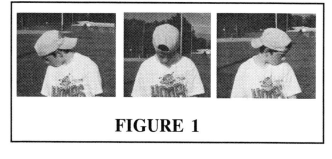

FIGURE 1

Exercise No.1- Neck Stretch

This stretching exercise is for the neck muscles. It is for all competitors because in many events you are twisting and turning your head around. From the standing position, put your hands down at your sides, turn to the right and put your chin on your right shoulder. Hold for two in and out breaths, then relax.

Next move your head back to center, then put your chin on your chest. Hold that position for two in and out breaths, then relax. Then turn to the left, and put your chin on your left shoulder. Hold that position for two in and out breaths, then relax. Repeat this at least five times, for all three of the positions. After you have been doing these every day for awhile, you can increase the number slightly for extra work if necessary *(SEE FIGURE 1)*.

Exercise No. 2- Fingers Stretch

This stretching exercise is for the fingers. All competitors except stand up start distance and cross country runners can benefit from using this stretch because they use their fingers in some way. From the standing position, put both your feet out about shoulder width apart. Than put both arms straight out in front. Next, with your fingers spread and pointing straight out, squeeze your fingers together in a fist, then extend them back out. Then keep squeezing and extending them over and over for about five seconds. Now while you are still squeezing your fingers in and out, move both arms overhead for about five seconds. Next while still squeezing in and out, raise both arms out to your sides for about five seconds. Now while still squeezing in and out repeat all three positions three times *(SEE FIGURE 2)*.

A   B   C

FIGURE 2

Exercise No. 3- Wrist Stretch

This stretching exercise is for the wrist muscles. All competitors except stand up start distance and cross country runners can benefit from using this stretch because they use their wrist in some way. From the standing position, put both your feet out about shoulder width apart. Then put both arms straight out at your sides. Next, with your fingers spread slightly apart and pointing straight out, roll both hands around in a circle at the wrist joint with fingers spread, go as far down and around as you can. Do this while doing your breathing, then relax your hands back down at your sides. After relaxing for about ten seconds repeat this again at least five times *(SEE FIGURE 3)*.

FIGURE 3

Exercise No.4- Forearm Extensor Stretch

This stretching exercise is for the forearm extensor muscles. All competitors except stand up start distance and cross country runners can benefit from using this stretch because they use their forearms in some way. From either a standing or sitting position, put your right arm straight out in front of you with your palm facing down. Then keeping the right hand rather stiff, take your left hand and grasp the back of the right hand and push it downward so that the hand is twisted a little towards the right. You should feel the stretch on the top side of the right forearm. Hold that position while doing your breathing, then let go and bring your arms back down. Relax for ten seconds in between each stretch. Repeat this at least five times for each arm *(SEE FIGURE 4)*.

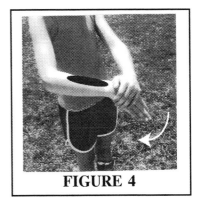

FIGURE 4

Exercise No.5- Forearm Flexor Stretch

This stretching exercise is for the forearm flexor muscles. All competitors except stand up start distance and cross country runners can benefit from using this stretch because they use their

FIGURE 5

forearms in some way. From either a standing or sitting position, put your right arm straight out in front of you with your palm facing down. Then take your left hand and grasp the fingers of your right hand, and pull it back so that the fingers are pointing upwards. You should feel the stretch on the underside of the right forearm. Hold that position while doing your breathing, then let go and bring the arms back down. Relax for ten seconds between each stretch. Repeat this at least five times for each arm *(SEE FIGURE 5)*.

Exercise No. 6- Triceps Stretch

This stretching exercise is for the triceps and rotator cuff muscles. All competitors except stand up start distance and cross country runners can benefit from using this stretch because they use their triceps in some way. From the standing position, put your right hand behind their head, and touch the top of the opposite (Left) shoulder blade. Next hold the elbow of your right hand using your left hand. Then gently push down on your elbow, pushing your right hand down your back. Hold that position while doing your breathing. Then totally relax for six seconds in between each stretch. Then switch arms and put your left arm behind you and touch the top of your right shoulder and push down. Repeat this at least five times for each arm *(SEE FIGURE 6)*.

FIGURE 6

Exercise No. 7- Biceps Stretch

This stretching exercise is for the biceps muscles. All competitors except stand up start distance and cross country runners can benefit from using this stretch because they use their biceps in some way. From the standing position, with your back to a wall and feet shoulder width apart, reach back and place both hands behind you against a wall at about shoulder height. Next bend both knees down until you feel the stretch in your front biceps area of your upper arm and shoulders. Hold that position while doing your breathing, then raise your knees back up to the starting position, put your arms down and relax for ten seconds between each stretch. Repeat this at least five times *(SEE FIGURE 7)*.

FIGURE 7

Exercise No. 8- Rear Shoulder Stretch

This stretching exercise is for the anterior and medial deltoid, and pectoral major muscles. All competitors except stand up start distance and cross country runners can benefit from using this stretch because they use their shoulders in some way.

FIGURE 8

From the standing position, with your legs apart, put both your arms straight down behind your back. Then grasp both hands together at the fingers. Next push down and rotate your shoulders up, keeping your arms straight. Hold that position while doing your breathing, then totally relax your arms and shoulders for four seconds in between each stretch. Repeat this at least five times *(SEE FIGURE 8)*.

Exercise No. 9- Front Shoulder Stretch

This stretching exercise is for the upper back trapezius, rhomboids, and posterior deltoid muscles. All competitors except stand up start distance and cross country runners can benefit from using this stretch because they use their shoulders in some way. From the standing position, with legs apart, put your left arm straight out to your right across your chest. Next make a fist and bend your right arm up towards your chin. Hold that position while you do your breathing, then bring both arms back down and totally relax for four seconds in between each stretch. Next switch arms and put your right arm out to your left. Then bend up your left arm and hold while doing your breathing. Repeat this at least five times for each arm *(SEE FIGURE 9)*.

FIGURE 9

Exercise No. 10- Side Torso Stretch

This stretching exercise is for side torso, upper back, and rib cage. All competitors can benefit from using this stretch because they use their torso in some way. From the standing position, put both your feet about shoulder width apart. Then put your right hand on your right hip. Next put your left arm straight up towards the sky and make a fist. Then keeping your arm as straight as possible, move it over to the right until it touches the top of your head. Next twist your wrist so the knuckles are pointing to the right. Then bend the whole upper body to the right, and hold that position while doing your breathing. Then put your arms down to your sides and relax for ten seconds between each stretch. Then switch and stretch the other side. Repeat at least five times with each arm *(SEE FIGURE 10)*.

FIGURE 10

Exercise No. 11- Waist & Stomach Stretch

This stretching exercise is for the waist and stomach muscles. All competitors can benefit from using this stretch because they use their waist and stomach in some way. From the standing position, with legs about shoulder width apart, put both arms straight out at your sides. Then twist your entire torso 90 degrees to the left, hold there while doing your breathing, then back to facing front. Now twist 90 degrees to the right and hold

FIGURE 11

while doing your breathing. Then put your hands down at your side, and relax for ten seconds. Repeat this at least five times to each side *(SEE FIGURE 11)*.

FIGURE 12

Exercise No. 12- Seated Pelvic Stretch

This stretching exercise is for the lower back, obliques, and gluteus maximus (butt). All competitors can benefit from using this stretch because they use their pelvis in some way. From the sitting position, put your left leg straight out in front with your toes up. Next put the right leg over the left, just back of he knee, with the toes pointed outward. Then put the left elbow on the right knee, with the hand on the right hip. Next put your right arm out to the side, and slightly back for balance. Turn your head to the right, then hold that position while doing your breathing. Then put your arms down and totally relax for ten seconds in between each stretch. Now switch legs and repeat at least five times to each side *(SEE FIGURE 12)*.

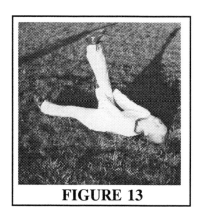

FIGURE 13

Exercise No. 13- Hip Extensor Stretch

This stretching exercise is for the hip extensor muscles. All competitors can benefit from using this stretch because they use their hips in some way. From the lying position, head up, put your left leg straight out in front with toes down. Next lift your right leg up, keeping it as straight as possible, with your foot flat. Grasp your right leg with both hands behind the knee and pull back towards your head. Hold that position while doing your breathing, then put your leg down. Now totally relax for about ten seconds in between each stretch. Switch, then lift up your left leg and repeat the pull. Repeat this at least five times with each leg *(SEE FIGURE 13)*.

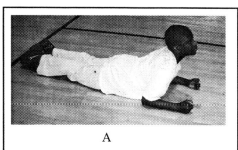

A

B

FIGURE 14

Exercise No. 14- Upper and Lower Back Stretch

This stretching exercise is for the upper and lower back muscles. All competitors can benefit from using this stretch because they use their back in some way. Lying on your stomach, spread you legs to hip width, and put the tops of your feet on the floor. Rest your forehead on the floor, then bend your elbows and put your forearms on the floor with palms down. As you inhale press your forearms against the floor and raise your chest and head. Keep your pelvis and thighs against the floor. Hold that position while doing your breathing, then as you exhale lower your head slowly back to the floor. This stretches your lower back *(SEE FIGURE 14-A)*. Now totally relax for about ten seconds in between each stretch. Do the same thing again, except this time raise up by pressing your palms against the floor *(SEE FIGURE 14-B)*. This stretches your upper back. Repeat this at least five times each for your upper and lower back.

Exercise No. 15- Seated Hamstring Stretch

This stretching exercise is for the "hamstrings", and quadriceps muscles. All competitors can benefit from using this stretch because they use their hamstrings when running and jumping. From the sitting position put both legs together out in front of you. The toes should be pointing straight up. Then keeping your knees down to the floor or ground, reach forward and touch your toes with both hands. Hold that position while you do your breathing, then lean back, put your hands out at your side, and totally relax for ten seconds in between each stretch. Repeat at least five times *(SEE FIGURE 15)*.

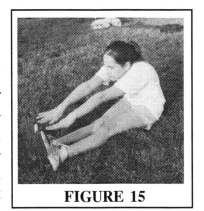
FIGURE 15

Exercise No. 16- Thigh Stretch

This is a stretching exercise for the front thigh quadriceps muscles. All competitors can benefit from using this stretch because they use their thighs when running and jumping. From the kneeling position, put your right leg out in front of you. Next put your right hand on your right thigh, and your left hand on your left waist. Put a towel or pad under the down knee for protection. Keeping your back straight shift your weight to your front leg. Then lean forward until you feel a stretch in the front of the hip and thigh of the leg you are kneeling on. Hold that position while doing your breathing, then lean back and totally relax for six seconds. Then switch legs and stretch the other thigh. Repeat this at least five times with each leg *(SEE FIGURE 16)*.

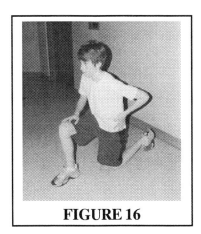
FIGURE 16

Exercise No. 17- Straddle Groin Stretch

This stretching exercise is for the inner thigh groin muscles. All competitors can benefit from using this stretch because they use their groin in some way when running and jumping. From the sitting position, put both legs way out to the side in front of you, toes up, keeping your knees down and straight. Next grasp both hands together at the thumbs, then keeping your arms straight, lean forward, and reach way out in front. While doing this, try to keep the back straight. Hold that position while doing your breathing. Then lean back and totally relax for ten seconds in between each stretch. Repeat this at least five times *(SEE FIGURE 17)*.

FIGURE 17

33

Exercise No. 18- Abductors Stretch

This stretching exercise is for abductors in the inner thigh. All competitors can benefit

FIGURE 18

from using this stretch because they use their legs in some way when running and jumping. From the standing position, put your right arm down at your side, and extend the left leg out to the top edge of a chair, bench or some other stationary item. Whatever the item is, the leg has to be as straight out to the side as possible. Then push lightly down, with the left hand just above the left knee. Hold that position while doing your breathing. Then put the leg down and totally relax for ten seconds, in between each stretch. Now put the right leg up, push down, and hold while doing your breathing. Repeat this five times for each leg *(SEE FIGURE 18)*.

Exercise No. 19- Knee to Chest Stretch

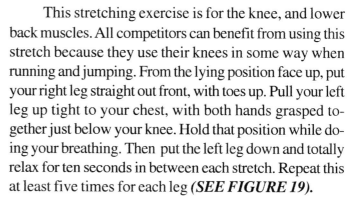
FIGURE 19

This stretching exercise is for the knee, and lower back muscles. All competitors can benefit from using this stretch because they use their knees in some way when running and jumping. From the lying position face up, put your right leg straight out front, with toes up. Pull your left leg up tight to your chest, with both hands grasped together just below your knee. Hold that position while doing your breathing. Then put the left leg down and totally relax for ten seconds in between each stretch. Repeat this at least five times for each leg *(SEE FIGURE 19)*.

Exercise No. -20 Calf Stretch

FIGURE 20

This stretching exercise is for the calf muscles. All competitors can benefit from using this stretch because they use their calf muscles when running and jumping. Stand in front of a wall and stagger your left foot in front of your right foot, with both heels flat on the floor. Next lean forward and put both of your hands against the wall, then bend the leading front leg down until you feel the pull in your right leg calf. Remember though you have to be far enough away from the wall so that you can feel the pull. When you feel the pull hold that position for about three seconds. Then stand up and relax for about ten seconds. Now lean back against the wall and stretch the calf in your left leg for three seconds. Repeat this at least three times for each leg *(SEE FIGURE 20)*.

Exercise No. 21- Ankle Stretch

This stretching exercise is for ankle area muscles. All competitors can benefit from using this stretch because they use their ankles when running and jumping. From the sitting position put both your feet, relaxed toes up, out in front of you with feet together. Arms out at your sides, for balance. Next keeping your legs flat to the floor or ground, roll both ankles forward, pushing your toes downward. Hold that position while you do your breathing, then relax your feet back to the starting position (up). Next, keeping your heels flat to the floor, roll both ankles back towards your head, with your toes pointing up. This should be a hard pull, with your toes hard towards your head. Hold that position while you do your breathing. Then totally relax your feet for ten seconds in between each stretch. Repeat this at least five times for each position *(SEE FIGURE 21)*.

FIGURE 21

Drills for Coordination and Agility

Explanation

These drills are designed to teach you how to move around on your feet better, without falling down. These drills will also help you improve your balance and agility in case you do fall or trip. They will also help you in field events like shot put, discus, hammer throw, high jump, pole vault, triple jumping and the steeplechase. If you will do the drills related to your event, every day even for a short while, you will notice your coordination improving after just a few weeks.

Drill No. 1 Crossover Foot (Carioca)

The Basics are

This is called the crossover foot, and side to side, or "carioca" exercise drill. This is agility and coordination core training to keep you from tripping over your feet while on the move. What it will do for you is amazing, believe me. It's very widely used in almost all sports now. The feet have to keep crossing over each other, from in front to behind. Its an old football drill, but it works great for coordination and agility training in any sport. All you young track field event competitors and cross country competitors need to work on this drill *(SEE FIGURE 22)*.

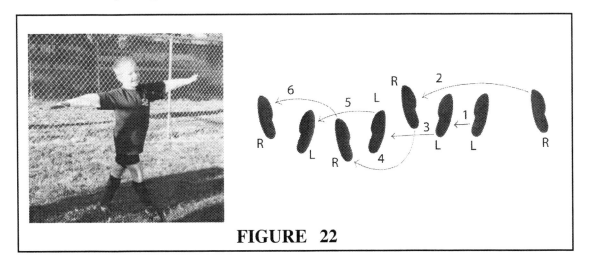

FIGURE 22

Practice

Get mom or dad to come out in the backyard with you, or down to the park where there is lots of thick grass. The thick grass will give you some cushioning in case you fall. Or you can even do this indoors. Have mom or dad stand in front of you, and both of you face each other, at about 2 or 3 yards apart. Have mom or dad do the same steps you are going to do, except they will start out to their right (a mirror image of the way you are going). Start out by both of you walking through this slowly until you learn how to move your feet, then speed up little by little until you both get better at it.

Start with your feet apart, then step to the left with your left foot. Next step to the left, with your right foot crossing over the top of your left foot. Then step again to the left, with your left foot crossing behind your right foot. Next step again to the left, with your right foot crossing behind your left foot. Then step again to the left, with your left foot over the top of your right foot. Then keep repeating this combination of steps to the left, over and over, for about 10 yards. Then stop and reverse these steps, going first to your right with your right foot, then with your left foot over your right, and so on, for about 10 yards back to the right. The better you get at doing this, you can speed the process up faster and faster. After a few weeks, you should be able to do this drill on a full run, and without falling down. A "*TIP*." If you put your arms straight out to your sides while moving, it will help you balance as you first start to do this drill. Keep working with mom or dad, and don't give up because you can learn how to do this. You should do this drill for at least five to ten minutes at a training session.

Drill No. 2- Running Backwards

The Basics are

This is called the running backwards coordination skill. This will help you just getting a better feel of the backwards and twisting movements for events like the shot put, discus and hammer throw. It will definitely help your body balance.

Practice

Find a very large backyard, a big area in a park with thick grass, or you can do this drill indoors in a big gymnasium. It's better outside in the grass though. The reason I am suggesting thick grass as a choice, it will cushion your fall a little if you accidentally fall backwards a lot when starting out. Get mom or dad to come out and help you, then both you line up side by side about

FIGURE 23

two or three yards apart, with at least about 30 yards of clear space behind you. Then both of you start running backwards while pumping your arms up and down *(SEE FIGURE 23)*. Do this for about 30 yards then stop, turn around, and repeat the drill for about 30 yards back to where you started. Usually you will fall down the first few times you try this activity. If either of you or your partner (mom or dad) fall down, laugh and make a joke out of it.

The secret for keeping your balance is raising your knees high while pumping your hands up and down as fast as you can. And once you can run fast for the 30 yards, and not fall down, your interest level will go up because you can do something your friends may not be able to do! When you do become good at this, then you can change the activity a little to make it harder. A suggestions on how to do this is run backwards about 10 or 15 yards, then have mom or dad blow a whistle, then you turn around without stopping, and run forward. Keep doing this, and change directions every 10 or 15 yards. This is one of the best skill activities for kids, that I have seen, that will really improve your running coordination and agility, and keep you from tripping over your own feet if you accidentally get turned around or tripped while running. You should do this drill for at least 10 to 15 minutes at a training session.

Drills for Controlled Falling & Field Presence

Explanation

These drills are designed to help you kids control your body, and react to falling so that you won't get hurt. No matter what running event you compete in, you should learn how to roll, jump, and control your body while falling. In any running event a competitor in front, or next to you, could fall and accidentally trip you. The more you do these drills, the more natural it will be for you to tumble, roll, or jump over a competitor if you start to fall. Repetition of these drills will make these reactions a habit (muscle memory). It may not seem important now, but if get tripped and get all skinned up, believe me you will wish you had learned how to do this.

Drill No. 3- Forward Roll (Somersaulting)
The Basics are

This is just a simple roll, or forward somersault. It is squatting down, putting your head between your legs, and rolling forward. This drill will help you to come up on your feet if you start to trip or fall. Once you master this drill, it will become a habit to you if you start to fall. This will be especially useful for cross country runners, and steeple chase runners.

Practice

Go out to the back yard, or park, where there is a heavy grass area, or go to a gym where they have tumbling pads to work on. Start out by doing this in slow motion. Stand with your feet slightly spread, and bend at your knees a little, then from your waist bend over, and put your hands on the ground. Next put your head between your legs, and just fall forward rolling over. Do this a lot in slow motion before doing it fast, especially if you are having trouble learning to do this.

After you get better at this, then do the drill from a short running start. If you are not good at this, then do the drill over and over, step by step until you do get better at it. You could jam your neck, or hurt your shoulder if you try to do this roll at a full run from the start. Make sure that you can do it naturally standing still before you ever try it at a full run. Start out your approach, at just a few steps head start, then increase the *run up distance* little by little *(SEE FIGURE 24).*

STEP 1 STEP 2

FIGURE 24

Drill No. 4- Over the Top Jumping

The Basics are

This is a jumping over someone drill. It is putting your hands on the back of someone in front of you, and propelling yourself over the top of them. This is a drill to teach you to go over the top of a competitor falling, or starting to fall, directly in front of you. Once you master this drill, it will become a habit for you if someone in front, or even slightly to the side of you, starts to fall. This will be especially useful for hurdlers, cross country runners, steeple chase runners and even distance running event competitors.

FIGURE 25

Practice

You will need a friend, about the same size as you, to practice this drill with. You will also need a thick soft grass area, in the yard or park, to work in. This is so you won't accidentally get hurt if another competitor falls near you. Have the friend stand, and bend over at the waist. Then you go behind them about two or three yards. Next start running at a medium speed, towards the back of the friend, and leap frog over the top of them.

Do this by jumping up, and placing both of your hands on the back of the friend. Then push down on their back using your hands, then swing the legs through as you vault over the top of the friends back. This may take some work with you younger kids. Or at first run slowly, put your hands down, and jump over an imaginary person until you get the feel of it. Then you can have the friend get down lower, on all fours, to make it easier for you to get over the top of them. You can speed up the running as you get better. Keep working on it until you master this drill *(SEE FIGURE 25)*.

Drill No. 5- Over the Rolling Body

The Basics are

This is a drill for jumping up and clearing a rolling body. What this does is teach you to go over the top of competitors on the ground, or rolling in front of you from the side. This will be especially useful for hurdlers, cross country runners, steeple chase runners and even distance runners.

FIGURE 26

Practice

You will need a friend, about the same size as you, to practice this drill with. You will need to find a thick soft grass area, in the yard or park, to work in. The grass is so you won't get hurt if you accidentally fall. Have the friend lay down on the ground, flat on their stomach. Then you stand about three yards to the left of the friend, and back about three yards. On the word "GO," have the friend roll over and over on the ground to their left, and straight in front of where you are standing. Also on the word "GO", you start to run slowly straight ahead. When you see the rolling friend start to pass to your right, you jump up and kick both feet backwards, then they let the friend roll underneath of you and on by. You should come down on all fours, push up with your hands, and start running forward again. The friend stops rolling, then you go back to the original starting position. Next on the word "GO," the friend starts rolling back to their right. At the same time you run forward, let the rolling friend pass underneath from your left side as you jump up and then come down on all fours. Then you Push up again, and run forward. As you get better at this drill, then always try to look straight ahead, and not look at the rolling friend. This helps you develop your peripheral vision *(SEE FIGURE 26)*.

Drills for Strength

Explanation

These drills are designed to build up your strength. They are not to build you into a muscle bound weight lifter, just enough to tone up your muscles so that you will be a little stronger. Many of you young kids these days just sit around at home a lot, and don't have a lot of chores to do as kids did years ago, possibly on a farm. And because you have very little to do with your arms like pitch hay or carry buckets of milk, your arms and legs are weak. It is important that you do some of these drills every day. If you get tired and quit for a week or two, the drills will not help you as much. Make sure you follow all breathing instructions for each drill because they are very important.

Because there are different parts of your body that need strengthening, we will break this down into the upper back, lower back, chest, shoulders, arms, abdominal, legs and how they will help you in the different events. For a good weight training program, a utility bench and a lightweight barbell set for kids would be great if your mom and dad can afford it. If not, at least get a dumbbell set. They are not that expensive. In fact you could find some work around your neighborhood and save enough to get a set of dumbells for yourself. You should start with 3.3 or 4 pound lightweight dumbbells at five years old, and work up to 6.6 or 7 pound dumbbells later.

UPPER BACK

Drill No. 6- Dumbbell Rowing
The Basics are

This exercise is pulling your hands up and down in a rowing type motion while using a dumbbell. This is good for strengthening the back of the arm muscles, the upper back, and the shoulder arm socket area. It is useful for the field event competitors such as, shot putters, discus throwers, hammer throwers, javelin throwers and pole vaulters.

Practice

Hold a dumbbell in your left hand, with the palm facing in, and to the left end of a utility bench, table or couch. Make sure the dumbbell is heavy enough for you to feel the pull on your muscles. It will depend on how old you are as to what the weight needs to be. Trial and error use

FIGURE 27

will determine the weight for you. Put your right hand on the top of the bench, table or couch, for support. Next bend forward at the hips until your back is parallel to the floor or ground and arched, with your knees bent slightly. Youir left arm with the dumbell should hang down. While in this position you pull the left arm up under your arm pit until the elbow is pointing up.

Then you lower the dumbbell slowly back down. You should feel a slight pull along the right outside of your back. This is working the Latissimus Dorsi muscles (Lats) along your back. Then turn around, switch the dumbbell to the right hand, and repeat this process. Take a deep breath just before you start to pull up, then let it out slowly as you let the dumbbell come back down. For you younger five year olds, you should do about five of these with each arm. As you get a little older and stronger you can increase this number and go to the heavier dumbbells *(SEE FIGURE 27)*.

LOWER BACK

Drill No. 7- Straight Leg Deadlift

The Basics are

This exercise is lifting up dumbbell's from the floor, by using your back and straightening up your legs. It is useful for field event competitors such as shot putters, discus throwers, hammer throwers, javelin throwers, high jumpers, long jumpers, triple jumpers and pole vaulters.

Practice

Stand straight up with a dumbbell in each hand, and with your palms facing your stomach. Your knees should be bent, with your legs about shoulder width apart. Next lower the dumbbells by bending over, using only your back and NOT your arms. Keep the dumbbells close to youir shins, and your head should be looking up and not down. Then you raise up, bringing the dumbbell's up, by straightening your legs and using your back. While you are doing this your hips should be moving forwards. Take a deep breath just as you start to bend down, then let it out slowly as you come back up to the straight up position. For you five year olds, start out with about five of these lifts, then increase the number later as you get stronger and older *(SEE FIGURE 28)*.

FIGURE 28

Drill No. 8- Back Extension (Superman)

The Basics are

This exercise is laying down, extending both the hands and the legs, then raising the feet and the hands up slightly off the floor or ground. It is useful for the field event competitors such as, shot putters, discus throwers, hammer throwers, javelin throwers, high jumpers, long jumpers, triple jumpers and pole vaulters. It is also useful for steeplechaser's.

Practice

Lay down on your stomach on a floor or flat surface, with both arms straight out in front of you. Face your palms down, and your legs straight out behind you. Next pull in your abdominal muscles, like you would be creating a small space between your stomach and the floor or ground. Then lift both arms and legs, just a few inches up off the floor. Hold that position for about five seconds.

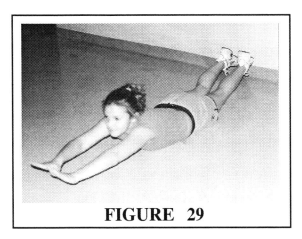
FIGURE 29

While doing this, you need to stretch out in front and in back as much as you can. Then lower the arms and legs slowly. Take a deep breath just as you lift up your arms and legs, then let it out slowly as you lower them. You should start out doing about five of these, then increase the number a little each time as you get older and stronger *(SEE FIGURE 29).*

CHEST

Drill No. 9- Chest Press

The Basics are

This exercise is for pressing, or pushing, up dumbbell's in each hand. This helps you build up your upper body chest strength. It is useful for the field event competitors such as shot putters, discus throwers, hammer throwers, and javelin throwers. It is also useful for pole vaulters.

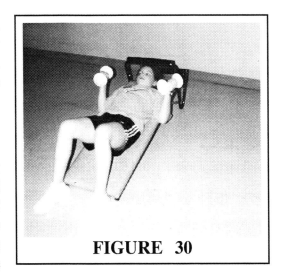
FIGURE 30

Practice

Lay down on some type of utility bench, or even on a mat, with a dumbbell in each hand, and with your feet on the floor, knees bent *(SEE FIGURE 30).* Then push both of your arms up directly over your shoulders, with your palms facing forward, and arms extended. Next bring the dumbbells back down slowly to your sides, with your elbows just a little lower than your shoulders. Then push the dumbbells back up again. While doing this you should pull in your stomach abdominal muscles, but don't push your back into the flat surface. All during the press, your shoulder blades should not raise up off the bench. Start out with five year olds doing about five of these, up through 12 year olds doing about 10. Take a deep breath before you push the dumbbells up, then let it out slowly as you bring your arms back down. For you 9 to 12 year olds, if you do have a barbell set, you can substitute the barbell weight for the equivalent dumbbells weight. I don't advise the barbells, for you little kids because it might be to much weight for you to handle. You can use barbells when you are a little bit older. You can do a few more repetitions also once you get a little bit older and stronger

SHOULDERS

Drill No. 10- The Shoulder Shrug

The Basics are

This is lifting or shrugging up dumbbell's in each hand, from a hanging down position up to the shoulder position. This helps you build up your upper body shoulder strength. It is useful for field event competitors such as shot putters, discus throwers, hammer throwers, javelin throwers, high jumpers, long jumpers, triple jumpers, and pole vaulters.

FIGURE 31

Practice:

Stand straight up, with your feet about shoulder width apart, and with a dumbbell in each hand. Your arms should hang straight down, turned with the palms facing your stomach in front of your thighs. Tuck in your chin towards your chest, and pull in your abdominal muscles. Youir knees should be relaxed. Next shrug (pull up) your shoulders up towards your ears, then slowly lower your shoulders back down to the arms hanging down position. Take a deep breath, just before you shrug and pull up your shoulders, then let it back out slowly as you lower your shoulders. Start out with you five year olds doing about five of these, up through the 12 year olds doing 10 of these. You can do a few more of these once you get a little older and stronger *(SEE FIGURE 31).*

Drill No. 11- Shoulder Front Raise

The Basics are

This is lifting up dumbbell's in each hand, from a hanging down position, to a straight out from the shoulders position. It is useful for the field event competitors such as, shot putters, javelin throwers, and especially hammer and discus throwers.

Practice

Stand straight up, with your feet about shoulder width apart, and with a dumbbell in each hand. Your arms should hang straight down, turned with the palms facing the stomach in front of youir thighs. Pull in your abdominal muscles, and have your knees relaxed. Next raise your right arm straight out in front of you, to about shoulder height, hold it there for five seconds, and then slowly lower it back down to the arm hanging position.

Take a deep breath just before you raise your arm, hold it, then let it out slowly as you lower your arm. Next you repeat the process with your left arm. Start out with you five year olds doing about five of these with each arm, up through 12 year olds doing about eight with each arm. You can do a few more of these once you get a little older and stronger *(SEE FIGURE 32)*.

FIGURE 32

ARMS

Drill No. 12- Wrist Curl

The Basics are

This exercise is rolling (lifting) up a dumbbell using your wrist, from the down position to the up position. It is useful for all starting block runners, relay runners, shot putters, discus throwers, hammer throwers, javelin throwers, and also pole vaulters.

Practice

Lifting weight should not hurt you if you don't over do it with too much weight. This drill should improve your wrist strength. Start with you five year olds using two 3.3 or 4 pound dumbbells, and then work up to 6.6 or 7 pound dumbbells as you get stronger and older. Its not so much the amount of the weight, but you are working your muscles and tendons. This drill can be done inside or outside of the house. Start by sitting on the edge of a utility bench, chair, or couch. Next spread your legs apart, then take the dumbbell in your right hand. Put your right elbow on the top of your right knee.

Next take your left hand, and use it to hold down your right hand right at the wrist *(SEE FIGURE 33)*. Start with your right palm facing up, then curl the dumbbell down towards the floor using your fingers, then back up again. Hold in the up position for five seconds. You five year olds should do this about five times with your right wrist, then switch to the left wrist reversing the positions, for about five times. 12 year olds should

FIGURE 33

start out doing about 10 of these with each wrist. As you get stronger, you can increase the number of repetitions with each wrist. Caution, do NOT over do it with too many repetitions, and hurt your wrist. If you are not strong enough at first, then reduce the number of repetitions and the weight until you get stronger. To judge how strong you are at first, make this observation, you should be just barely able to do the last curl lift, on each set, for each wrist. And last, take a deep breath and hold it just before you start on the upward curl motion, and then letting it out slowly as you move your wrist back to the down position.

Drill No. 13- Biceps Curl

The Basics are

This exercise is lifting up a dumbbell from the down position to the up position. It is useful for all starting block runners, relay runners, shot putters, discus throwers, hammer throwers, javelin throwers, and pole vaulters.

Practice

Stand straight up, with your feet about shoulder width apart, and with a dumbbell in each hand. Then let your arms hang down at your thighs, with your palms facing in. Next you pull in your abdominal muscles and stand up straight, with your knees slightly relaxed. Start by curling up your right arm to your shoulder, with the barbell just touching your shoulder at the top of the movement. Next you slowly lower your arm back down to the starting position.

FIGURE 34

Then repeat the same process with your left arm. You 5 year olds should do about four of these with each arm if you can, and you 12 year olds doing about eight with each arm. If you 10 to 12 year olds have a light weight barbell set, you can substitute it to do your curls. Caution, don't put too much weight on the barbell that will keep you from easily doing at least eight curls. You can do a few more when you get a little older or stronger. Take a deep breath, just before you start to curl up the dumbbell, or barbell, and let it out slowly as you start on the downward motion to lower your arm *(SEE FIGURE 34).*

ABDOMINALS

Drill No. 14- Sit Up Crunches

The Basics are

This exercise is just partially sitting up from a lying down on your back position, with your knees bent. It is for all competitors because at some time or another you will use those abdominal muscles in an event.

Practice

Lay down on the floor or ground on your back, with both knees bent up about 10 to 12 inches high, feet flat on the floor or ground. Then fold both arms together across your chest. Next raise up just enough to get your neck, and the top of your shoulders, off the floor or ground a little bit. Hold it there for seven seconds, then slowly lower back down to the lying position. Each time, just before you raise up, take a deep breath and hold it for about five seconds while you are in the raised up position. Then let it out slowly as you come back down into the lying position. For you five year olds, you should do about seven of these. For you 12 year olds, do about 15. If you can't do that many, then do as many as you can without struggling. Then increase the number a little each time as you get older and stronger *(SEE FIGURE 35)*.

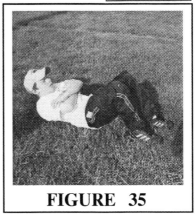

FIGURE   35

LEGS, TOES, ANKLES

Drill No. 15- Toe Raise
The Basics are

    This exercise is raising way up on your toes and holding that position for a few seconds, to strengthen the lower legs, toes, and ankles. It is for all competitors because at some time you will use your feet and ankles.

Practice

    Stand up straight with your feet about shoulder width apart, and arms out at your sides for balance. Then you raise up on your toes as high as you can go. Hold that position for five seconds. Then come slowly back down to the starting position. Five year olds should start out doing about five of these, with 12 year olds doing about eight. Increase the number of repetitions by a few as they get older and stronger. Take a deep breath before you start to push up, then let it out slowly as you come back down to the standing position *(SEE FIGURE 36)*.

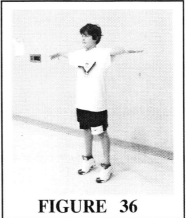

FIGURE   36

Drill No. 16- Cone Jumping
The Basics are

    This exercise is standing at one end of a line of cones, then jump hopping over each one through to the end of the row. This improves on your ability to get out of the starting blocks quicker. It is for all competitors because at some time you will use your legs to propel you in some event.

Practice

    This is another alternative drill to strengthen your thigh and leg muscles. This is safer for you younger kids than running the stairs. This should help give you more leg strength for any of the

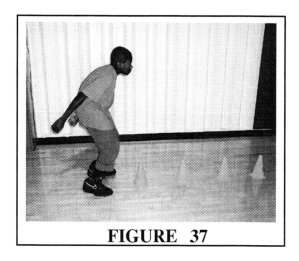

FIGURE 37

running and jumping events. It's worked for me. First you get a set of six of the nine inch tapered orange cones that are available in many stores now. And they are not that expensive. Set them out in a row, spaced at about 18 to 24 inches apart, depending on your size. Stand at one end right in front of the first cone, and face the row. Now hop, landing with both feet together, over each cone all the way through to the end of the row. This is *a core training drill.*

The object is for you to jump up as high as you can, and go all the way through to the end of the row as quickly as you can *(SEE FIGURE 37)*. Now on the way back turn around and hop all the way through, landing on both feet each time. Focus on going through each time jumping higher and faster than you did the last time. Try to do one set of down and back every other day if possible. Then you will notice how much quicker you are becoming.

THIGHS

Drill No. 17- Wall Sits
The Basics are

This exercise is to strengthen the quadriceps (front thigh), and also the hamstrings, gluteal (buttocks), and back muscles. It is for all competitors because at some time or another you will use these muscles in a track and field event.

Practice

Stand next to a wall, then put both feet about shoulder width apart and about 1-1/2 feet out in front of you. Put both hands up, and out to your sides, palms up, then your back slides down the wall until your thighs are parallel to the floor. Take a deep breath before you slide down the wall,

FIGURE 38

then hold the down position for at least ten seconds. Let me point out that you should slide down the wall far enough, to feel a tightening in your front and back thigh muscles. Then as you straighten back up to the starting position, you slowly expel the air, then they relax for half a minute or so.

Start out by doing about 3 or 5 of these. If you are a large boy or girl, still carrying a lot of baby fat, you may not be able to do that many. In that case start out with the most you can easily do, without struggling too much, then increase the number as you get older and stronger *(SEE FIGURE 38)*.

46

Drill No. 18- Stair Climbing

The Basics are

This is an exercise is to strengthen the thigh and leg muscles using an ordinary wall. It is for all competitors because at some time or another you will use these muscles in a track and field event.

Practice

Find some steps somewhere convenient, maybe a nearby high school stadium after school, or a three or four story building someplace nearby. You can try this several ways. One, is hit each stair with one foot then the next step with the other foot. This developes quick feet while building leg strength and endurance. Another way is, both feet step on one step. This will help your coordination and develop quick feet also. The last way is, run up the steps two at a time. This will lengthen your stride abilities. You can run down the stairs in the same ways. It will help in developing a different area of the quadricep muscle. Running up, and down, the stairs is effective in developing all four quadricep muscles. A note of *caution*. If you are under 11 years old DO NOT use this drill. Either your mom or dad, a coach, or adult, should be there at all times while you run the stairs in case you accidentally fall. You could be seriously hurt and no one would be around to help you.

General Drills for Running

Drill No. 19- Wind Sprint Ladders Running (Suicides)

The Basics are

This exercise is for running out to a set distance, touching down, and going back to the starting point. Then touching down at the starting point, and running out to a the next longer distance, touching down, and running back to the starting point. The distance you run out keeps increasing as you touch the starting point *(SEE FIGURE 39)*. This drill is for all competitors because at some time or another you will need to use quickness and endurance in a track event.

Practice

If you don't have a football field close by, with white yard line markers, this will take a little work to set up. *Beware*, before you even start this drill, jog around then yard for two to three minutes to get your muscles properly warmed up. Next, since this is an explosive type drill, do at least eight to ten hamstring and calf stretches *(SEE EXERCISE 15, 20)* to keep you from getting hurt by pulling a muscle. To make the yard line markers, try using old white plastic milk bottles filled with sand, kitty litter, or water, to weight it down.

Mom or dad can probably help you on this. Take a wide tip black felt permanent marker, and mark 0, 10, 20, 30, 40, on the milk bottles in great

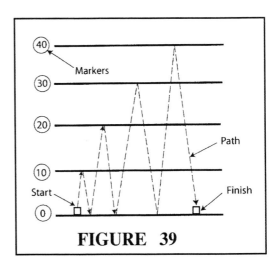

FIGURE 39

big letters. They make great yard markers, and you are "recycling" for the environment. Next estimate, or measure out a 40 yard distance. Put one bottle, marked "0", down at the starting point. Then go down about 40 yards, and put another one down marked "40". Now in your mind divide the distance between the two bottles into 4 equal spaces, of about 10 yards long. Then go out from the start 10 yards, put down the bottle marked "10", then out another 10 yards and put down the bottle marked "20", then 10 more yards and the bottle marked 30. Now you have a 40 yard course set out for running ladders.

Here is how ladders work. Go to the starting point. On the command "GO," from mom or dad, you charge out straight ahead at full sprint for 10 yards, then you stop quickly and touch either hand down on the ground, turn and sprint back to the starting line. You will know when you have gone 10 yards, by looking over at the milk bottle. And always looking over at the milk bottles will tell you about where to touch down. Now, at the starting point, you stop again, quickly touch either hand down, then turn and sprint out to the 20 yard marker. Again you touch down, then turn quickly and run all the way back to the starting point. Then you touch down again, turn, and sprint out to the 30 yard marker. Then you touch down again, turn, and run back to the starting point. In other words you will be increasing the distance you run, by 10 yards, each time you touch down at the starting point. The last time you will be sprinting the whole 40 yards, then touching down, and sprinting back the 40 yards to the starting point. Try to do at least one set of these, every time you practice this drill. Later on if you can do more than one set, and you are not too tired, its OK.

Drill No. 20- Speed Burst Running for Quickness
The Basics are

This exercise is explode out sprinting to a set distance, stopping and walking back to the marker. Resting for a few seconds, then explode out sprinting back to the starting point. Next resting at the starting point for a few seconds, then explode sprinting out to the next longer distance. Then resting again, and explode sprinting back to the starting point. The distance you run out keeps increasing as you explode run out from the starting point. The distance you run for this drill can be tailored to specific training needs (20-30-40 yards) depending on your age. Also if you can find a gradually sloping hill with a reasonable incline, this drill can be run up hill to develop even better lung capacity, and endurance. After you have been doing this drill for a while, you can speed up the drill and further improve on your quickness. The beauty of this drill is when you run in your first meet, and you see how fast you have become when compared to the other kids your own age, then you will feel good about all the work you did on this excercise. It is for all competitors because at some time or another you will all need to use quickness and endurance. But it is especially good for sprinters, relay runners, and all the jumping events competitors.

Practice

This is a special quickness, and endurance, running drill. It is called speed bursts. It is a drill that is somewhat like ladders *(SEE FIGURE 39)*. There are several variations, but I like this one best for young boys or girls. I have always ended up coaching the littlest kids, so that's why I am recommending this drill to you, and because I know it works. ***Beware*** before you ever start this drill, jog around the yard or park a few times, to get your muscles warmed up properly. Next do at least four or five hamstring and calf stretches. This is to keep you from possibly getting hurt with a bad muscle pull. Start off by marking a 20 yard coarse similar to the one in Drill No.19 *(SEE FIGURE 39)*, except put your yard markers at five yard intervals instead of ten yards apart. When you have your course marked, then go to the starting point of yard "0". On the command "GO," you explode out from the starting line. Then you sprint as fast as you can for five yards while pumping your knees, and hands, up and down as high as you can.

Then at the five yard marker, stop and catch your breath, turn, and walk back to the five yard marker. Next take a minute to rest, then say "GO," and sprint as fast as you can back to the "0" yard marker. Then you turn, and walk back to the "0" yard marker while catching your breath. Then stand there at the "0" yard marker, and rest a minute. Then say "Go," and you sprint out to the ten yard marker the same way and stop, then turn, and come back to the ten yard marker. Rest a minute, then say "GO," and run back to the "0" yard marker. You keep doing this until you get all the way out to the last yard marker and back to "0," going five yards more each time. Make sure you pump your hands up and down, and get your knees up as high as you can.

If you get too tired, stop the drill until you can build up your stamina enough to get all the way through one complete set. This drill will be very tough, on boys or girls that are big for their age, or overweight, so be patient and keep working. If you are having trouble, then try going just a little bit farther each day or week as you see that your endurance is building up. One time through the whole 20-40 yards once a day should be more than enough if you are only five years old. That would be a big accomplishment, for even the best of five year olds.

Drill No. 21- Indian Runs

The Basics are

This drill is a very different way to run laps. Basically a group of four or more runners get in a "single file line," then start to jog slowly around the track. Then the runner in the back of the group sprints to the front of the group. Next, after about 15-20 yards, the new back runner sprints to the front of the group. And all the way around the track the back runner keeps leap frogging around the others to the front about every 15 -20 yards *(SEE FIGURE 40)*. This will make your laps running not such a drudgery, and it helps develop your running endurance. It is for all competitors, but it especially helps longer distance runners and cross country runners. It also really helps five to eight year olds build up their running endurance.

Practice

To do this drill you will need to find a 1/4 mile oval track someplace, possibly at a high school near you. Also sometimes your local "YMCA" has an oval track you might use. You will need to find at least three of your friends to help out. All four of you start to jog *SLOWLY* around the track in single file, at about two arms distance apart.

As soon as you get down the track about 20 yards or so, the runner at the back of the line (original No.4) sprints as fast as they can around all the other runners and takes the leader position in front of the group. Then the whole group slowly keeps

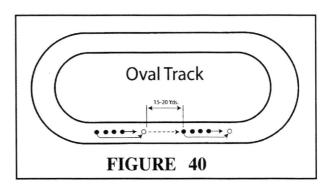

FIGURE 40

jogging single file for about 20 more yards. Then the next runner in the back of the group (original No. 3) sprints to the front of the group. The group slowly jogs about another 20 yards. Then the back runner (original No. 2) sprints to the front. Followed by the back runner (original No. 1) sprinting to the front after about another 20 yards. Then it starts all over again. And this keeps going on this way all the way around the track until the number of laps you are running is over. Remember though when you get to the front just jog, do not run fast.

SPRINTING

Explanation

Sprinting is a special kind of running. In youth track & field sprinting means the 50m, 100m, 200m, and 400m races. For you younger kids it means only the 50m and the 100m. Not everyone is a natural sprinter. You need to learn how to be very quick to get out of the starting line or blocks. Good sprinters usually have very large well developed strong legs, from the waist down. You also need to learn how to "lean" right at the finish line. Learning the best way how to come out of the starting line is very important. There is more than one way! To continue to develop, you need to work on **Drill No. 18 Stair Climbing**, **Drill No. 20 Speed Burst Running and Drill No. 16 Cone Jumping.** Sprints are an anaerobic activity. Because you run all out, and at full speed when sprinting, you need to develop your anaerobic endurance capacity. Sprinters also need to learn how to run at top speed while staying as relaxed and smooth as possible.

This is more mental than physical. It means staying focused from start to finish of a race. Since the track & field and cross country season is very short in some parts of the USA because of the weather, you need to work three or four months ahead of time on your techniques training.

FIGURE 41

Concentrate on basic sprinting technique, and learning how to relax while sprinting. **Before** you attempt to do any explosive sprinting, make sure you get properly warmed up, and stretch out your "hamstring" and "calf" muscles. Begin each training session with light easy running, then flexibility exercises, then fast striding, short sprints, and last practice starts. Properly warming up is very important when the weather is cold, to prevent injury to your muscles.

Here is an idea to practice starting. Have mom or dad help you to make what is called a "starting clapper" **(SEE FIGURE 41)**. It is made up of two boards hinged at the base, with half of a black and white disk attached to each board. In the center of each board is a handle. Mom or dad or whoever starts you will use the handles to grab the boards. The "crack" of the boards when they are brought together gives a sound similar to a "starting pistol." Also when brought together the black and white halves of the disk form a visual signal for starting stopwatches. If possible have mom or dad get you a good stop watch to accurately keep track of your times.

Drill No. 22- Accelerating out of the Starting Line
The Basics are
The Starters Commands

There are 3 positions to starting a race at the starting line. They are *"on your mark," "get set,"* and *"the sound of the starting pistol."* In the ***"On your mark"*** position command you will get down in a runners stance down position with both feet in on the ground, in starting blocks, or in a stand up start that some young kids use. When you are in the down position, you are relaxed and your back is down. Your head and butt are down, and your mind is focusing on the start. Arms are shoulder width apart. Shoulders are rotated forward. Your hands are down, and fingers just touching the back edge of the starting line. The thumb and fingers form a "Vee" ***(SEE FIGURE 42)***. The power (stronger) leg drives from in front. It is usually 1-3/4 to 2 of the competitors foot lengths from the starting line. To find out which is your strongest (power) leg ***SEE DRILL NO.44***. Your back foot can be anywhere from "0" to 1-1/2 of your foot lengths behind your front foot, depending on your size and age.

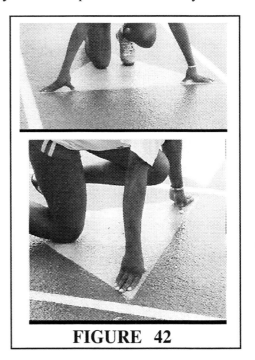

FIGURE 42

On the command *"**Get set**"* your seat (butt) is raised up, and you lean forward. At this point the angle of your leading leg is about 90 degrees, at the knee, to the ground. You are coiled like a spring, with your body weight equally supported by your arms and legs. Your head is forward and towards the ground, your mind is focused on hearing the starting gun. Your shoulders are just a little ahead of your hands. At this point you take a deep breath, and hold it.

When you hear the ***"gun go off,"*** the front leg pushes off and extends. The back leg drives out as hard as possible with an explosive step move. Your body is still leaning forward. You stay low and swing or thrust the arm on your lead foot side forward and stretched out far as hard as possible. There are basically three foot positions for starting ***(SEE FIGURE 43)***. Which position you choose will depend on the length of your legs, and what you are comfortable with.

Foot Positioning

The elongated position (No.1) is mostly used by sprinters with long legs. The bunched position (No.3) is mostly used by sprinters with short legs. The medium position (No.2) is for everyone in between. Starting blocks are adjustable if you use them. So you might have to use some trial and error to get the most advantageous foot positions. Notice the foot lengths

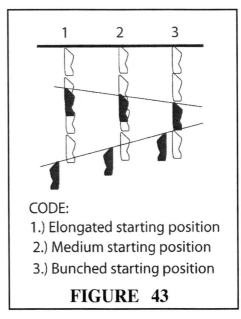

CODE:
1.) Elongated starting position
2.) Medium starting position
3.) Bunched starting position

FIGURE 43

back for your guide. Once you figure out your foot positions in the blocks, make a mental note and mark your blocks. Many of you beginning kids may be coached to use the standing start now *(SEE FIGURE 58)* because it takes less leg strength and it's just easier for you. However, it is not the fastest sprint start.

Positioning of Starting Blocks

Even though you may not be using starting blocks yet, you should know how to use them. They are not that hard to use. You just need to know how to use them. The hands and feet are basically positioned using the same technique as the down "runners" start. The difference is how

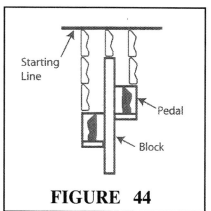

FIGURE 44

do you place the "blocks," and how do you get into them. Place the front of the blocks rail one foot length from the starting line *(SEE FIGURE 44)*. As a starting place put the front pedal two foot lengths from the starting line. Place the rear or back pedal three foot lengths from the starting line. Or you can place the front pedal 1-1/2 to 2 foot lengths, and the rear pedal 2-1/2 to 3 foot lengths. It's going to depend on whether you have long or short legs *(SEE FIGURE 43)*. If you have short legs you can start in the 1-1/2 foot length position.

Determining Foot Placement

You will need to make adjustments from these starting positions when you find your exact placement comfort zone. As you grow older each year, these positions may change a little because of your new size. Now put both your knees down on the track as close to the starting line as you can without touching it. Bend your knees to 90 degrees. Next get down on all fours with you body extended over the starting line, hands out in front. The hands will be out about 1-1/2 to 2 feet in front of the starting line. Keep your hands directly under your shoulders, and your toes are curled under. Place the blocks down if not already there. Put your power foot in the front block. Mark it's position. All of this placement starts by keeping your knees in the same spot. Now you have your "power foot" placement marked. Adjust the pedal to your foot placement if necessary, and lock it down.

To determine the rear foot placement, stay on all fours after marking the power foot location. Now stand up and measure one foot (12 inches) back from your power foot. Make a mark. That's where your back foot is placed. Adjust the pedal to your foot if necessary, and lock

FIGURE 45

it down. Now measure the placement of both toes with respect to the starting line. Why are you doing all this? When you travel for competition the starting blocks may be different. However, now you will know how to adjust and set the starting blocks to always be just about the same place you want them. Some are a little different, but they all adjust.

Getting Into the Blocks

After you have your blocks set, stand up and walk a little behind them. Shake both legs to keep them loose. Wait for the command while standing behind your blocks. When the starter starts the first command, jump up high with both heels to your butt two times with some intensity (flicks). This starts firing up your muscular and neurological system. Now go up and place your hands on the track, to make the adjustments with you feet. When the starter says, "On your mark," you extend and shake out your power foot again, then place it in the front pedal, heels off the pedal, toes curled and touching the track. Shake out the back leg and place it in the pedal. Now you are ready *(SEE FIGURE 45)*.

Practice

To practice this drill you will need mom or dad to purchase you some good track shoes. Maybe for your Birthday or Christmas. You can get some starting blocks when you get a little older. Why? You need good traction on coming out of the starting line position! Before actually getting in the starting position, there are several good drills to prepare you to reach your maximum ability to explode out. These are known as "plyometric" or jump-training type drills. Some are in the warm up or submaximal plyometric category, and some are full plyometric.

The first one is the *"LEANING DRILL."* This is a submaximal warm up type drill. You will need to some kind of a line, on the ground, for you to come up to. Maybe it's some tape, or a string, down on a non dirt track, or just a line scratched on a dirt track. This is so you can get your toes right up on a line. Lean forward as far as you can, without stumbling, then begin sprinting for only about five to ten yards. Then stop, come back to the line and do it again. Keep your knees driving straight forward when you start to run. Learn to drive out hard with your legs, and lift your knees as high as possible. Then lift your elbows as high as possible to the rear, with each arm swing. This works for both the "standing" and the "down" on two hands start. Do this five times, or more, each day if possible *(SEE FIGURE 46)*. I call these "lean outs."

| STEP 1 | STEP 2 | STEP 3 |

FIGURE 46

The second drill is called *"TOUCH the GROUND DRILL."* This is a submaximal warm up type drill. You will probably need to find a track someplace to work on this drill. Start out jogging slowly in a straight line. On mom or dads or your own signal of "touch," you bend down and touch the ground with both hands, for just a few seconds to simulate the "set position." Then you immediately pop up and sprint for 10 -15 yards. After that you continue to jog slowly on around the track until you hear or you say "touch," then you repeat the 2 part process again of touching and sprinting *(SEE FIGURE 47)*. Keep doing this all the way around the track, for at least one lap (about 400 meters). I call these "touch downs."

STEP 1   STEP 2   STEP 3   STEP 4
FIGURE 47

The third drill is called the "*JUMP and TOUCH DRILL.*" This is a regular plyometric drill. You will probably need to find a track someplace to work on this drill. Start out jogging slowly in a straight line. On mom or dads or your own signal of "jump," you make a small jump in the air and rotate 180 degrees to your rear. The drop down, with both hands on the ground, into the "set position" for a few seconds. Then you immediately pop up and sprint for 10 - 15 yards. Then you go back to jogging until you hear or say "jump" again. At which time you repeat the whole three step process all over again *(SEE FIGURE 48)*. Keep doing this all the way around the track, for at least one lap (about 400 Meters). I call these "pop up touches."

STEP 1   STEP 2   STEP 3   STEP 4
FIGURE 48

The forth drill is getting in the down position, with or without blocks, or in the standing position and practicing your start. Get into your position, and get your feet adjusted. Then have mom or dad say "on your mark" *(SEE FIGURE 49-A & B or 58-A)*, then say "get set" *(SEE FIGURE 49-C or 58-A)*. As you go through each position, have mom or dad check that your body is positioned correctly. At this point mom or dad would clap the "starting clappers" for you. Then you need to explode out low and sprint for 10 -15 yards *(SEE FIGURE 49- D & E)*. Then come back an do it again. If you have access to an oval track (your high school), then practice starting on a curve as well as the straightaway. This is because some of the longer sprints are started on a curve, and you need to get the feel of running on the curve. If you are already a sprinter you should do at least six of the starts a day if possible, with half of them on a curve if available.

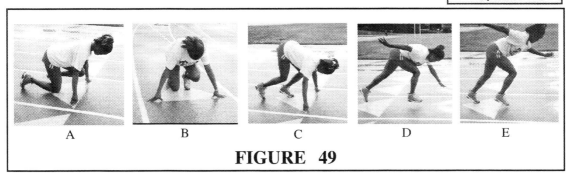

A   B   C   D   E

FIGURE 49

Drill No. 23- Middle of the Race

The Basics are

The middle of the race technique is also very important. Once you have come up out of the starting line, and you have ran four or five strides, you should be sprinting at top speed. Learn how to run on the balls of your feet *(SEE FIGURE 50)*. The upper body can be straight up, or leaning forward slightly *(SEE FIGURE 48, STEP 4 & FIGURE 50)*. It just depends on which style you are most comfortable with. The arm swing should be straight ahead in the direction of the run, with the elbows driven way up high on the back swing *(SEE FIGURE 50)*. *Not* across your body from side to side like a washing machine. Your front, or strongest leg, should be extended and driving with the knee lifted to a horizontal position *(SEE*

FIGURE 50

FIGURE 50). The facial muscles, hands, and shoulders should be relaxed. Your line of vision should be straight ahead, *not* side to side. The body should be leaning inward slightly, when running the curve. Focus on keeping your head as still as possible, and staying in the middle of your lane.

Practice

To practice the middle of the race technique, you can work in a large back yard, park, or on an oval track. The track is preferable because it has curves. There are several good submaximal (preparetory) "plyometric" drills to prepare you to reach your maximum sprinting ability during the middle of the race.

STEP 1   STEP 2   STEP 3

FIGURE 51

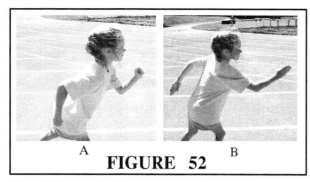
FIGURE 52

The first one is "*HIGH KNEE MARCHING.*" Start out by slowly marching forward. On each step you take, you raise your knees up to the horizontal position. And as you step, you push up hard on their toes. The arms work straight ahead, forward and backward, *not* across the body *(SEE FIGURE 51)*. The hands can be extended straight, or in a fist just for this exercise. Some runners do make a fist with their hands, but I am *NOT* recommending it. Usually the fist means you are pressing, and are not relaxed while running *(SEE FIGURE 52-A)*. The extended hand and fingers position may also be much better, aerodynamically speaking, for moving down the track *(SEE FIGURE 52-B)*.

A variation of this drill is "*HIGH KNEE MARCHING with LOWER LEG EXTENSION.*" The difference is the lower leg is extended after the thigh is raised to the horizontal position. To start lift up your right thigh to the horizontal position, then kick and extend the lower part of the right leg. Next they bring the leg back down to the ground. Then you relax and step forward normally with the left leg. Then they repeat this again with the right leg. Do about four or five of these with the right leg. Then turn around and repeat the same action, but lift the left leg, step, and repeat all the way back to the starting point. This should give them about four or five times with each leg *(SEE FIGURE 53)*.

STEP 1   STEP 2   STEP 3
FIGURE 53

The second one is "*HIGH KNEE SKIPPING with LOWER LEG EXTENSION.*" This is going to be hard for little kids to do it right. What you need to do is make one repetition, then rest. The skipping action is similar to skipping a rope. Except instead of walking as in the first drill, you do the right leg action followed by the left leg action (a 1-2), then rest, all in a skipping motion *(SEE FIGURE 54)*. Then repeat again once with each leg, then rest again. The action is the same as the marching with the knee lift, then lower leg kick extension. The concentration and focus is on the leg action though and not your arms. So don't worry to much at first with what your arms are doing. You should do a total of about four or five of these two leg sequences at a session. Add your arm action after you have mastered the leg action. Try to get in a rhythm of "up and extend," "up and extend." If you get strong enough, you can do more repetitions at a time without resting. Go slow at first, don't wear yourself out on this.

STEP 1 STEP 2 STEP 3 STEP 4

FIGURE 54

A variation of this is, do the same drill at a slow run, instead of walking. Set up your rhythm by doing this running in place. Then when your rhythm gets going, move forward at a slow jogging pace. Increase the speed of your leg movement as you get better at this.

The third one is *"SEAT (BUTT) KICKING"*. Move slowly forward in a straight line. Then kick up your heels to the rear, and attempt to hit your buttocks, first with one leg then the other *(SEE FIGURE 55)*. Start by running slowly in place, and kicking up your heels nice and easy. Don't worry about making contact, just start to move slowly forward kicking up your heels higher as you go. Then concentrate and focus on getting the heels up to your buttocks. Do this for about 10-15 yards, then stop, turn around and repeat all the way back to the starting point. Once all the way through this sequence at a session, should be good enough for you young kids. As you get stronger, you can do more.

FIGURE 55

The fourth drill is *"SITTING ARM EXTENSION"* movements. What this does is get you used to moving your arms in the correct way (muscle memory). Sit down, extend both legs together out in front of you, your head is looking straight ahead. Now extend your fingers out on both hands *(SEE FIGURE 52-B)* and start a pumping piston like action with both hands going back and forth. Just like running, but sitting still on the ground or floor *(SEE FIGURE 56)*. Do this for about one or two minutes, then rest your arms. Then do another one to two minute set of these.

Last running short *"TEN YARD SPEED BURSTS"* going up a hill, will also help you build up your endurance for middle of the race sprinting. The plyometric "long stride bounding drill" *(SEE FIGURE 90)* used by the high jumpers also will help you with the middle part of the race.

FIGURE 56

Drill No. 24- Finish of the Race

The Basics are

The finish is basically all in your technique and form. The position of the CHEST when thrust forward (lean) at the tape is very important. That is the part of the body that is observed going across the line first, not your hands or your feet. The other technique is learn to focus, then continue sprinting two or three yards beyond the finish line. A good technique for this is visualize in your mind, the finish line as two or three yards beyond the actual finish line itself.

Practice

To practice your lean at the finish line, you will need to set up a string or tape across two points. However, make sure it is something that will break or fall away when you pass through it. You need to also mark a line or use cones as a marker, about two or three yards past the finish line. This is so that you will get used to running to that point past the tape every time. Then go out about 15 - 20 yards out in front of the line, and start sprinting towards it. Getting the lean at just the right time is really a timing problem. You don't want to start your lean too soon, or it may slow you

FIGURE   57

down a little. The best thing to do is before you start your sprint, walk through your lean right in front of the tape. Stand back about 1/2 yard away from the tape. Then lift your left leg, and lean into the tape or string (just there for practice). Then take a couple of steps forward, and then go back and do it again. Line yourself up with mom or dad or friends holding a string, then have the string holders watch to see you are doing it correctly *(SEE FIGURE 57)*.

When you have mastered the technique, then go back and practice sprinting towards the tape. Make sure you are continuing to run past the finish line tape to the marked line, without slowing down. You must learn to do this so that your speed will not be reduced as you pass the finish line. Then when you have practiced all three parts of the sprint race, then run the full distance, and have mom or dad time you with a "stopwatch." Make sure whoever times you, to be sure and click the stop watch just as the front of your torso (chest) crosses the plain of the finish line *(SEE FIGURE 57)*.

Note:
DO NOT lean to soon. Start your lean about a yard to a half yard before the finish line

Check *TABLE 1* to see some comparison performance times for you to achieve in order to be competitive. The main records are "*American outdoor*" youth track & field records, but we have also added the local "*CYC*" and national "*CYO*" records for a comparison.

COMPARISON PERFORMANCE TIMES - SPRINTS

BOYS		DISTANCE							
Age Division		50m	Record	100m	Record	200m	Record	400m	Record
6 - 8 (Primary)	Satisfactory	10.0		18.0	*□16.09	32.0	△30.40	1:30.0	*☆1:09.18
	Good	9.0	△9.87	16.0	*☆14.25	31.0	*☆28.93	1:10.0	△1:07.42
	Excellent	8.0	*□7.31	15.0	13.73	30.0	28.43	1:06.0	1:05.90
9-10 (Bantam) (Roadrunner)	Satisfactory			15.0	#14.02	30.0	#29.94	1:08.0	#1:06.52
	Good			14.0	*12.96	28.0	*27.18	1:04.0	*1:03.37
	Excellent		N/A	13.0	12.71	27.0	25.83	59.80	58.76
11-12 (Midget) (Cub)	Satisfactory			14.7	#12.34	28.5	#25.54	1:06.0	#1:00.03
	Good			12.7	*12.15	26.5	*25.03	58.6	*57.56
	Excellent		N/A	12.0	11.7	25.5	23.74	57.6	52.90
13-14 (Youth) (Cadet)	Satisfactory			14.0	#11.74	27.0	*&24.53	58.0	*&56.09
	Good			12.4	*$11.5	24.5	#23.64	54.0	#54.04
	Excellent		N/A	11.4	10.94	23.5	21.84	52.0	47.16
GIRLS		DISTANCE							
Age Division		50m	Record	100m	Record	200m	Record	400m	Record
6 - 8 (Primary)	Satisfactory	11.0		18.0	*□16.90	35 0	△33.89	1:30.0	△1:19.09
	Good	9.0	△9.49	16.5	*☆14.85	32.0	*☆30.89	1:12.0	*☆1:10.53
	Excellent	8.0	*□7.78	15.5	14.11	31.0	29.05	1:08.0	1:07.21
9-10 (Bantam) (Roadrunner)	Satisfactory			15.5	#14.39	32.0	#31.12	1:13.0	#1:11.77
	Good			14.5	*13.80	29.0	*28.55	1:09.0	*1:07.82
	Excellent		N/A	13.5	12.85	28.0	26.50	1:04.0	59.81
11-12 (Midget) (Cub)	Satisfactory			15.0	*13.40	29.5	#27.94	1:12.0	#1:04.18
	Good			14.0	#13.24	27.5	*26.96	1:04.0	*1:02.94
	Excellent		N/A	13.0	12.10	26.5	24.47	1:00.0	54.73
13-14 (Youth) (Cadet)	Satisfactory			14.5	*$13.02	29.0	#27.04	1:10.0	#58.68
	Good			13.5	#12.54	27.0	*&25.85	59.0	*&57.60
	Excellent		N/A	12.5	11.74	25.0	23.81	58.0	53.10

N/A = Not applicable or available in this age group.

All times are measured in seconds or minutes and seconds.

Unless otherwise noted all records are "American AAU/ USATF National Outdoor" youth (2002-2007).

△ = AAU/ USATF Private Track Club Record.

= A "CYO" (Catholic Youth Organization) National record or performance time (2007).

* = A "CYC" (Catholic Youth Council, St. Louis, MO.) record or performance time (2007).

□ = For 6 year olds.   ☆ = For 7-8 year olds. $ = For Sub Youth 13 year olds.   & = For 14-15 year olds.

TABLE 1

RELAYS

Explanation

Relays are like a sprint game. In youth track & field relays mean the 4 x 100m, the 4 x 200m, the 4 x 400m, and the 4 x 800m races. It is one competitor handing off a baton to a team mate, continuously all the way around the track, to see which team can get to the finish line first. There are several methods for passing the baton. There are also techniques for switching the baton from hand to hand after the pass is made. There are exchange and acceleration zones. The baton is typically exchanged within a 10m exchange zone. The acceleration zone is for the handoff team mate to accelerate in, prior to the handoff. In the 4 x 100m relay the receiver does not look back. Looking back slows you down. The 4 x 100m relay has three exchange zones, each one 10m in length, they are located on a stagger. Most tracks have a 10m acceleration zone marked with triangles. In the 4 x 400m relay, and longer distances, the first lap of the race is run in lanes. The second lap runner stays in their lane all the way to the 300m mark then they can move down to lane one. The rest of the race is basically finished in lane one, except at the finish line. In the youth 4 x 400m and 4 x 800 relays the receiver sometimes looks back for a visual exchange of the baton in the acceleration zone. Otherwise you look straight ahead and feel for the baton.

Drill No. 25- Start of the Race

The Basics are

The competitors start out in the first leg lined up just as they would for a regular sprint race, except they are staggered. The only difference between a regular sprint race and a relay race start is the competitors carry a baton. This makes it a little hard for you beginning kids because you don't want to drop the baton on your start. Holding the baton the correct way at the start can be

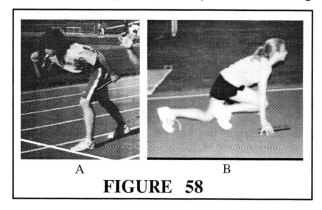

A   B
FIGURE 58

critical for you (*SEE FIGURE 58-A & B*). Also the coach will have to decide which hand they want the team to start with, then change to on each exchange. See the section on *Sprints* on how to get down into, or stand up at the start of the race. The starter (first leg runner) has to be very good at starting, no false starts. You also need to be a good curve runner, and very good at handing off the baton.

Practice

Except for holding the baton, practice for the start is the same as for the sprints. Get into your starting position (on your mark). Start out with the baton in your right hand, but make sure you practice holding it in your left hand also. The fingers are in the "Vee" position (*SEE FIGURE 59-A*) for a down start. The baton should be positioned so you will be holding it at the very rear end of the baton (*SEE FIGURE 59 A & B*), with the front end facing forward. This is so that when you come out of the set position you can drive your hand straight up and not have to turn it. You grasp the baton with your fingers as you push off, so that it slides right into position between the thumb and fingers. Then have mom or dad or a friend say, "Set," and you immediately raise your butt up into the set position (*SEE FIGURE 49-C*).

For the stand up position you grab the baton down at the end and face it straight ahead. (*SEE FIGURE 59-B*). Make sure you practice both the down position and the stand up position. Have mom or dad use your "clappers" so that you get used to exploding out at the starters

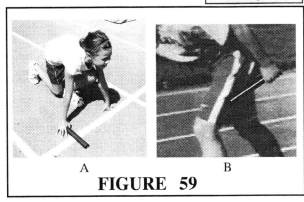

A   B
FIGURE   59

"gun sound." Once you explode out you only need to run about ten yards. Then stop and come back to the starting point. Probably the best thing for you to do is walk through both types of starts several times slowly at first so that you have the idea of what you will be doing. You should practice both start positions at least five times at a session.

Drill No. 26- Middle of the First Leg of the Race
The Basics are

For this part of the race the coach will have to decide whether they want an outside or inside exchange. This determines whether you will run to the inside or outside of the lane during the exchange. Learning the "technique" is very important, in fact critical to be successful. At the exchange point, it is the responsibility of baton carrier (you) to correctly put the baton into the hands of the receiver. On an outside exchange the carrier holds the baton in their left hand. The receiver receives the baton with the right hand. This means the starter has to run on the outside part of the lane during the exchange while the receiver waits to the inside of the lane.

On an inside exchange the carrier holds the baton in the right hand. The receiver receives the baton in their left hand, and waits on the outside part of their lane. This means the starter has to run on the inside part of the lane during the exchange. Each technique has advantages and disadvantages. As you (the carrier) come up to the exchange point you need to make a smooth exchange in order to not slow down the receiver. This part of a 4 x 100m race is run with the starter staying in their lane all the way, and using good technique (fast runner) to get the lead in the first leg of the race. In the 4 x 400m relay and longer distances the runners need to stay in their lanes for the the entire first lap and the first bend at the 300m mark of the second lap. Then all the competitors can move down. The exchange zone is where relay races are won or lost. Make sure you learn how to do it right.

Practice

You will need to get a "baton" and a friend to practice these techniques with. Before you start, sit down with mom or dad and go over exactly what you will be doing in the exchange zone. This is to make sure you beginning kids understand. Next decide where you want to practice running in the lane (inside or outside). I suggest practicing both so that you will be ready to run on either the inside or the outside of the lane. Sort of like a switch hitter in baseball.

The Outside of the lane exchange

Get into either your up or down set position, with the baton in the left hand, then have mom,

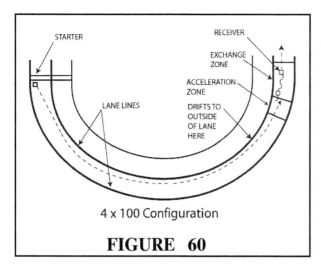

STARTER

RECEIVER

EXCHANGE
ZONE

ACCELERATION
ZONE

LANE LINES

DRIFTS TO
OUTSIDE
OF LANE
HERE

4 x 100 Configuration

FIGURE 60

dad or a friend say, "GO," then you run immediately to the inside part of the lane. You don't need to use a clapper because this is just practicing the middle part of the run. When you start to approach the acceleration zone you move to the outside part of the lane *(SEE FIGURE 60)*. To practice this you will probably need to find a high school track with the lanes and zones marked. Start out practicing on the curve. Every time you get into the up or down "set" position, have mom or dad check and make sure you are holding the baton correctly at the end. You only need to run about 15 or 20 yards on the curve, then drift to the outside of the lane, stop, and come back to the starting position. You can practice the exchange technique on the next drill. In the actual race you would go to the outside of the lane as you approach the acceleration zone *(SEE FIGURE 60)*. You should practice this middle of the race technique at least five times at a session.

The Inside of the lane exchange

Get down into either your up or down set position with the baton in your right hand, then have mom, dad, or a friend say, "GO," then run immediately to the inside part of the lane. In the actual race as you start to come around and approach the acceleration zone *(SEE FIGURE 60)* the receiver would move towards the outside of the lane to take your exchange. For this practice you run the same as you did in the outside exchange, except you stay on the inside of the lane, stop, turn around and walk back to the starting position

In the 4 x 400m the starter always runs the whole lap leg while staying in their lane, but the second lap leg runners stay in their lane only through the first bend to the 300m mark after the exchange, then they can move out of their lane down to the inside lane number "one" of the track.

Drill No. 27- The Baton Exchanges
The Basics are

For both the 4 x 100m and the 4 x 400m races the exchange from runner to runner must be made in a 10m long exchange zone between the large triangles. Usually a gold triangle to gold triangle for the 4 x 100m race. For the 4 x 400m race, and longer distances, the exchange is made in a 10m area between triangles, but the triangles may be different colors depending on how the field is marked. In the 4 x 100m exchange the receivers usually take blind passes, and they need to know ahead of time whether it will be an inside or outside exchange. This is so that you know what side of the lane to be in, and which hand to extend back to take the pass in. In the 4 x 400m exchange the receivers look back for the pass, but they still have to know which side of the lane to be on, and which hand to take the pass in. The receivers take the passes by reaching back and making a "vee" between their thumb and the fingers *(SEE FIGURE 61)*.

Both the carrier and the receiver also need to know whether the exchange will be made using the "upsweep" or the "downsweep" handoff technique in order to hold their hand in the right

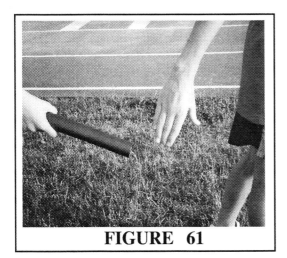

FIGURE 61

position. Receivers can use either one of two crouched starting positions *(SEE FIGURE 68)*. It will depend on which one your coach wants to use. The smaller triangles on the track, or check marks, are used in the 4 x 400m and longer distance races, to position the receiver for acceleration up to the start of the exchange zone.

Carriers can make verbal calls in order to let the receiver know exactly when to start accelerating. *After* making the exchange in the 4x100m race only, the carrier must stop and stay in their lane until all carriers in the race have past. This is for safety reasons because all lanes might have a carrier running in that lane. For longer races the excahange is made in lane one, and the carrier should watch then leave immediately to the right for safety reasons.

The "second leg" runner must be good at receiving and handing off the baton. You need to be able to sprint fast over long distances. You can be on the tall side in the 4 x 100m because there are no curves to run. The "third leg" runner must be good at receiving and handing off the baton. They have to be a good curve runner, and they need to be able to sprint fast over long distances. The "forth leg" runner must to be good at receiving the baton, and they need to be able to take the pressure of finishing the race. They are usually the fastest runner on the team because some of the time you need to come from behind to win at the finish line.

Practice

You will need to get a "baton", and a helper friend about the same size as you, to practice these techniques. I suggest you begining kids get mom or dad to come out and direct you, to be sure you are doing it correctly. Before you start, sit down with mom or dad and let them explain to you exactly what you will be doing during the exchange. You will also need to find a high school track with marked lanes. "CYC" six year olds do not have a relay event. Sub Bantam (seven & eight year olds) runners can start their practice by working on the 4 x 100m exchange first. Then work on your 4 x 200m exchanges. Bantam (nine & ten year olds) runners can work on 4 x 400m exchanges. Find the starting line (stagger designations), and the the two zones, for whichever relay you will be in. You will probably be located on the curve at one of the track ends *(SEE FIGURE 60)*.

The Elementary Outside of the Lane Exchange

Have your helper go to the inside of the lane at start line of the acceleration zone. Have them face straight ahead because these will be blind (no look) passes from the rear. Then you go to an inside of the lane spot on the curve about five or six yards back of the helper, and hold the baton in your left hand *(SEE FIGURE 60)*. Make sure you hold it way down at the bottom, with the rest of it sticking out in front *(SEE FIGURE 61)*. Both you and the helper walk through the drill first so that you both know exactly what to do when you run through it. Have mom or dad say, "GO," and you start walking. You will be handing it off with your left hand into the right hand of the friend on this drill. So as you get close to the receiver then start to move from the inside of the lane towards the outside of the lane *(SEE FIGURE 60)*. The helper needs to go through the

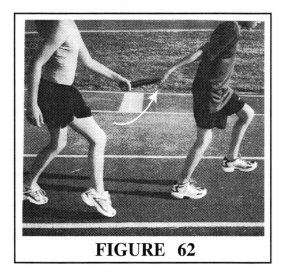

FIGURE 62

FIGURE 63

acceleration zone and into the exchange zone where they move to the inside of the lane where the exchange will take place. This is all timing so the exchange can be made just before the end of the exchange zone. Since you are both walking for this exchange, the helper will need to walk slower than you in order for you to catch up with them right near the end of the exchange zone.

The helper looks straight ahead and puts their right hand back, palm down, to the rear, making a "vee" with the thumb and fingers. For this exchange use the "upsweep" technique. With an up swing motion, you put the baton into the "vee" of the helpers hand *(SEE FIGURE 62)*. After both of you have walked through this a few times, then speed it up a little each time until you get the timing right, and can run through it at full speed. To learn both positions, take turns at being the "carrier" and the "receiver."

After you make the exchange, the receiver only needs to run another ten yards or so, then they can stop and come back. There is another exchange technique called the "downsweep." This is where the carriers hand goes up with the arm swing, then comes down into the receivers hand, which is palm up *(SEE FIGURE 63)*. Work on both of these techniques for practice. Also in the "elementary outside exchange," the receiver needs to change hands after the exchange, and move the baton to their left hand for the next exchange *(SEE FIGURE 64)*.

There are two distinct advantages to this technique. One, the receiver always receives the baton in the most favored right hand. Two, the exchange is always the same for each team member, then the coach can easily move team members from one position in the race to another. Three, this method is much easier for you beginning kids to learn. There are disadvantages though. One, it

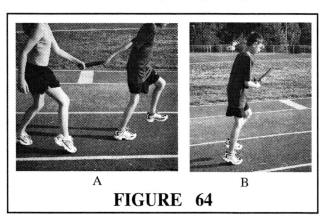

A B
FIGURE 64

slows down the second and third leg runners when making a hand switch. Two, the first and third leg runners (on the curves) have to run further than they would usuing the "inside exchange." When you are the carrier, use a code word, such as "blue" or their "name," to signal the receiver to start their acceleration run.

Also just for practice have the carrier always slow down, stop, and remain in the lane after the exchange until the receiver walks back to them. This is for safety reasons, and it needs to become a habit for the carriers. Second leg, third leg, and fourth leg runners need to work on this technique. You should practice this exchange technique at least five times each session.

The Elementary Inside of the Lane Exchange

The inside exchange is almost like the outside exchange, except the carrier puts the baton in their right hand, stays to the inside of the lane, and hands off to the receivers left hand after the receiver has moved to the outside of the exchange zone. The receiver then switches the baton to their right hand for the next exchange. Practice this technique just like the "outside exchange" method. Also practice using both the "upsweep", and the "downsweep" techniques, for handing off. There are several advantages to this technique. One, the "upsweep" exchange method complements the carriers sprint arm action. Two, the method of exchange is the same for the whole team, which makes it easy for your coach to substitute and move team members around. Third, the 1st and 3rd leg runners run shorter distances than they would using the outside exchange technique. The disadvantages are the 2nd and 3rd leg runners are slowed down a little bit by shifting the baton from one hand to the other. Also the receiver receives the baton in the left hand, which is not the most favored hand. 2nd leg, 3rd leg, and 4th leg runners also need to work on this technique. If you are using this technique, you should practice it at least five times at a session.

The Alternate Upsweep and Downsweep Advanced Exchanges

Many world class relay teams use these advanced exchanges. In the *"advanced alternate upsweep"* exchange technique *(SEE FIGURE 61)*, the only difference between this technique and the others is the carrier always uses the "upsweep" technique. You start out with the baton in your right hand. And the receiver does not switch hands after receiving the baton in their right hand. The tricky part of this technique is the carrier has to give as much of the baton to the receivers hand as possible. When the receiver gets the baton, they need to have as much of the baton sticking out in front of their hand as they can. To do this the carriers hand, and the receivers hand need to touch on the exchange. There are several advantages to this technique. One, the sprint times for the second and third leg runners is going to be faster because they don't have to switch hands. Two, they run the shortest distance for their leg of the race. Three, the upward sweeping motion of the arm at the exchange complements the sprinting arm action.

The disadvantages are; one, rearranging team members is a little more difficult. Two, each receiver of the baton has less and less of the baton to hold onto. Occasionally this forces the next receiver to readjust their grip on the baton. In the process the baton may accidentally get dropped,

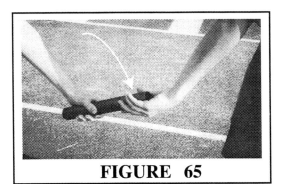

FIGURE 65

especially in the very last exchange (fourth leg). I'm not really sure you little kids need to work on this technique until you are over 12 years old. But you can go over it with mom or dad, to get familiar with the technique.

In the *"advanced alternate downsweep"* exchange technique the carrier grasps the base of the baton and hands it off with a pushing downsweep motion. *(SEE FIGURE 65)*. The receiver has to grasp the baton way up on the upper portion. After the receiver gets the baton, the receiving hand is rotated down and forward so that end sticks way out and is ready for the next exchange. There are several advantages to this technique; One, this type of exchange allows the greatest distance between team mates at the exchange point. This means the receiver has a shorter distance to run on their leg of the race. This applies to both the second and third leg runners. It makes their time faster because there is no slight slowdown from shifting the baton from hand to hand.

The disadvantages of this technique are; One, the pushing downsweep action is not complementary to sprint arm action. Two, sometimes the arm stretch and baton distance between team mates can cause a loss of rhythm and speed while making the exchange. Three, substituting and moving runners into another leg is more difficult. You younger kids don't need to work on this technique either until you are over 12 years old. But you can sit down with mom or dad and go over it so that you are familiar with how this technique works.

Positioning of the team members in the lanes and the zones is the same for both the "upsweep" and "downsweep" alternate techniques. The starter always carries the baton in their right hand, runs on the inside of the lane, and hands off on the inside part of the lane. The second leg receiver accelerates to the outside of the lane, takes the hand off with the left hand, and continues to run on the outside part of the lane until the hand off. The third leg runner accelerates along the inside of the lane, receives the baton in the right hand, and continues to run along the inside of the lane until the hand off. The fourth leg runner accelerates on the outside of the lane, receives the baton in the left hand, and continues to run on the outside part of the lane all the way to the finish. Elite world class relay teams *prefer* the "alternate downsweep" technique.

The Push Press-Open Palm Exchanges

This technique is growing more popular, especially with elite college 4 x 100m teams. It is different though. And it takes more training because of the arm position at the exchange point. And although different it is considered to be an advancemrnt of the other techniques. In this exchange the receivers arm is extended, but the elbow is bent with the palm open *(SEE FIGURE 66)*. This does put more pressure on the carrier to push extend the baton into the receivers palm. The receiver runs in the exchage zone then on verbal command extends the arm back with their palm open, thumb down, fingers slightly spread and pointing away from the body. The carriers arm motion brings the baton up into an almost vertical position.

FIGURE 66

When the arm and baton gets to the right position they push extend the baton into the receivers hand *(SEE FIGURE 67)*. The receiver grabs the very top of the baton so that the next receiver has the top part of the baton available to grab. When done right this is a very smooth quick exchange. This method makes it easier to steer and then place the baton into the receivers hand. This technique can be used with the alternate left-right handoff, or it can be used with a right hand to right hand handoff method.

I like the right hand to right hand handoff because it has more advantages than disadvantages. The runners are always running on the inside of the lane, and they don't need to switch hands for the handoff. It just takes more practice.

One thing I like about this technique is it seems more natural because it fits in with the normal sprint action arm movements which allows for smoother baton passing, and it lets the runners have more speed through the exchange zone. Some coaches call this the natural exchange technique.

The Look Back Receiver Techniques

There are three different receiver semi-blind techniques for the "look back"stance. All of these stances are to help the receiver look over their shoulder or under their arm pit for the incoming carrier and start their acceleration run. One is called "the sprint crouch start" technique, the second is called "the regular crouch start," the third is called "the under the arm start" technique.

FIGURE 67

the Regular Over the Shoulder Crouch Start

You can practice this technique on the track, out in the back yard, or even out in the park. You would only use this technique for longer relays like the 4 x 400m or longer distances. Stand with your right foot out in front of your left, then crouch down, bend at the knees, look back over your left shoulder *(SEE FIGURE 68-A)*. This is how you would stand if you are waiting on the outside of the lane to start your acceleration into the exchange zone. You would flip flop and look over your right shoulder if you are waiting on the inside of the lane. Have mom or dad or a friend say, "Go," and you turn back to the front and start to accelerate straight ahead.

When you have sprinted for four or five yards have mom or dad yell "blue left" at you (if thats the signal) and you make a blind reach way back with the "left" arm while continuing to look and run straight ahead. Or you can accelerate for two or three strides

A **FIGURE 68** B

then look back and make a visual reach for the baton while still accelerating into the exchange zone. Then after a few steps pretend (for practice only) to grasp a baton and continue sprinting straight for another four or five yards, then slow down, stop, and come back to the starting point. The next time switch and have them look back over the right shoulder, and reach back with the right arm and hand for practice. Second leg, third leg, and fourth leg runners need to work on this technique. You should practice this exchange technique at least five times at a session.

The Sprint Crouch Start

You can practice this technique at the same places as the regular crouch. Get down into your sprinters start stance, except with only the right arm down, then turn and look back over your left shoulder *(SEE FIGURE 66-B)*. This is how you would stand if you are waiting on the outside of the lane to start your acceleration into the exchange zone. You would flip flop and look over your right shoulder, with the left arm down if they are waiting on the inside of the lane. The rest of the practice is the same as for the "regular crouch" start. Second leg, third leg, and fourth leg runners need to work on this technique. Practice this exchange technique at least 5 times at a session.

The Under the Arm Pit Start

This technique is not one you see much, but it does have an advantage. It does not take as long to turn your head around. You look back and see the carrier coming so you start to accelerate, after about three or four strides you look back under yor arm pit and extend your hand back for

FIGURE 69

the baton *(SEE FIGURE 69)*. Your palm may be down, up, or facing in, depending on which technique you and the carrier are using for the exchange move. Then you can do a blind exchange or look back for a visual exchange as you continue to accelerate ahead. Your head only moves from bent down to up and straight ahead. You should practice this exchange technique at least five times at a session.

Summation

Which one of these look back techniques to use will either be what your coach wants you to do, or which one is more comfortable and works best for you. These techniques are fotr the longer distance relays. Normally they would not be used in a 4 x 100m relay race.

Sprint Arm Action Static Exchange

This is a very good practice drill you can work on at home. You will need to find two or three of your friends to come over and help you out on this drill. You may want to have mom or dad come out and observe to see if you are doing the drill correctly. You and your friends all get in a

FIGURE 70

straight line, one behind the other, about 1.5 meters (about five feet) apart. All of you face straight ahead, and lean slightly forward. Start out with the last person in the line. Have them start out with the baton in their right hand. Have mom or dad say, "GO," then the last person in line starts swinging their arms back and forth as if running, except they stay in place. Everyone in line *stays in place*. Make sure they are holding the baton down at the bottom *(SEE FIGURE 65)*. After about two or three arm swings the last person calls "Blue," and passes the baton to the person in front of them. When the receiver hears the call "blue", they reach back with their right arm for the baton. Use the "downsweep" method as it is the more popular. When the second person in line gets the baton, they shift it from the right hand to the left hand. Each carrier has to make sure while shifting the baton to grasp it down at the bottom. Then they start swinging their arms back and forth while staying in place. After two or three arm swings, they make the call "blue", and pass the baton off to the person (third) in front of them. That person reaches back with their left hand, when they hear the call. Then they take the baton, switch it to their right hand, and keep swinging their arms while staying in place. Keep doing this up to the front of the line. Then go back to the starting point and the whole drill starts all over again when mom or dad says, "GO." Work on getting a rhythm going. This drill teaches you all the actions, and the rhythm of the exchange *(SEE FIGURE 70)*.

Drill No. 28- The Middle of the 2nd & 3rd Legs of the Race
The Basics are
For this part of the race the coach will have to decide whether they want you to use an outside or inside baton exchange. This determines whether you will run to the inside or outside of the lane during the next exchange. You also have to be ready for your coded "call," and which technique will be used for the hand off (upsweep, downsweep, or push press). Other than that you just use good sprint technique, run as fast as you can, and don't drop the baton.

Practice
Practice this the same as the sprint practices *(SEE DRILL NO. 23,* except work on your exchange techniques.

Drill No. 29- The Finish of the Race
The Basics are
The fourth leg runner has to finish the race. You must use good exchange techniques, good sprinting techniques, and lean at the tape (finish line).

Practice
Practice this the same way you would practice for a "sprint" race and finish *(SEE DRILLS 23 & 24)*, except also practice and work on your exchange techniques *(SEE DRILL 27)*. The fourth leg runner is usually the best sprinters and athlete on the team. You need to have a lot of "heart," to do your best if your team is behind in the race.

Check *TABLE 2* to see some comparison performance times for you to achieve in order to be competitive. The main records are "*American outdoor*" youth track & field records, but we have also added the local "*CYC*" and national "*CYO*" records for a comparison.

COMPARISON PERFORMANCE TIMES - RELAYS

BOYS		DISTANCE							
Age Division		4 x 100m	Record	4 x 200m	Record	4 x 400m	Record	4 x 800m	Record
6 - 8 (Primary)	Satisfactory	1:20.0	Δ60.80	3:00.0		6:00.0			
	Good	1:10.0	*1:01.78	2:30.0	Δ2:22.40	5:40.0			
	Excellent	1:05.0	Δ1:01.50	2:20.0	*2:17.04	5:30.0	Δ5:26.80		N/A
9 -10 (Bantam) (Roadrunner)	Satisfactory	1:10.0	#1:01.17	2:20.0		5:10.0	Δ4:58.22		
	Good	1:00.0	*59.74	2:10.0	*2:05.28	4:35.0	#4:30.24		
	Excellent	52.00	51.63	2:00.0	Δ1:55.20	4:15.0	4:11.54		N/A
11 -12 (Midget) (Cub)	Satisfactory	56.00	#53.54	2:12.0		5:00.0	#4:46.11	12:00.0	Δ10:28.36
	Good	54.00	*52.69	2:02.0	#1:59.74	4:40.0	Δ4:38.44	11:00.0	Δ9:27.78
	Excellent	52.00	47.54	1:52.0	*1:50.06	4:00.0	3:47.50	10:00.0	9:20.82
13 - 14 (Youth) (Cadet)	Satisfactory	1:08.0	*48.31	2:10.0		4:30.0	Δ3:45.77	10:00.0	Δ9:08.13
	Good	58.00	#47.94	2:00.0	#1:45.66	4:00.0	Δ3:28.68	9:00.0	Δ8:30.0
	Excellent	48.00	43.25	1:50.0	*1:40.78	3:26.0	3:23.96	8:26.0	8:24.03

GIRLS		DISTANCE							
Age Division		4 x 100m	Record	4 x 200m	Record	4 x 400m	Record	4 x 800m	Record
6 - 8 (Primary)	Satisfactory	1:25.0	Δ1:12.10	3:00.0		6:00.0			
	Good	1:11.0	*1:02.08	2:35.0	Δ2:17.60	5:30.0			
	Excellent	1:06.0	Δ60.02	2:25.0	*2:23.68	5:20.0	Δ5:00.5		N/A
9 -10 (Bantam) (Roadrunner)	Satisfactory	1:10.0	#1:03.25	2:30.0	*2:07.56	5:30.0	Δ6:05.4		
	Good	1:07.0	*1:00.09	2:20.0	Δ2:01.24	4:42.0	Δ4:36.39		
	Excellent	55.0	53.62	2:10.0	Δ1:59.90	4:22.0	4:19.00		N/A
11 -12 (Midget) (Cub)	Satisfactory	57.00	#55.64	2:22.0	#2:03.93	5:20.0	#4:40.04	12:12.0	Δ11:13.87
	Good	55.00	*54.69	2:12.0	*1:58.17	4:40.0	Δ4:35.59	10:52.0	Δ10:39.98
	Excellent	53.00	49.17	2:02.0	Δ1:49.50	4:00.0	3:57.26	9:32.0	9:30.72
13 - 14 (Youth) (Cadet)	Satisfactory	58.00	*55.19	2:20.0		5:10.0	#4:25.52	12:00.0	Δ10:58.70
	Good	53.00	#52.14	2:10.0	*1:58.18	4:30.0	Δ4:14.60	10:40.0	Δ10:14.09
	Excellent	48.00	46.58	2:00.0	#1:57.57	3:50.0	3:45.90	9:20.0	9:15.68

N/A = Not applicable or available in this age group.

All times are measured in seconds or minutes and seconds.

Unless otherwise noted all records are "American AAU/ USATF National Outdoor" youth (2002-2007).

Δ = AAU/ USATF Private Track Club Record.

= A "CYO" (Catholic Youth Organization) National record or performance time (2007).

* = A "CYC" (Catholic Youth Council, St. Louis, MO.) record or performance time (2007).

TABLE 2

DISTANCE RUNNING

Explanation

In youth track & field, distance running means the 800m, the 1500m, the 1600m, the 3000m, or cross country. The 800m is considered a short distance race, the 1500m and 1600m a middle distance race, and 3000m and beyond are long distance races for kids. Distance running requires anaerobic and aerobic endurance. The energy demands for distance running training are shown in *DIAGRAM 2* The anaerobic endurance you will need has to do with a runners muscular system capacity to operate using the fuel stored in the muscles. Anaerobic endurance training is when a vigorus all out effort is used over a short distance. The aerobic endurance you will need has to do with the ability of a runners circulatory system to supply oxygen to your muscles using a sustained effort over a long distance.

As you can see by the table, you need to build up both types of endurances by different amounts, for different races. You young kids that run in distance races need to work, and train, in the off season as well as during track season. Always make sure you get "*warmed up,*" and "*stretched out*" before any training sessions. And maybe some light flexibility exercises after that.

When you train will depend on when your competitive track & field season takes place. It is usually spring or summer for outdoor distance racing, and fall to winter for indoor track racing and cross country racing. Start your training with some easy running where

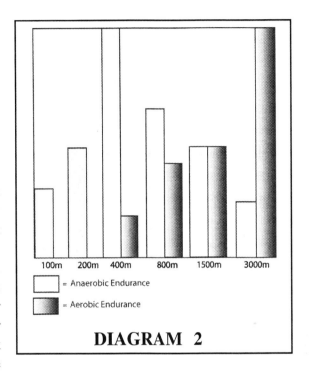

= Anaerobic Endurance

= Aerobic Endurance

DIAGRAM 2

stretching out and striding is emphasized. And you can mix in some acceleration drills to get your legs in shape. Some general guidelines for how to train, and set up a program, in the different seasons are:

OFF SEASON	**BETWEEN SEASONS**	**COMPETITIVE SEASON**
1. Emphasize mostly aerobics	Mix of anaerobics and aerobics	Emphasize mostly aerobics
2. Long distances	None	Short distances
3. Light intensity	Moderate intensity	Heavy intensity
4. A few repetitions	Many repetitions	A few repetitions

If you are noticing some soreness and feeling like you need to avoid any running, your approach to your training may be wrong. Try making it more fun with some variety, and with a more progressive development approach. In other words you may be working too hard. We will give you some ideas, and ways, to make it more fun.

Drill No. 30- Start of the Race

The Basics are

Distance race starts are fairly simple. They are usually "stand up" starts because the long distances *do not* not require getting down into starting blocks for a quick start. However, your coach may want you to get out fast. If they do, you need to learn how to do this.

Practice

All you need to practice this is a back yard patio or a drive way. You will need a strip of white tape, or a strip of cloth on the ground, to simulate the starting line. The reason is to emphasize to you that the toe on the power leg foot has to be just behind the edge of the line *(SEE FIGURE 71)*. Come up to just behind the line edge, with the toe of your power leg, and bend at the knee. You get your push from the power leg. To find out which leg is your power leg or foot *(SEE DRILL NO.44)*. Your trail leg is back and ready to take a big step forward at the start. The arm on the power leg side is bent and to the rear, ready to swing forward hard on the first step (left power leg shown) *SEE FIGURE 72-A*. The arm on the trail side leg is foward, and ready to swing very hard to the rear on the first trail leg step. The back can be bent down, nearly parallel to ground, for a faster come out low start *SEE FIGURE 72-A*. Or the back can be up more, at about a 60 degree angle, for a more relaxed, I'm not in a hurry start *SEE FIGURE 72-B*. For a just kind of stand there, make them think you are going out fast, then let everyone else go out first start *SEE FIGURE 72-C*.

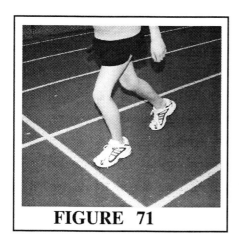

FIGURE 71

Three different start forms, for left and right foot starts, are shown in the illustration. Some very good long distance and cross country running coaches like to have their runners start out slow at the start, then stay at the back of the pack, to avoid getting tripped or falling down in the bunched up group of runners. However, most coaches want their runners to go out fast at the start to avoid problems. It't going to depend on what strategy your coach thinks is best for you. There is one exception to the starts. If you know you are going to be running a cross country race, and the trail is mostly narrow, establish a front position as soon as possible. This means passing is going to be very hard, so sprint at the start if possible to get to the front of the pack.

For practice go up to the starting line and have mom or dad say, "GO," then work on your fast start first, then a slow start. For a fast start you need to work on driving the trail leg forward very hard, and the power leg side rear

A   B   C
FIGURE 72

arm forward very hard. This is what gets your momentum started quickly. After you come off the starting line, you only need to run about five to ten yards for practice, then come back to the starting line for another start. You should practice this start technique at least five times a training session. All 800m, 1500m, 1600m, 3000m and cross country runners, need to work on this drill.

Drill No. 31- Beginning of the Race

The Basics are

On the short distance race (800m) it may be better to start off slow at the back of the pack just until everyone is stretched out a bit in the first 1/4 lap. However, since it's a two lap race, you may want to start to move closer to the leaders as soon as possible before they get too far ahead. For you young kids a two lap race is going to be at a pretty fast pace. If you sprint out too fast at the start, to get ahead of everyone, you may get" burnt out" for the finish of the race. It's going to depend on your running ability, and how much aerobic stamina you have for a fast pace two lap race. If you have the stamina it's probably better to go out fast.

A distance runners technique is to run in a more upright body position. Some forward lean is OK when you are accelerating, or finishing. In a short distance race yourstride length should be moderate to long. In a middle or long distance race, your stride length should be shorter and more fluid, without a lot of head bounce. The runner should be pacing and running as relaxed as possible.

FIGURE 73

The jaw and face are loose, and *no* clenched fists if you can help it. And your arm action should always balance the motion of your legs *(SEE FIGURE 73)*. It should be very vigorous when sprinting, and moderate to slow action in the non sprinting part of the race.

Practice

There are several drills and games you can play with your friends to get ready for this part of the race. I am going to start with the runs first. It's best to run with one or two of your friends as a team. It makes the running seem less of a drudgery. Don't go on long runs or run on consecutive days. Mix in other technique training and games in between. The games will also help make it more fun for you. Run some of the time on an oval track, and some of the time straight ahead. This would be back and forth across a soccer field, or out on a street or side walk. Mix it up, it helps believe me. Have mom or dad always accompany you, especially when you are out on the streets.

Run - Walk

You little kids can start out training with a run, then a walk routine. Run at a moderate speed for about 1/4 of a mile (one lap around on a track), then walk for about 1/4 of a mile (1 lap). After you have made the first run and have stopped, and you are walking, notice if you are gasping for breath or they have a flushed face (redish color). If you can't tell, then have mom or dad look at your face for you. These are signs of discomfort and fatigue. This means you must cut back on the distance and speed a little until you get into better aerobic shape. If you are in good shape, go ahead and run- walk for about three cycles (about 1-1/2 miles or six laps on an oval track). No sprinting early in your training, it's too demanding on on your body system when you are starting to train for distance running. The sprinting can come later in the training cycle.

Long Runs

You need to do some long distance running to build up your aerobic endurance. These long runs should be only about 1-1/2 to 1-3/4 miles long. You can do this on roads, trails, or fields, but only at slow to moderate speeds. *Do not* make these runs on consecutive days. And you need to also take some safety precautions:

1. Run with a buddy or friend, not alone.
2. Have an adult run with you, or have them follow you in a car, so you are supervised.
3. Plot a course that doesn't cut across traffic lanes if possible. Here is how to do that. Run way down the street, then turn around and come back on the same side.
4. Check out any cross country courses ahead of time for hidden or visible dangers such as potholes, tree roots, and sharp rocks.
5. When running on roads oe streets, run towards the traffic.
6. Check what the weather will be before you leave so that you are prepared.
7. Wear the proper clothing, for what the season of the year dictates.
8. If it's hot, make sure you have "gatoraid" or water for fluid replacement.
9. Wear comfortable loose clothing, it will make the run more enjoyable.
10. Make sure you are running with good quality running shoes.
11. Make sure you are properly *warmed up* and *stretched out* before you start.

Drill No. 32- Chase and Tag Game
The Game Basics Are

This is a running game you can play to help you with your acceleration, quickness, speed and explosiveness. All competitor's can benefit from playing this game. Here is how it works. You will need to have mom or dad to come and help. Then you need to find at least 3 to 5 of your friends to come over and play the game with you. You will need some cones to mark the lines. Team "A" lines up on one side, and team "B" lines up on the opposite side *(SEE FIGURE 74)*. To start mom or dad you say, "GO" and each member of team "A" runs slowly to a line 15 yards ahead. Then as they get to the line, they touch it, turn and sprint back to the starting line. Members on team "B" get into a "stand up start" position on the line 5 yards away, then chase them and try to tag them before they back to their starting point line *(SEE FIGURE 74)*.

Playing the Game

After their opponents on team "A" touch the line, a team "B" member opposite of them takes off and attempts to tag them before they get back to the safety of their starting line. To make

74

it easy to tell if a player gets tagged, you can put a loosly tucked in handkerchief in their rear pocket, belt, or waist. Then it will be obvious when someone grabs their handkercheif, that they have been tagged or caught.

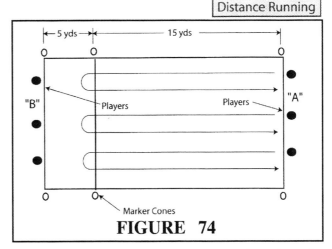

FIGURE 74

After about ten minutes of playing all the players on both teams rest for a minute or so, then rotate and swap sides by sending the players on team "B" over to become team "A." players. Some *TIPS* for team "A" players. Run slowly to the line, you don't have to sprint. When you get close to the line, you straighten their body up for the turn around. What you don't want to do is get caught leaning because then it takes longer to turn around and sprint back. Pivot as quick as you can, then accelerate quickly back to your starting line. Some *TIPS* for team "B" players. As your opponent comes up to the line, keep your eyes on the turn around line. As soon as the opponent touches that line, you blast out after them and accelerate quickly. Try to tag them or grab their handkerchief before the team "A" player gets back to their safe starting line.

For some variation to the game, all the players on team "B" get in a kneeling position, especially if they seem to always be catching the team "A" players before they get back to safety. It will "level the playing field" so to speak. Have mom or dad, just for fun and competition, keep track with a pad of paper of how many times each team is caught. You can swap sides about four times, then go on to another activity, drill or game.

Drill No. 33- The Shadow Game
The Game Basics Are

This is a moving game you can play to help you with your movement while in a croud of bunched up runners (muscle memory). All competitor's running in distance races can benefit from playing this game. Here is how it works. You will need to find at least three or five of your friends to come over and play the game with you. And you will also need some cones to mark an area of confinement. Play this game in an area of confinement, or everyone will be running all over town. I suggest an area of about of about 20 or 30 yards square for four to six players.

It can be adjusted to a larger area square if need be, to give you a little more room to maneuver in. Pair up in groups of two. Player "B" shadows player "A" within tagging distance. In other words player "B" goes everywhere player "A" goes, but does not run into them *(SEE FIGURE 75)*.

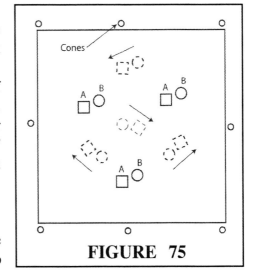

FIGURE 75

Playing the Game

You can start this off by having mom or dad come out and say, "GO," or blowing a whistle. They can also help supervise. Each team of "B" player's need to shadow (follow) their team "A" partner's wherever they go, but without running into their "A" partner or the other teams of two. The object of the game is for the players on one team to get rid of their shadow. Some *TIPS* for team "A" players. Try to get rid of, or shake off, your shadow by suddenly accelerating and by changing directions. Some *TIPS* for both team "A", and team "B" players. Keep your eyes on everyone around you, so that you avoid collisions with the other players (peripherial vision). Play this game for about 2 or 3 minutes at a time, then stop and let the players rest. Then switch and player "B" (shadow) becomes player "A". Play the game for another two or three minutes , then stop again. Have mom or dad, for fun and competition, keep track of how many times the player's on team "A" get away from their shadow. Then go to another skill activity, drill, exercise or game.

Drill No. 34- The Shuttle Relay Game
The Game Basics Are

This is a moving game you can play to help you with your speed in getting away from a croud of bunched up runners. All competitor's running in distance races can benefit from playing this game. Here is how it works. You will need to find at least three or five of your friends to come

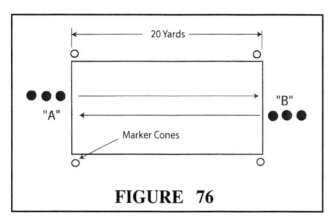

FIGURE 76

over and play the game with you. Have mom or dad come out and help by supervising. You will need cones to mark an area of confinement, and the end lines. Get into two groups, team "A" and team "B," to have a competition going. On "GO," or a whistle, the front member of team "A" sprints down to a line 20 yards away. They tag the hand of the front member of team "B", who then sprints down and tags the hand of the new front member of team "A" *(SEE FIGURE 76)*.

Playing the Game

Mom or dad blows a whistle or says, "GO" to get the game going. The object of the game is to see which team is the fastest. This goes on until all the members of team "A" are down at the same end. That team is the winner. Then all of you rest a few minutes. Do this for four or five minutes, then swap team members around so they are paired with different kids. Then run the game again. You should go through this at least four times. A "variation" of this game is pass a baton back and forth instead of slapping hands. Have mom or dad, just for fun and competition, keep track of the time for each group to see who was the fastest. Play the game for no more than 20 minutes. Then go to another skill activity, drill, exercise or game.

Drill No. 35- Middle of the Race
The Basics are

This is just using good "technique" to help you start moving up in the pack, towards the front in distance running. This puts you in a good position for the finish. Some power and resistance training is needed in the off season, mostly to build up the strength in your legs. This doesn't mean build big bulky muscles, but just some light weight training for strength. This can also be accomplished by running up hills, in sand, or in water. "Tempo" (pace) training is very important to keep you running at a particular speed for long distances. "Interval" training should be used along with "tempo" training. This is where a runner performs a series of runs, then takes a short recovery period after each run. Most forms of interval training now use an incomplete or partial recovery period after each run. What this means is, your heart rate is not allowed to return to a full rest.

By continuously placing a specific work load on your cardiovascular system, it responds by becoming more efficient and powerful. You young kids need to be very careful though to

FIGURE 77

not put too much of a load on your system. For cross country runners, "Fartlek" training is used (this is a swedish word meaning "speed play"). Fartlek is a special course that provides a variation in the terrain, and running intensity. A lot of work on this course should be performed in the off season, and just before your outdoor track season starts.

Practice

Start out by working on your power and resistance training in the off season. You can do some light weight training by doing half squats *(SEE FIGURE 77)*. The half squats build up your thigh muscles. Go half way down, hold there for five seconds, then come up and relax for a few seconds. Do at least ten of these at a session. They will help you when running uphill. Follow that by actually doing some uphill running if you can find a short hill. Then start to work on a mix of aerobic and anaerobic training in the middle of the off season, and going into your track season. In some parts of the USA I know it will be hard to work outside during winter. If this is the case, look for a YMCA to do your running indoors. Or get outside as soon as you can in late winter or early spring.

Light Weight Training

You will need dumbbells for this exercise. Usually five or six pound dumbbells will do. Get in a standing position and take a dumbbell in each hand. Then go into a half squat and hold for five seconds *(SEE FIGURE 78)*. Take a deep breath just before squating, then slowly letting it out as you come back up into the standing position. Do at least 20 of these going down into the half squat, then straightening back up. Use ten seconds (count by 1000s) rest then go right into the next squat. This is within the guidelines for short recovery periods, lots of repetitions.

Running Up Hill

Find a nearby road or street, with an up hill incline *(SEE FIGURE 79)*. Maybe a 10-15 degree slope, but not steeper like 45 degrees. Run this at a moderate pace for at least one mile for you younger kids, to two miles for 12 and olds. If you don't want to go out to the street or road, then find a short hill somewhere nearby, and run up and down the hill about 20 times.

FIGURE 78

FIGURE 79

Tempo (Pace) Training

Before you start, have mom or dad get you a stopwatch or a regular watch to use. Then sit down with your mom or dad and tell them when a certain amout of seconds have gone by. Mom or dad can say, "GO," then you tell them without looking at a clock or watch when you guess 20 seconds have gone by. Just raise your hand, when you think that many seconds have past. Compare your estimate with the correct amount of time, then have mom or dad let you know how far you are off. Then try to guess when 30 seconds and 45 seconds have gone by. What you are doing is learning how to estimate time.

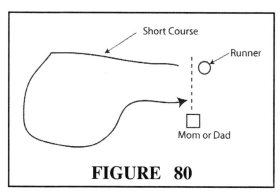

FIGURE 80

A *TIP* is close your eyes and visualize the second hand going around on a clock. This is all a test for understanding "tempo" and "pace." I suggest getting one of your friends to run with you while you are training. It makes running a little more fun. Now go out to the back yard or park, and plot a short course around the area *(SEE FIGURE 80)*. Mark a starting point then have mom or dad say, "GO," and you run around the short course and try to come back to the starting point in exactly 45 seconds. You need to keep working on this until you can get back in exactly 45 seconds. All of this is training you to estimate the duration of a run. Next go out on a track, back yard (if you have the room), sidewalk or the street, and run 50 yards in 20 seconds.

Mark a 50 yard long measured course, and mom or dad can time you. Have mom or dad

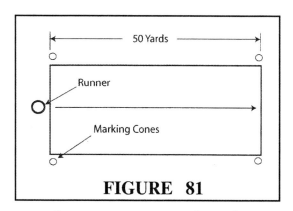

FIGURE 81

stand at the end of the course and say, "GO," then call out your time as they go by the finish line *(SEE FIGURE 81)*. *DO NOT* suddenly increase your speed at the end to get to finish line in the 20 seconds. You need to learn to adjust your pace to get there right at 20 seconds. You should run doing this drill three to five times at a session in order to get the feel of the required pace. As you progress in your training, you can can use different timing for the 50 yards, so you can practice faster and slower "paces" of running.

Once you get your pace down, then go to a "triangular" course, to make the running a little different. It helps break up the monotony of a straight or oval course all the time. Mark each leg (side) of the triangle to be 50 yards long *(SEE FIGURE 82)*. Get a couple of your friends to run with you as a group. It will be more fun. And more like a game than running. Now all of you go down to one corner of the triangle. Then say, "GO," or have mom or dad blow a whistle, and the whole group has to run 50 yards down to the next corner.

Before you start, pick a certain target time to get there in. For the first time make it 40 seconds. Then you, mom or dad, or someone set your watch or stop watch, for 40 seconds. When 40 seconds is up have them blow whistle. The object for you is to get there in exactly 40 seconds. If you get there early you have to jog in place, and wait for the slower runners to get there and catch up. When the whole group gets there, you all jog in place resting for about 30 seconds. Have mom or dad tell you this time if you need to adjust your pace, to get there right at 40 seconds. Then say, "GO," again and then all of you start out to the next corner. Have mom or dad reset the stop watch, then blow the whistle at 40 seconds again.

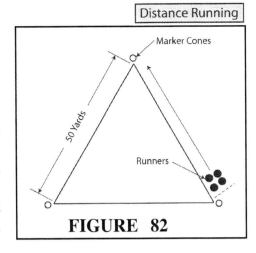

FIGURE 82

This time you should all get closer to the correct steady pace, to get you there in 40 seconds. Keep doing this until you get the pace down, always resting for about 30 seconds at each corner. When you get the 40 second down, you can change the pace to 20 seconds between corners. This will really help you learn tempo running. Two or three times, around all three sides, should be enough for one session. When you get better at tempo running, you can vary the distance to a triangle side, and the time or "pace" you need to work on.

Interval Training

For interval training it would be a good idea for you to get two or three of your friends to come over and run with you. Have mom or dad come out and help. For you young kids, set up a square course with 50 yards to a side. Mark each corner with a cone, or a flag. Have the group all go down to one corner *(SEE FIGURE 83)*. Then have mom or dad say, "GO," or blow a whistle and the group has to run 50 yards down to the next corner just like the "triangle" drill. At first all of you try to run it in 20 seconds, then mom or dad blows a whistle so that you will all know when 20 seconds has passed.

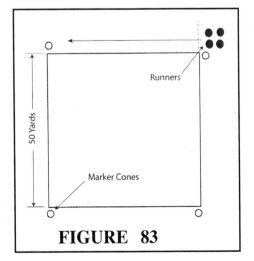

Then you all stop and rest for a 30 second interval, then mom or dad blows the whistle and times you on the next leg, just like the first leg. The object is for all of you to get there in just exactly 20 seconds while running at a constant speed, rest then procede to the next corner. After one time all the way around, change the rest interval to 15 seconds. After two times around all four sides, you all walk slowly around the whole course twice for a recovery period. This should be enough for a one session.

FIGURE 83

Cross Country "Fartlek" Training

Some "Fartlek" training can help the longer distance runners (1500m and 3000m). Mostly though it's for "cross country" runners. Instead of trying to set up your own Fartlek course, it will be a lot easier to go to your local high school and ask the "track & field" coach if you can use their course. Fartlek courses provide a course with a variation in terrain, areas for calisthenics, walking,

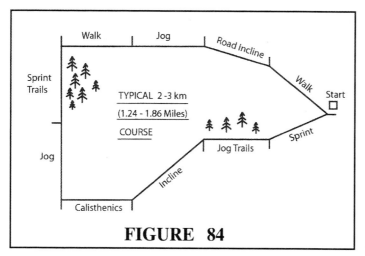

FIGURE 84

jogging, rugged trails, and sprinting *(SEE FIGURE 84)*. Get the layout from your high school track coach, then go with mom or dad out to the start point. It's a good idea to get several of your friends to go along with you. You younger kids, DO NOT go all by yourself. For younger kids, each leg should be organized so the whole course lasts about 20 minutes.

For 12 year olds and up, it's up to you as to how fast you sprint, and at what speed you jog or run. For you younger kids, walk the first leg, then do the incline legs, the jog legs, and the trail legs, at moderate speeds. You can do jumping jacks for the calisthenics. You need to end up by sprinting at about 80 % of all out speed. Since there are ten legs to the course, that leaves two minutes a leg at about 218 yards per leg. This means your runing "pace" should be just about the same as it was in the interval training square course drill on page 79.

After you have been through the course a few times, you will have a better idea of what your "pace" should be. However, if you younger kids take 30 minutes on the course, it's OK. The time is just suggested, not written on stone. Also if possible have mom or dad accompany you on the course. Or at least tell them to stay close by where they can see you, for *safety* reasons. Once or twice a week through this course should be enough. But it's probably going to depend on when the course is empty as to when you can use it. You younger kids stay off the course when older high school kids are using it because of the safety issue.

Drill No. 36- Finish of the Race

The Basics are

Finishing a race is basically sprinting the last 50m or so to the finish line on oval tracks. And if you see there is going to be a close finish between you and an opponent, then you will need to lean going across the finish line. The finish for the cross country is a little different. One of the better coaches reccomends starting to accelerate in the last 1/4 of the cross country race distance. Then finish with a "kick sprint" at 300m from the finish line. This is where all that anaerobic training comes in handy.

Practice

Use the same practice routine and methods as in the "sprinting" section *(SEE DRILL 23)* for the 800m, 1500m, 1600m and 3000m races. There is one other thing to work on in finishing a distance race that we have not talked about. And that is "kick sprinting". It's a little different from the style of sprinting in 100m, and 200m races. In those type of short races it's more of getting lots of high knee lift. Kick sprinting is running hard, but striding out a bit further and pushing off forward with your toes, then kind of kicking the leg hard as it goes forward instead of pumping *(SEE FIGURE 73)*. If your coach wants you to kick sprint finish, instead of hard pumping, it's up to them because they will know which style will work best for you. First decide the distance you want to work on for "kick sprinting." Then go out to the track and start running down the track. Go about 5 yards then say to yourself, "GO," and you immediately start kick sprinting for about 20 yards, then stop and come back. Do this at least five times at a session.

Check **TABLE 3** to see some comparison performance times for you to achieve in order to be competitive. The main records are "**American outdoor**" youth track & field records, but we have also added the local "**CYC**" and national "**CYO**" records for a comparison.

COMPARISON PERFORMANCE TIMES - DISTANCE RUNNING

BOYS		DISTANCE							
Age Division		800m	Record	1500m	Record	1600m	Record	3000m	Record
6 - 8 (Primary)	Satisfactory	3:40.0	△2:54.14						
	Good	3:00.0	△2:39.50						
	Excellent	2:40.0	*2:26.92		N/A		N/A		N/A
9-10 (Bantam) (Roadrunner)	Satisfactory	3:10.0	△2:42.44	7:00.0	#5:24.44	8:00.0	△8:20.00		
	Good	2:40.0	2:20.28	5:40.0	△4:57.47	6:00.0	△6:39.00		
	Excellent	2:20.0	2:19.0	5:00.0	4:43.70	5:30.0	*5:32.09		N/A
11 -12 (Midget) (Cub)	Satisfactory	3:00.0	#2:20.54	6:00.0	△4:43.30	7:00.0		12:50.0	△12:27.31
	Good	2:25.0	*2:16.17	5:10.0	#4:51.16	5:55.0	△5:59.00	11.35.0	#9:58.60
	Excellent	2:15.0	2:07.21	4:40.0	4:22.58	5:15.0	*4:58.88	10:20.0	9:38.52
13 - 14 (Youth) (Cadet)	Satisfactory	2:50.0	#2:08.34	5:50.0	△5:37.35	6:25.0	△5:59.00	12:10.0	△9:53.34
	Good	2:15.0	*2:10.93	4:50.0	#4:20.24	5:45.0	#4:53.97	10:00.0	△9:14.13
	Excellent	2:05.0	1:56.36	4:20.0	4:04.72	5:05.0	*4:51.27	9:40.0	9:08.86
GIRLS		DISTANCE							
Age Division		800m	Record	1500m	Record	1600m	Record	3000m	Record
6 - 8 (Primary)	Satisfactory	3:40.0	△2:51.90						
	Good	3:20.0	*2:44.96						
	Excellent	3:00.0	2:34.82		N/A		N/A		N/A
9 -10 (Bantam) (Roadrunner)	Satisfactory	3:30.0	*2:44.96	6:20.0	#5:47.67	7:50.0			
	Good	3:10.0	△2:33.10	5:50.0	△5:00.95	7:10.0	△6:30.50		
	Excellent	2:50.0	2:23.98	5:20.0	4:51.28	6:30.0	*6:03.97		N/A
11 -12 (Midget) (Cub)	Satisfactory	3:10.0	*2:34.97	6:00.0	#5:07.84	7:40.0		12:00.0	#11:09.84
	Good	2:50.0	#2:30.44	5:30.0	△4:58.36	7:00.0	△6:48.00	11.00.0	△10:35.93
	Excellent	2:30.0	2:13.56	5:00.0	4:41.62	6:20.0	*5:49.56	10:30.0	10:03.54
13 - 14 (Youth) (Cadet)	Satisfactory	3:00.0	*2:37.54	5:50.0	#4:49.93	7:00.0	△6:29.00	11:50.0	△10:34.36
	Good	2:40.0	#2:24.94	5:05.0	△4:42.60	6:30.0	#5:40.38	11:00.0	△10:33.66
	Excellent	2:20.0	2:09.00	4:50.0	4:28.61	6:00.0	*5:30.37	10:00.0	9:35.12

N/A = Not applicable or available in this age group.
All times are measured in minutes and seconds.
Unless otherwise noted all records are "American AAU/ USATF National Outdoor" youth (2002-2007).
△ = AAU/ USATF Private Track Club Record.
= A "CYO" (Catholic Youth Organization) National record or performance time (2007).
* = A "CYC" (Catholic Youth Council, St. Louis, MO.) record or performance time (2007).

TABLE 3

HIGH JUMPING

Explanation

    High jumping has been around in the olympics almost since the start of modern day olympics. All you young kids like to jump. It's not too dangerous for you younger kids, mainly because you don't get too high up in the air. However, when using the "Fosbury flop" technique there is always a danger of landing wrong on your neck. Dick Fosbury developed this technique in the 1960's, which revolutionized high jumping. There are several other techniques. They are the "scissors" style, and the "western roll" style. Now almost everyone uses the flop technique. This is probably because of several reasons. One it's not too hard to learn, and two the possibility of the jumper going higher than either of the other two older styles. If you use the approved landing pad that every high school uses, the landing becomes safer. Of course there is always the danger of accidents

H   G   **FIGURE 85**   F   E

so I can't say it's entirely safe, but very close. If you follow the proper training development stages first, the danger probability is very low. The best thing to do is use your local high school's bar and jump pit if possible.

    You could build your own pit area in your back yard if you really want to become a serious high jumper. To buy a good jumping pit pad, weather cover, bar, and standards, you are looking at anywhere from $600 all the way up to $3400. Or you could buy a good pad and cover, then make your own standards, and bar. I'm *NOT reccomending* you do this, but you could if you do it right. What I am definately *NOT* suggesting you do is dig a big pit hole in your back yard and fill it with sand or sawdust, like they used to have at playgrounds. This type of jumping is just to *dangerous*.

    High jumping these days is about technique and leg strength. The "Flop" is the best, so we will concentrate on that technique. "Short" run-ups, and the longer "curved" run-ups will be defined as well as good drills to use. We will start with the jumping techniques first, then lead-ups last to develop your jumping and lift abilities (core training).

Drill No. 37- Fosbury Flop Technique

The Basics are

    This is basically jumping up off "one foot" only, turning your back to the bar, then going over it backwards, with a little kick up of the feet as you go over the bar *(SEE FIGURE 85)*. The lift you need (vertical leap), to get way up in the air, is sometimes referred to as raising your "center of gravity." Have mom or dad get you some high jumping shoes if you are going to be serious about becoming a good high jumper. The jumping shoe has spikes on the sole as well as the heel, to prevent slipping on the takeoff. Some jumpers use short spikes, or none at all, on the leading leg (closest to the bar). Spikes on the sole and heel of the push off leg are critical for good traction on the takeoff. Good back arch as you go over the bar is another critical skill that you need to develop. Gymnastic type flexibility exercises are used to develop this skill. And lift, along with leg strength, must be worked on and developed. Howerver, the arch and kick won't help your foot drag (Which knocks down the bar), unless you have a 100 % spin rate revolving around the bar *(SEE FIGURE 89)*. There are a number of drills that have been developed to enhance each one of these skills. Use all of these drills and you will become a successful high jumper.

Practice

The key to flop jumping is technique. So you start practice by working on the basic technique itself. That is going over the bar backwards. If you can't learn how to go over the bar backwards, and be comfortable with it, then forget about "flop" jumping.

D   C   B   A
(Continued)   **FIGURE 85**

Backward Jumping

If you are a young beginner you will need to get mom or dad to come out and help. Start out by learning the basic orientation to backward jumping. First you need to find a place to practice with an approved landing pad which is probably gong to be at your nearest high school. Stand about two foot lengths from the edge of the landing pad *(SEE FIGURE 86-A)*, then turn around with your back to the pad. Next bend down at your knees, and put both arms down and back behind you. The next step is, push upwards very hard with both feet, swing your arms upward and

C   B   A
FIGURE 86

backwards hard, and jump backwards way up onto the pad *(SEE FIGURE 86-B)*. Then as you get up in the air kick both feet upwards very hard, so just as your back and shoulders hit the pad your feet are sticking way up *(SEE FIGURE 86-C)*. Make sure that as you make contact with the pad, your back and shoulders are flat with your arms at your sides. You can land this way by learning to push back at your waist hard, flex your hips, and straightening your back while bringing your arms to your sides to help break the fall. Because of the height of the pad, you need to learn to land this way every time, and not straight down on your neck. When you are beginning do this drill at least five times at every session (to train muscle memory).

   The second part of this training is "jumping with leg elevation." Stand in the same position as before, with your back to the pad *(SEE FIGURE 87-A)*. Except this time land with your legs way up, knees bent and pulled in slightly to your chest *(SEE FIGURE 87-C)*. Also make sure that as you jump, and get up into the air, you arch your back and flex your hips *(SEE FIGURE 87-B)*. A "Tip." Imagine an upward and backward jump with a "sit" in the air. Also learn to relax your whole body as you land on the pad. Learn to not just fall back on the pad, but jump up so you just drop your back onto the pad. When you are beginning you need to do this drill at least five times at every session (to train muscle memory).

C   B   A

FIGURE 87

   Now for the third part of the training add in a cross bar and standards (bar holders). For this part of the training you will need mom and dad or two other people to help you. You will also need a string or a flexible type rubber tubing cross bar. This is for safety reasons. For the initial bar setting, set it at just a little above a heigth you can easily jump *(SEE FIGURE 88-A)*. This drill is to get you used to the heigth when jumping (It's a muscle memory-Anti fear thing). The best way to do this is jump off a "box stand" if possible. The box stand only needs to be about 10 or 12 inches high. Or if you don't have a stand then move back about two foot lengths away from the pad, then lower the bar to a height you can jump from ground height. Next jump backwards over the bar and try to clear it, using all the techniques you just learned in the previous drills.

Spin Rate

   You need to get 100 % spin rate as you go over and around the bar. What you need to do is just as you go over the bar with your back arched, and your legs starting to kick up *(SEE*

84

FIGURE 88-B), is thrust your hips up and back as fast and as hard as you can towards your head. This is to get the spin around the bar, with the bar as the pivot point *(SEE FIGURE 89)*. If you look at the diagram, you can see what happens to your feet when you get even 25% too low on your spin rate. The spin is what gets your feet over so they don't drag.

To work on this you will need to go out someplace where they have a high jump pad. Then get a broom stick or even a long baseball bat, and get mom, dad, or a friend to act as a "spotter," to hold it where the bar would be.

Place the broom stick or bat at a height of about where your belt line would be as you stand straight up right in front of the jump pad *(SEE FIGURE 88-B)*. Now stand right up against the stick or bat, so it is touching

A   B
FIGURE 88

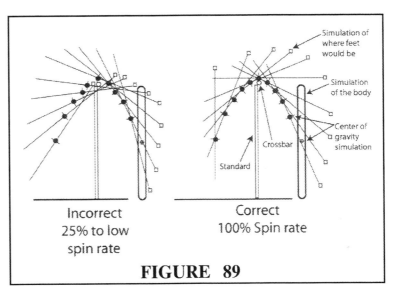

Incorrect
25% to low
spin rate

Correct
100% Spin rate

FIGURE 89

right at the top of your hips or belt line on your back side.

Now do the "flop" jump back over the stick or bat while mom or dad holds it still. Next as you kick up your feet and start to go over, you thrust you hips up and backward while rotating your shoulders downward. If you are not rotating around the stick fast enough, then have mom or dad use the stick to kind of boost and flip you on over and around the stick. Coaches in gymnastics do this to help kids flip over, and they call it spotting. All of this is to have you get the feel of fast rotation around a bar. You need to do at least five of these at a session. You will need to continue doing this drill many many times, to train your body and feet to do the fast rotation (muscle memory). A *"TIP."* Just before you jump up and kick, close your eyes and focus real hard on what you need to do. Your brain will take care of the rest of your move. I have coached and watched many of you young kids learning to high jump, and one of the biggest problems most of them have is foot drag and hitting the bar. They get their back and arms way over the bar, but the feet drag and hit the bar or come down on it.

Drill No. 38- Bar Lead Ups

The Basics are

Now lets go through all the lead ups to the bar, to help build up the strengths and skills you will need. Lead ups are different methods and approaches to get you to the bar. You can't just stand flat footed in front of the bar and expect to jump up over it. You need lead up momentum. There are drills you need to work on that build up your leg strength and lift. Drills to work on are:

- High knee marching *(SEE FIGURE 51, 53, 54)*.
- Long stride bounding *(SEE FIGURE 90, 91)*.
- Jump and touch the ball *(SEE FIGURE 92)*.
- Squat jump over a bar *(SEE FIGURE 93)*.
- Cone jumping *(SEE FIGURE 37)*.

Practice
High Knee Marching

Do each one of the three marching drills two times, going about 10 yards down and back.

Long Stride Bounding

Long stride bounding is taking a little running start, then driving forward and upward to cover as much distance as possible. How this works is run about three steps, then bound by pushing off upward and driving or thrusting your leading leg thigh to a horizontal position. Use a lot of arm swing to help get momentum for the bound. Stretch out at the midpoint of each bound to get the longest stride stretch possible. And try to momentarily get the feeling of floating just at the midpoint of each bound, almost dong the splits. Land on your leading leg, then make a couple of short steps and bound again *(SEE FIGURE 90)*.

FIGURE 90

A variation of this is "bounding with arm swings." This is where you swing your arms forward on one stride, jump up, then swing them backward on the next stride *(SEE FIGURE 91)*. This drill teaches you to rotate your arms forward while simultaneously moving in a forward direction and bounding (muscle memory). Do this bound about three or four times over a 20 yard distance. Then go back to the starting point, and go through the sequence again. Doing two or three repetitions of this drill will probably be enough of either of these drills at a session for you young beginning kids. You can do more reps as you get older, stronger, and get used to bounding.

A   B   C

FIGURE 91

Jump and Touch the Ball

This is a drill to train your muscle memory to lift or propell you straight up. In this drill you just take a few short steps, then jump up and touch a ball with the top of your head *(SEE FIGURE 92)*. If you have a basketball hoop on your garage, you could use that to suspend the ball from.

The ball can be a light weight beach ball. Tie some twine, or heavy string permenently around it, and suspend it so that it is about one to two feet above your head. Then get about six or eight feet away from the suspended ball, take a few short steps to get your momentum going, then push off straight up in the air, and try to touch the bottom of the ball with the top of your head.

Lean slightly backward just before you take off on your jump. Make sure you jump *UP* as much as possible, and not outward from your momentum. Swing the leading

A   B

FIGURE 92

leg, and your arms, upward as hard as possible, to get upward momentum. This is a drill that helps you learn how to raise your "center of gravity." Do this at least five times at a practice session.

Squat Jump over the Bar

The object of this drill is training you to jump directly upwards.On this drill you can use the rubber cross bar, standards (bar holders), and a sand pit. You wil also need mom, dad, or a few friends to come out and help youon this drill. If you have your own bar and standards, take them over to the long jump pit at your local high school, and set up there. If you don't then you will need two people to hold the rubber cross bar for you to jump over. Also bring a rake so you can smooth out, and level, the sand after each jump. If you are using standards to hold the cross bar, then bring some weights to hold the base of the standards down. First go up to the bar and measure one arms length away. This is the takeoff point *(SEE FIGURE 93-A)*. Then mark that distance away

SAND PIT   Bar

1 ARMS LENGTH   Takeoff Point Line

A   B   C

FIGURE 93

with tape or sting so that you can visually see the takeoff point as you come up to the bar. Next face the bar, then get back one or two steps back away from the takeoff point. Take a short run up, push off with the non-power leg *(SEE FIGURE 93-B)* at the takeoff line, swing both arms up, and make the squat jump over the bar. Start with the bar at about waist high, then adjust it accordingly up or down, so you can make it over the bar. As you progress, you can raise it up. You could also use a hurdle, we used one just for illustration purposes. Here are some *"Tips."* Drive and push up off the ground with some power. Stretch up and extend your body upward at the takeoff. Keep your head up, and don't lean forward while in your jump. And last as you takeoff, bring your knees all the way up towards your chest so that your feet clear the bar *(SEE FIGURE 93-C)*. Do this drill at least five times at a practice session.

Drill No. 39- Run -Up Approach Techniques
The Basics are

Run-ups are the starting approaches to the bar in order to get the mementum, angle, and lift required to get you over the bar for the flop technique. Your approach is the most important, overlooked part of the flop technique. Every high jumper has slightly different skills that are related to their success in "flopping." Run-ups can be from the right, from the left, a straight angle to the bar, straight on with a curve, or they can be off to the side right or left with a curve at the end. The "elementary or basic run-up" is at an angle of 35 to 40 degrees to the bar, and uses a straight at the bar three stride run. The "straight on, curve at the end," technique uses a four to eight strides straight ahead from the front start, with a five stride tight curve at the end. And last the "elementary from the side curve" run-up uses a straight ahead two stride, with a three stride at an angle to bar gentle curve at the end. This is sometimes referred to as the "J" technique.

As you get better at jumping, you will need to increase the length of the run-up, and you will need to mark your starting point and where the start of your curved run begins. This is so that when your run-up is adjusted to just where you want it, then it is always the same. After you have been jumping for a few years, you will probably need to make some adjustments to your marks. Modern coaches say a 3/4 speed run-up with a sprint at the end is a better technique for most of you young jumpers to learn and work on.

Practice

Lets start with the basic elementary run-up, then go to the more complicated run-ups. If you have enough room you can practice these run-ups out in your back yard.

Elementary Run-Up

If you can, go to your high school "high jumping" area to practice because you will get a better feel for how this works. Even if they don't have their standards or pad out, you can still practice in front of where the bar would be. First get out in front of the landing pad. By now you should know which side you want to come in from. If not, then determine which is your power foot (strongest foot). To see how to find out which is your strongest leg and foot *SEE DRILL 44.* This will be the foot you plant or takeoff on. This is referred to as the "touchdown point." The power foot is planted on the outside farthest away from the pit. The trail leg provides the upward thrust, and is closest to the pit. If your power foot is your right foot, you should come in from the LEFT side. If it's your left foot, you come in from the RIGHT side. Then measure one arms distance out from the bar on that side, and 1/4 of the bars length in from the end, then mark that spot with an "X" or a square with tape or some kind of a marker you they can see. Chalk works good because it washes or rubs off later naturally. This will be your takeoff mark for your power foot, and you need to be able to visually see the mark *(SEE FIGURE 94)*.

Occasionally young beginning jumpers will go to the correct side that gives them their best power takeoff. What happens though is after a few jumps they find out it does not feel right to them when they jump from that side. So they go on their own to the other side. However, when you do that you are not pushing up (takeoff) with your strongest foot. This means you will not get up as high in the air as possible, which is critical if you want to be successful. If that happens to you, and you insist on coming from the opposite side, here is what you should do. Start doing lots of hops, or one leg push ups, with your week leg. In other words build it up to be your power leg.

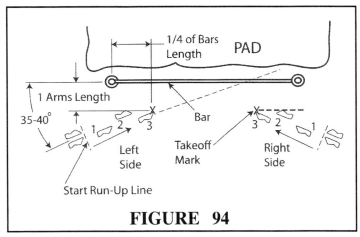

FIGURE 94

Now come out at about 35 to 40 degrees, and at about three strides out from the takeoff, and mark your start point for the run-up. Remember though the three stride run-up is just for the low height jumps to learn the technique. To go up in height you need longer run-ups. To make this easier for you, walk through the run- up first, and visualize the whole run-up and jump in your mind. Do this by standing at the start point, then close your eyes and visualize yourself running up, jumping up, turning in the air, and going over the bar. This will progam the jump in your mind, and help you focus better before you jump. Some coaches say focus on the top of the far side post while jumping. When you are young it's probably going to depend on which technique works best for you. Next set the bar down to a heigth you can easily go over, then start practicing the jump. You should make at least five of these elementary run up jumps at a training session.

Straight Ahead Curve at the End Run-Up

Go to the nearest high school high jumping area to practice this technique also. This is where you will get a better feel for how this technique works. First get out in front of the landing pad. Mark the takeoff point ("X"), left or right, just like in *FIGURE 94*. Then go back from that point

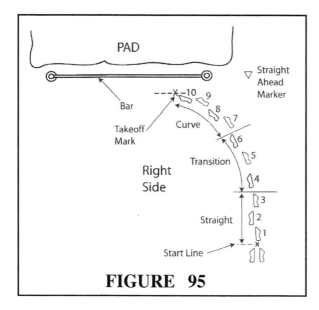

FIGURE 95

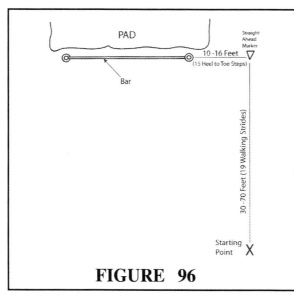

FIGURE 96

about seven curved strides and make a mark that you will be able to visually see. Then go back from that mark about another three strides straight back and make another mark *(SEE FIGURE 95)*. This will approximately be the starting point for your run-up. Now how do you mark your straight ahead marker. First go out 15 heel to toe steps to the right (or left) of the bar standard *(SEE FIGURE 96)*. Next go straight out 19 walking strides, then make a mark. Now compare the two marks. Where they come together or line up is your first starting point. I say the first because you may need to make adjustments later after a few run up approaches.

To make this easier for you, walk through this 10 step run-up first. Then go back to the starting point, close your eyes, and visualize the whole run-up and jump in your mind. Next set the bar down to a heigth you can easily go over, and start practicing the jump using this run-up. After a few jumps, make any necessary adjustments, then take some colored chalk and mark your starting point and your takeoff point. In competition, put your initals next to your marks. Then you won't have any confusion between yours and some other jumpers marks. Write down how many heel to toe steps and walking strides it takes to get to your starting point. This is where you mark your locations every time you go out to jump. Make at least five practice jumps at a training session.

Summation

There is some additional practice to go through, to improve on your curved run-up approach technique. It is called "curved running." You also need to learn to lean just a little forward at the start of your run-up. Also during the curved part of your run-up, you need to lean slightly away from the bar *(SEE FIGURE 97)*. The "circle run" will improve your lean skill. After doing your circle runs, then go to your starting mark and do some leaning runs around in front of the bar *(SEE FIGURE 99)*. Always do your leaning run throughs exactly in your ten step normal pattern. Do not run a wide or narrow pattern. Do at least five leaning runs at a practice session.

Curved Running & Sprinting

Use this drill to help improve your curved run-up approach technique. Set this up for a round circle *(SEE FIGURE 98)*. Mark a circle about 18 feet in diameter. You can do this by using cones, or you could use old white one gallon milk containers and fill them with sand, water, or kitty litter. Actually the cones will probably cost less. With the milk containers though, you are recycling. Say "GO" and run around the inside of the circle of cones two times at approximately 3/4 speed. Then you exit the circle *SPRINTING* straight out to the side for about four or five yards. Run around the inside of the circle the same direction you come into the bar, either around to your right or to your left. Do this drill at least two times at a practice session.

FIGURE 97

Circle Run With a Lean

This drill will also help improve on your "lean" for the curved part of your run-up. Use the same 18 foot circle as in *FIGURE 98*. In the single circle drill, jumpers that approach the bar from the left side will start out with the right foot, and run clockwise around the circle. This simulates the start of your run, and lean towards the inside of the circle. Jumpers that approach the bar from the right side will start out with the left foot, and run counterclockwise around.

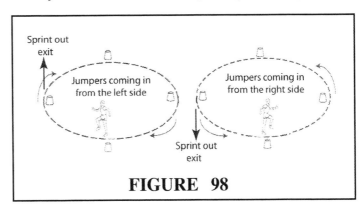

FIGURE 98

This drill is excellant training for the run-up approach and take off. Run fast around the inside of the circle leaning inward at least three times at a session. If you do this just before you jump, it programs your muscle memory to *AUTOMATICALLY* lean in your jump practice. Try it!

Drill No. 40- Pop-Up Arm Action & Body Positioning for Takeoff
The Basics are

These drills will help you improve on your arm action and body position just prior to your takeoff. First walk through the last 5 strides with your arm swinging before your takeoff so that you get the feel of what your arms and your body will doing on the takeoff. Just walk though and don't jump up yet. After you have walked through this several times, and you have your footwork correct, then you can speed up the drill. These are called "*pop-ups*." For this drill start your pop-up runs about where the last five

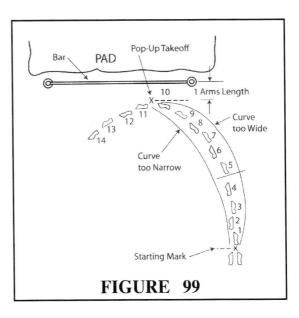

FIGURE 99

91

FIGURE 100

strides begin *(SEE FIGURE 99)*. Don't worry about the curve right now because this is just "form" training. Since many jumpers come in from the right side, and push up off of their left foot, then lets start from there *(SEE FIGURE 100)*.

- Start out with your left foot forward, arms down near your sides at step position five.
- First with the left foot forward, take one medium size stride with arms still at your sides.
- Next you take three long strides, and simultaneously swing both arms from backwards to forward at the last stride.
- Then you step forward one short stride with your left foot, plant it, then push up very hard with your left foot, simultaneously turn your back to the bar and tilt the upper part of your body a little backward.
- The last move is at the same time you swing and drive your right foot straight up hard, and jump straight up in the air bringing both hands way up over your head.
- Since this is only "form and technique" practice, the jump up need only be about one to two feet in the air.

Jumping from the left side is just the opposite, or flip flopped in technique. You would come in from the left side, push up off of your right foot. You can do this drill in your back yard if you have enough room. The best place though is where a bar and a landing pad are located. You don't need the bar for this training. Doing the drill in front of the pad and bar will help you with your takeoff technique, and maybe answer any questions you might have. This especially applies to young five through eight year olds. Do five of these complete run through "pop-ups" at a practice session.

FIGURE 101

Jump Rope

Jumping rope for about five minutes at a practice session will also help you with your arm swing. But bring the rope over your head from front to back. Beginners need to work on this.

Blocking

Using both arms and your free leg is called blocking, which is a stopping of one or more body parts in order to accelerate another body part. This means throwing or swinging both arms up as hard as you can while driving upward with your free leg thigh *(SEE FIGURE 101)*. The thigh should drive up parallel to the ground or higher. And if possible the thigh should end up parallel to the bar. DO NOT drive your knee across your body to turn your back to the bar. If you are running your approach curve correctly, your free leg will have to start behind and inside of your touchdown takeoff leg. And it will move in a circular path around your touchdown leg. This causes enough transverse rotation to turn your back to the bar. If the last part of your approach curve is flat or straight, you will need to drive your knee across your body in order to get the necessary transvers rotation to get turned. And this will cause a loss of height to get over the bar. When you do your pop-up drills make sure you are driving your free leg knee up correctly.

The other part of blocking is swinging your arms up. Your arm swing helps drive you straight up to get the height you need to get over the bar. As you start to swing them up think of doing a swimming brest stroke, it's very similar. Without the arm swing and knee drive, it's hard to go straight up vertically. Just as you take off on your touuchdown foot, your body needs to be straight up.

Drill No. 41- Bar Clearance

The Basics are

These drills will help you improve on getting over the bar once you get up in the air. One of the keys to bar clearance is keep both your legs and arms in closer to your body. Your spin rate and rotation over and around the bar is slowed down when your arms and leg are out farther away

from the center of your body mass. So keep those arms and legs in tighter as you start to go over the bar *(SEE FIGURE 88-B)*. Your head and shoulders are also important. Your head needs to stay balanced on your shoulders. If you tilt your head back into the bar to look at or see the bar, your shoulder and hip on that side will drop. In other words look up at the sky and don't look back at the bar. Your knees should be bent and your feet should be as close to your buttocks as possible. You need to arch your back by driving your hips up *(SEE FIGURE 102)*. Just as your hips go over the bar is when your rotation or spin has to be the fastest.

Just as your hips start to clear the bar, you need to raise your hamstrings. Bring your chin to your chest and

FIGURE 102

lower your hips, which will raise your hamstrings. This will also raise your knees and put them in a position to clear your feet. Then with your knees up, straightening your legs will clear your feet over the bar (the kick). After you clear the bar you need to slow your rotation as you drop towards the pit (pad). As you drop you keep your legs straight and extend your arms out away from your body. You need to land on the pad on your upper back and not your neck, to make sure you have a safe landing.

Practice

You practice your bar clearance using all these little techniques when you do your jumps over the bar from standing on the box *(SEE DRILL 37 SPIN RATE & FIGURES 88, 89)*.

Check *TABLE 4* to see some comparison jumping heights for you to achieve in order to be competitive. The main records are "*American outdoor*" youth track & field records, but we have also added the local "*CYC*" and national "*CYO*" records for a comparison.

COMPARISON PERFORMANCE DISTANCES -HIGH JUMP

BOYS		DISTANCE	
Age Division		Meters (Feet - Inches)	Record - Meters (Feet - Inches)
6 - 8 (Primary)	Satisfactory	.91m (3 Ft. - 0 In.)	
6 - 8 (Primary)	Good	1.04m (3 Ft. - 5 In.)	N/A
6 - 8 (Primary)	Excellent	1.17m (3 Ft. - 10 In.)	
9 -10 (Bantam) (Roadrunner)	Satisfactory	1.22m (4 Ft. - 10 In.)	Sub = 1.23m (4 Ft. - 0.5 In.)
9 -10 (Bantam) (Roadrunner)	Good	1.37m (4 Ft. - 6 In.)	* 1.42m (4 Ft. - 8 In.)
9 -10 (Bantam) (Roadrunner)	Excellent	1.52m (5 Ft. - 0 In.)	1.55m (5 Ft. - 1 In.)
11 -12 (Midget) (Cub)	Satisfactory	1.17m (3 Ft. - 10 In.)	# 1.58m (5 Ft. - 2 In.)
11 -12 (Midget) (Cub)	Good	1.55m (5 Ft. - 1 In.)	* 1.63m (5 Ft. - 4 In.)
11 -12 (Midget) (Cub)	Excellent	1.63m (5 Ft. - 4 In.)	1.75m (5 Ft. - 8.75 In.)
13 - 14 (Youth) (Cadet)	Satisfactory	1.52m (5 Ft. - 0 In.)	# 1.78m (5 Ft. - 10 In.)
13 - 14 (Youth) (Cadet)	Good	1.68m (5 Ft. - 6 In.)	* 1.73m (5 Ft. - 8 In.)
13 - 14 (Youth) (Cadet)	Excellent	1.83m (6 Ft. - 0 In.)	1.94m (6 Ft. - 4.25 In.)
GIRLS		DISTANCE	
Age Division		Meters (Feet - Inches)	Record - Meters (Feet - Inches)
6 - 8 (Primary)	Satisfactory	.71m 2 Ft. - 4 In.)	
6 - 8 (Primary)	Good	.81m (2 Ft. - 8 In.)	△ .76m (2 Ft. - 5.92 In.)
6 - 8 (Primary)	Excellent	.91m (3 Ft. - 0 In.)	
9 -10 (Bantam) (Roadrunner)	Satisfactory	1.17m (3 Ft. - 10 In.)	Sub = 1.27m (4 Ft. - 2 In.)
9 -10 (Bantam) (Roadrunner)	Good	1.30m (4 Ft. - 3 In.)	* 1.35m (4 Ft. - 5 In.)
9 -10 (Bantam) (Roadrunner)	Excellent	1.42m (4 Ft. - 8 In.)	1.47m (4 Ft. - 10 In.)
11 -12 (Midget) (Cub)	Satisfactory	1.37m (4 Ft. - 6 In.)	# 1.49m (4 Ft. - 10.5 In.)
11 -12 (Midget) (Cub)	Good	1.47m (4 Ft. - 10 In.)	* 1.45m (4 Ft. - 9 In.)
11 -12 (Midget) (Cub)	Excellent	1.58m (5 Ft. - 2 In.)	1.68m (5 Ft. - 6 In.)
13 - 14 (Youth) (Cadet)	Satisfactory	1.47m (4 Ft. - 10 In.)	# 1.58m (5 Ft. - 2 In.)
13 - 14 (Youth) (Cadet)	Good	1.58m (5 Ft. - 2 In.)	* 1.52m (5 Ft. - 0 In.)
13 - 14 (Youth) (Cadet)	Excellent	1.68m (5 Ft. - 6 In.)	1.74m (5 Ft. - 8.5 In.)

N/A = Records not applicable or available in this age group.

All distances are measured in meters or feet and inches.

Unless otherwise noted all records are "American AAU/ USATF National Outdoor " youth (2002-2007).

△ = AAU/ USATF Private track club record.

* = A "CYC" (Catholic Youth Council, St. Louis, MO.) record or performance height (2007).

= A "CYO" (Catholic Youth Organization) National record or performance height (2007).

TABLE 4

LONG JUMPING

Explanation

Long jumping has been around in the olympics almost since the start of modern day olympics. All of you young kids like to jump. I know because I have been coaching you for years. Many sprinters are also long jumpers because their running speed skills helps them get a lot of forward momentum down the runway for the jump. Long jumping can be broken down into four phases:

- Approach run.
- The last two strides.
- The takeoff.
- Action in the air and the landing.

The four techniques mostly used around the world now are the "hitch kick" technique, the "hang" technique, the "Sail" technique and the "stride" technique. The "hitch kick" technique seems to be the most popular right now. However, all of the other techniques have been used successfully by some world class jumpers, to attain some very long distances. Some German coaches are recomending the "stride" technique for young beginners. All the techniques use a fast run-up, and similar body positions at the takoff point. The approach run and the takeoff are the most important techniques to learn. The most important skills a jumper needs are speed, lots of leg strength and spring on the takeoff. If you already have these skills, what you do in the air may not even matter that much. However, by trying allof these different techniques, you may find one of these techniques that will help you get just a little more distance on a jump.

Long jumpers jump into a sand pit. You could make your own, but your local high school already has one. If you ask, they can tell you when they are not using it. Week ends, or the team is away for a meet, are both possibilities. If you do use the high school sand pit, bring a rake with you, and leave it smoothed out when you are through using it. Also for safety reasons rake it, and check for debris or other objects in it before and after you use it. If you do make your own pit, it's going to take a lot of room in your back yard, and it could get a little expensive. We will go into the approach run first (most important), then the lead-ups, the takeoff, and last the different techniques (action) in the air.

In all of our pictures and examples we will use a jumper starting with their left foot forward, and using their right (power) foot for their takeoff. You can use your right foot forward to start, but it changes the number of steps by minus one (-1).

Drill No. 42- The Approach Run
The Basics are

The idea in your approach run is to start out be gradually accelerating with your first few strides and ending with maximum acceleration at takeoff. However, this is a controlled run. Very fast, but smooth like a sprint race. The run breaks down into the length of your approach, your speed, acceleration, and your last two strides.

Length of Approach

The length of a beginners or inexperienced approach should be in the 13-17 steps range *(SEE FIGURE 103)*. The longer your approach run is, the harder it is to develp a consistant stride pattern. If you are small, short and stocky build, use the shorter 13 step run-up. If you are tall with a long legs build, use the 17 step run-up. The thing you need to learn is accelerate quick, run fast, run smooth, and stay under control as you go down the runway. If you are not too good at running go to the "sprint" section and find out how you need to train and practice to go fast. You need to always start out on the same foot, and use the same stride length in order to hit the takeoff

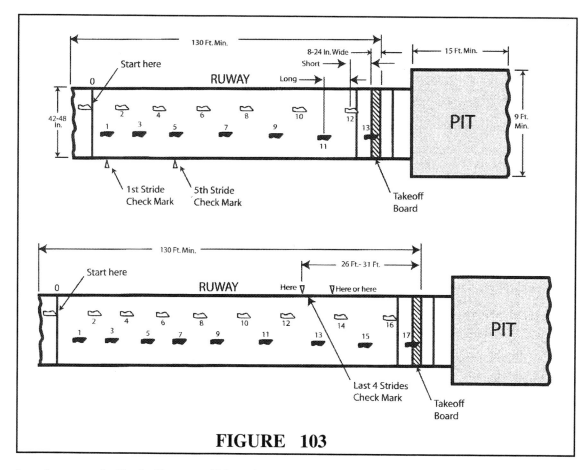

FIGURE   103

board accurately. Basically you will be using a stand up runners start *(SEE FIGURE 72)*. Hitting the takeoff board or line corectly is also important so that a good jump is not cancelled by a foul. You need to adjust your run-up so that your takeoff (power foot) lands as close as possible to the leading edge of the board or line *(SEE FIGURE 105)*.

Some long jump experts recomend a 12-16 stride run-up for beginning young kids. However, some young jumpers do use a longer run-up. From track to track some runways are longer than others, but it has to be at least 130 feet long. So it comes down to the jumper, and how many strides your coach wants you to use. Many world class jumpers use check marks *(SEE FIGURE 103)* at different spots down the runway to aid in their run-up.

Practice

To practice this drill go out to your starting point and practice some run-ups. Don't jump out in the pit though. First measure where the 13 or 17 strides comes out to by reversing your run. Start by standing in the middle of the takeoff board, in a full stride position with your favored (power) leg out in front touching the middle of the takeoff board. Your other leg is way back. Now move the toe of your power leg to the leading (front) edge of the takeoff board. Next run an all out fast as you can 13 or 17 strides down the runway. Have mom or dad or someone go down there near the end of the runway to place a mark where your last stride lands. Get some of those colored markers at the athletic equipment store. They make them so that they can be pushed into the ground out at the edge of the runway. Use them to mark your last stride. As you are running call out "One," "Two," "Three," and so on, every time one of your feet hits the ground. Do this all the way down the runway. This is so the person marking the spot has a check on your last stride. The person making the mark can count your strides as you run, for another check also.

There is another way to do this. Lay a 165 foot tape down along the edge of the runway. Put the end of the tape at the front edge of the takeoff board or line, have someone hold onto it, then stretch the rest of the tape out all the way down the runway. Have another person go down to the other end and hold it. Then you make your 13 or 17 stride run, and and they record the distance. Then you will always have that distance to mark the next time you long jump. I suggest you make three runs, mark the spots, then take an average if they come out slightly different.

A typical 13 stride run-up, with visual check marks for the first and fifth strides, is shown in *FIGURE 103*. Next thing to do is go down to the mark and make a practice jump out into the pit. Then have mom or dad, or someone, stand near the takeoff point and see where your toe actually lands on your takeoff. Don't look down to see, it will slow you down. Let the observer tell you. Make any necessary adjustment to the starting mark and distance, then try another jump. Keep making adjustments until the takeoff foot is hitting at just the right spot on the takeoff board or line. Make sure you are running at the same speed every time, or the takeoff point will vary.

Once this is all accomplished, then measure the corrected starting point again and record it in a little notebook. I like the second method with the tape because wherever you are jumping you can stretch out a tape and measure exactly where to mark your starting point and check marks for the run-up. Once you know this distance, then make at least five jumps at a practice session.

Drill No. 43- Acceleration and Speed Down the Runway
The Basics are
Drive off the line but slowly accelerate so that you are at top speed at the takeoff board. If you accelerate too fast at the start, then you will start to slow down a little at the takeoff board. At first don't jump out into the pit, just work on your rhythm and a consistant stride pattern, all the way to the takeoff board.

The Last Two Strides
The last two strides are important because it sets you up for your takeoff. In these last two strides you stay in a full sprinting position by pushing down hard on the runway. DO NOT slow down in these last two to four strides. Your next to last stride with your left foot is called penultimate stride. In this stride you lower your center of gravity slightly *(SEE FIGURE 104)*. You gather up your energy in this stride for the takeoff with your power foot. This how you prepare for the takeoff. The last stride with your right foot is slightly shorter than your penultimate stride.

FIGURE   104

On the last stride you come from the slightly lower penultimate stride and raise your center of gravity. As your takeoff foot hits, it needs to be flat and slightly in front of your body so that you can get a good solid push upward. Then just before your foot hits you slightly flex your takeoff leg. Remember your last two strides by thinking long-short. DO NOT reach out on your last stride because it is like putting the brakes on. Again, think short as you gather your energy.

Practice

To practice this drill go out to your starting point and practice some run-ups. Don't jump out in the pit though. First just run down the runway several times and work on a slower starting acceleration and a consistant stride. Make at least three of these type of runs at a practice session. Next go out about five strides from the takeoff board. Have markers for your last two strides. Use these two markers to work on your long-short strides. Do at least 3 of these type of strides at a practice session. On the last stride focus on a gathering and flexing of your takeoff leg.

Drill No. 44- Determining the Power (Favored) Leg
The Basics are

One of the first things you need to do in track & field is find your ***Power Leg*** because this is the leg you will use to get the maximum push off for running and jumping. To get a true test to determine which leg is the strongest (favored), take three one leg hops in succesion from a standing start. Mark where you start, then hop first with only your right leg, then measure the distance for the three hops. Then hop only with your left leg, and measure the distance of the three hops. Whichever is the farthest distance, is your strongest (power) leg. For most of you this will be your right leg. Remember this is when we ask you to use your power leg or foot to start or jump with.

Drill No. 45- The Takeoff
The Basics are

What you need to learn how to do in your takeoff is load up your takeoff leg to create a vertical push up through your center of gravity.

Takeoff Foot Ground Contact

As your takeoff foot hits the ground you need to load it up with energy. This vertical push or lift from your takeoff leg is what projects your body upwards and out into the air. The expert coaches say, "Focus on your jumping up at takeoff, and then the running." Focusing only on running up and out off the ground tends to cause you to not "load up" your takeoff leg. You need to get that hard ground contact that pushes you up in the air.

Placement of Your Foot

Your takeoff foot needs to be placed flat on landing, and in front of your body to get the maximum vertical lift *(SEE FIGURE 105)*. If you place your heel first as your foot lands, this will cause a braking or slowing down. If you land your takeoff foot up on your toes, it causes your leg to buckle and colapse. As your body moves through your takeoff and up into the air, you need to continue to move out and up off the ground. Look up and think "up-and-out."

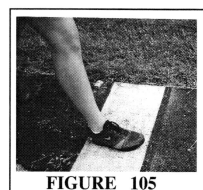

FIGURE 105

Your Body Position

At takeoff your body needs to be upright to the ground *(SEE FIGURE 106)*. And again you need to be looking up and out, NOT at the takeoff board or down at the sand pit.

Practice

To practice this drill use a shorter five step run-up, focusing on your last two steps. The shorter run-up will conserve some energy. This will let you take take more run-ups at a practice session. Work on your whole takeoff technique. The flat foot landing, the power leg flexing, and looking up and not down. Don't worry about your action in the air yet, just focus on your last two steps and a correct takeoff. Do at least three of these takeoff practices at every training session.

FIGURE 106

Drill No. 46- Your Action in the Air
The Basics are

Once you get up in the air after takeoff, you need to rotate your body into an efficient landing position. When you are up in the air you can't do anything about your center of gravity flight path. But you can move your arms and legs around your center of gravity to counteract your forward raotation, and get in the best position for landing. Right now there are four different techniques being used around the world. They are the "hang" technique (easiest to teach young beginning kids), the "hitch-kick" technique (favored in the USA), the "sail" technique, and the "stride" technique (a new one being used in Germany).

FIGURE 107

The Hang Technique

It is called the 'hang" technique because right in the middle and highest point in the air the jumper looks like they are hanging from a bar with their legs bent back. The hang technique works like this, at the takeoff your leading

FIGURE 108

FIGURE 109

leg is flexed and driven up hard. Your leading leg is then extended and brought backward to join your takeoff leg. Next both your legs in their extended position, are then bent and brought upwards toward the rear of your body *(SEE FIGURE 107)*.

Your arms circle from in front, to downward, to upward at the rear of your body. Following that your arms rotate from over your head to forward. Simultaneously your feet come forward to a sitting position. Then you kind of momentarily hang in the air in this sitting position. And last both of your legs are flexed then kicked hard forward as you are dropping for your landing. Simultaneously your arms circle from over your head, and downward, to extended in front of you. *SEE FIGURE 108, 109* for the whole hang technique sequence.

The Hitch Kick Technique

It is called the "hitch kick" technique because right in the middle and highest point in the air the jumper make a little cycling type kick. This technique is a little different in the air than the "hang" technique.

FIGURE 110

The big difference is the way your legs make this little kick. This is how the technique works, at the takeoff the leading leg is flexed at the thigh, and then is extended so both legs are in a stretched out stride. The leading leg is then rotated backward, and bent slightly up (the hitch) while the other leg kicks forward for the cycling action *(SEE FIGURE 110)*. Simultaneously the arms rotate forward, then backward around to the rear, and then on upward.

This balances the leg action and helps the jumper thrust forward. Next both of the legs are flexed and come forward, to almost in a sitting position. And at the same time the arms circle around and over the head from back to front so that they are extended. Last the legs are extended forward for the landing. For the whole hitch kick sequence *SEE FIGURE 111, 112*.

FIGURE 111

The Sail Technique

It is called the "sail" technique because right after takeoff the legs are extended out forward in a toe touching position with your hands *(SEE FIGURE 113)*. This lets the body kind of sail through the air in a compact position instead of your arms and legs moving all around. This technique puts you in a landing position early and on through the jump. This is a pretty elementary simple type of jump that you younger beginning kids should be able to learn fairly easy.

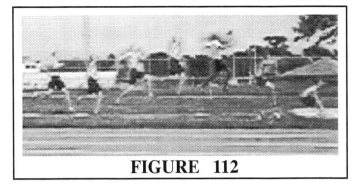

FIGURE   112

The Stride Technique

It is called the "stride" technique because right after takeoff the right leg pushes off and the left leg does a big bounding stride out in the air. Then as you get to the middle, or highest point of your jump, you rotate both arms forward. Then you bring your right foot up along side of your extended strided out left leg, and go into a regular type landing *(SEE FIGURE 114)*. Make sure you bend at your waist and rotate your body forward so that your hands and butt don't drag.

FIGURE   113

FIGURE   114

Practice

To practice your different actions in the air you will have to go out to a long jump pit at your nearest high school. Have mom or dad go with you to observe and let you know if you are doing your foot and arm moves correctly. I would practice all of these techniques using a three step run-up, push off at the takeoff board, get up in the air, then make your different foot and arm moves and rotations. When you think you have the moves figured out, the hang, the hitch kick, the sail and the stride, then go back and try them with a full run-up. I would try each one twice if you trying them all out. If you are working on just one technique, then do at least three attempts at a practice session. Pick the technique that is the easiest for you, and one that will give you the most distance.

Drill No. 47- Your Landing
The Basics are

Your landing is important because if you make a mistake it could cause you to lose from one to two feet of distance. As an example, you have made a great jump but your your hands fall back behind you and drag instead of extending out in front of you, or your butt hits or drags. These are going to be a loss of distance. Just before contact with the sand is made, your arms need to swing

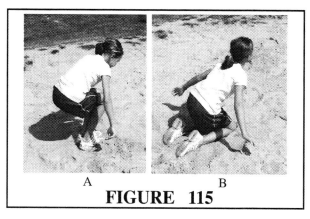

A   B

FIGURE   115

forward to drive you beyond where the first leg contact with the sand was made *(SEE FIGURE 115)*. Your legs are brought forward as quickly as possible, then you keep them straight but not stiff.

Just as your heels hit the sand your knee joints flex. Right at this time you straighten up your body just a little which allows your hips to come forward. As your hips move forward, shift your body weight over your supporting legs and keep your butt up high to keep from touching. Your arms need to come forward in enough time though to keep from hand dragging. Otherwise they measure behind you where the hand touched, causing your jump to be measured short. Also during this action you need to rotate your shoulders forward so that you do not fall back

Here is the key to prevent this from happening. As mentioned, just as contact with the sand is made, your legs must flex and bend at the knees, your upper body moves forward and over your legs and extended hands. This cushions the impact, keeps everything going forward.

Practice

To practice your landing you will need to find a sand pit. The best place is your local high school. Have mom or dad come out with for observation and helping. They can watch your form and tell you if you are making the right moves. This is important. It is core training for your technique. A bad landing can ruin a great jump. At first stand at the edge of the sand pit, right in front of the takeoff board. Squat down, then jump way out into the sand. Get up high so that you have room to work on your landing. Pay particular attention to the part of the technique that rotates you forward over your feet. Always make sure your arms rotate and go out in front of you. This changes your center of gravity, and helps you rotate forward over your feet. Do about three of these standing jumps, then go back about four or five steps, get a running start and make at least three landings at a practice session.

Long Jump Problem Solving

Explanation

You need to learn how to solve any problems you might be having with your long jumping. Get mom or dad to come out and observe, they can help you with another set of eyes. This means making any necessary corrections on the spot to solve the problem. If you don't solve your problem right away, you will just keep reinforcing any bad habits you may have.

Takeoff Problem Solving

You need to learn how to solve any problems you might be having with your takeoff. Here are some problems and errors and their corrections or solutions:

1. *Problem or error-* Looking up and you have a hollow back.

Correction- You need to learn to look straight ahead, and focus on not arching your back as you push upward.

2. *Problem or error-* You have a backward lean.

Correction- Focus on keeping the trunk of your body upright as you push upward.

3. *Problem or error-* You have too much of a forward lean, which is usually associated with your lead leg.

Correction- This is usually because you don't drive and lift your lead leg up high enough. You need to really focus on pushing straight up which takes strength. This means build up your legs.

In Flight Problem Solving

You need to learn how to solve any problems you might be having in flight. Here are some problems and errors and their corrections or solutions:

1. *Problem or error-* Too much forward lean with your lead leg dropped after your takeoff.

Correction- Focus on staying in your upright position as you first start to go up in the air. Even a slight backward lean is better. You need to start bringing your lead leg towards the position it needs to be in for whichever technique you are using. Concentrate on not leaving your lead leg down.

2. *Problem or error-* Your legs are dropped too low for an efficient landing.

Correction- Focus on getting into the jack-knife position, with your upper body leaning over your knees. Both legs need to be stretched out at the same height *(SEE FIGURE 113)*.

FIGURE 116

3. *Problem or error-* You are holding your body in the outdated crouch position *(SEE FIGURE 116)*, which you should only use in the "sail" technique.

Correction- Focus on getting into a jack-knife position instead of the crouch position .

Landing Problem Solving

Here are some problems and errors and their corrections or solutions:

1. *Problem or error-* Both feet not landing at the same level, resulting in a loss of inches in your jump.

Correction- Focus on bringing both legs together while you are still in the air *(SEE FIGURE 115-A)*.

2. *Problem or error-* Your knee joints are too stiff, which is causing you to fall backwards.

Correction- Just as your heels hit the sand, relax and bend both knees, don't flex and stiffen your legs *(SEE FIGURE 115-B)*.

Landing Problem Solving (continued)

3. *Problem or error-* Touching the sand with your butt, or falling backwards.

Correction- Don't place your feet too far forward just before you hit the sand. Bend them just a little before your feet hit the sand *(SEE FIGURE 115-A)*.

4. *Problem or error-* You dive or over rotate forward head first as you land.

Correction- Focus on not dropping your feet DOWN too early just before they hit in the sand. In other words your in too much of an upright position as you start to drop from the high point of your jump.

Miscellaneous Lead In Training

Explanation

These are a series of drills to help with your core training and muscle memory. They are all designed to help you improve the different phases of your long jumping. It's best to go down to your local high school long jump sand pit for these drills. Have mom or dad come down with you for another set of eyes. They can notice things you don't while you are jumping. For a typical sequence **SEE FIGURE 117**.

Drill No. 48- Two Legged Takeoff Standing Jump

The Basics are

This is a drill to build up your "springing" abilities and skills. It is basically standing flat footed, knees bent slightly, arms back, and making one big jump forward out into the sand pit, for as much heigth and distance as possible.

FIGURE 117

Practice

Go to the edge of the long jump pit in front of the takeoff board. Put both feet up close to the edge of the pit. Then bend both of your knees slightly, put your arms back, and make the jump. Go forward as far out and as high into the pit as you can. To make a good jump, you need to push and thrust with your legs as hard and powerfully as possible. At the same time swinging both of your arms forward as hard as possible, then rotating them back. Just after you push up, you bend both legs back underneath of you, then kick them out forward and bend them *(SEE FIGURE 117)*. Next, just as you start to make contact with the sand you bend your legs and keep your arms rotating forward. At the same time the center of gravity of your body needs to rotate foward, almost in a "praying" position *(SEE FIGURE 115-B)*. You younger kids should make at least three of these jumps, followed by a short rest, then three more jumps only at each practice session.

Alternative No.1

Every now and then vary this drill by making standing one legged takeoff jumps. This is very similar to the bounding, except you bring the thigh of the leading leg up to the horizontal. Next you swing and kick your push off (power) leg forward as hard as possible. Simultaneously both arms

104

drive forward to the upward position. Then you extend both legs forward for the landing, just like the two legged jump *(SEE FIGURE 115-A)*. You young kids should make at least three of these jumps, followed by a short rest, then three more jumps at a training session. You can do more when they get older and stronger.

Alternative No.2

Another alternative to this drill is "standing jumps over a mound of sand." This is to encourage you to get heigth to your jumps *(SEE FIGURE 118)*. Try to jump over as high as you can. It may even be encouraging and fun for you to get a friend or two to come out and jump with you. When you work on this drill be sure and bring a rake with you to make the mound, then to leave the pit smoothed out flat when you leave. You young kids should make at least three of these jumps, followed by a short rest, then 2 more jumps during a training session. You can do more when you get older and stronger.

FIGURE   118

Drill No. 49- Driving the Hips
The Basics are

This is a drill to teach you how to push your hips forward. This is most usefull in the "hang" technique jumping style. While in flight the jumper pushes their hips (the front of the lower abdomen) forward as much as possible.

Practice

For practice you can use a shorter run-up. Then have mom or dad stand just off to the side and out in front of the takeoff point. Take a broom handle or a bamboo stick, then have mom or dad hold it loosely out in front of you about where their stomach would be as they go by in the air. Now go back to your start point and make a jump. What you do in the air is arch your back and push your hips forward to contact the broom handle *(SEE FIGURE 119)*. Tell mom or dad to make sure and hold the broom handle loose enough so that it pushes out of the way as you go by. It's there just for the feel.

Another variation of this drill is find two friends, have them stand about one yard back of the takeoff point. One is on each side, then they turn sideways and stretch out one arm each to make a sort of double gate. You push your hips forward as you jump, to open the gate so to speak. Whichever method you use, do at least five of these at a practice session.

FIGURE   119

Drill No. 50- Arm Action
The Basics are

This is a drill to work on your arm action. Emphasizing arm action is very important for young jumpers. This is because it's a little unusual to use your arms in this manner. After you take off and drive upward, your arms swing from in front to upward and backward. Then you circle them forward, down, and in back. After doing this flex your legs, but bend them at the knees just before your feet hit the sand. Then rotate forward over your legs for the landing. This drill will help you in both the "hang" and the "hitch Kick" techniques.

Practice

To practice this you will need a fairly high box or jumping stand to use as a jump off. Jumping off the elevated box gets you higher up in the air. And it gives you more time to do the arm

FIGURE 120

action as well as get the feel for your body control way up in the air. Stand up on the box, with the leading (strong) push off leg up slightly forward, then put your arms forward. Next you push off with your leading leg, jump way up and out, throw your hands up and back, then bend both knees back. Then while still in the air swing your arms forward, then down. Simultaneously you bring the legs around to forward, flex them, then bend them for the landing *(SEE FIGURE 120)*. Do at least five of these at a practice session.

Drill No. 51- Scissoring the Legs
The Basics are

This is a drill to get you used to scissoring your legs in flight. It is very usefull in learning the "hitch kick" technique. It will also be helpfull when using the "stride" technique. After you take off in the air you scissor kick your legs while in flight. Then on the landing they go to the praying position *(SEE FIGURE 115-B)*.

Practice

To practice this you will need a box or jumping stand to jump off. Jumping off an elevated box gets you higher up in the air. And it gives you more time to do the scissors kick. If there is a springboard available, you can use it to jump on the box which will ley you get up even higher in the air. However, I do not advise this technique for you younger kids. To easy for you to get hurt. You can use it when you are 12 years old or more, or you are very experienced with the springboard technique.

First when you spring up and your power foot touches the top of the box, you drive your thigh of your power leg up, straighten it, then swing it backwards while in the air. Simultaneously

106

FIGURE 121

the other leg comes forward (the scissors effect), then is flexed and bent for the "praying" type landing *(SEE FIGURE 121)*. Since this practice is just for scissoring, you can land in the kneeling position. However, dont get too used to the kneeling position because it become a bad habit (foot drag). While scissoring, your arms rotate back and forth to counteract your leg action, and give balance to the scissors motion. This will probably be very hard for you younger kids to learn. But keep working with mom or dad on this drill because you need to learn how to do this movement for the "hitch kick" technique, which will get you more distance. The landing should end up with the takeoff (power) leg ahead when using a kneeling position landing. Do at least 5 of these at a session.

Drill No. 52- Leading Leg Action

The Basics are

This drill is for building up your leading (power) leg in the jump. This drill is usefull for all long jumpers . From a short run-up you jump from the edge of the end of the runway out into the sand. You bring your leading (power) leg up to the horizontal position, and leave it there all the way to the kneeling landing position *(SEE FIGURE 122)*.

Practice

To practice this go out about three strides from the takeoff line, then start your run-up. This drill is *core training* and *muscle memory* for just what your leading leg does, so don't worry about where you hit the takeoff line. When you get to the takoff point you push off and bring your leading (power) leg up to a horizontal position. Then you keep it in that position all the way to the landing. The back foot follows, and ends up down in the sand in the kneeling position. The arms swing through toward the front *(SEE FIGURE 122)*. Do at least of five of these at a practice session.

FIGURE 122

Drill No. 53- Acceleration Wall Series
The Basics are

This is a group of acceleration drills called the "wall series." They are called that because your hands are against a wall. For long jumping you need a fast explosive start. You usually accelerate to your maximum speed in four to six steps. Basically the slower you are the faster you will get to your top speed. You faster runners will take longer to get to your top speed. The rest of your steps to your takeoff are done at a cotrollable maximum speed. What that means is once you get to your maximum speed, you run nice and smooth and straight while maintaining that speed. These drills are designed to help you accomplish this.

FIGURE 123

The Regular Wall Series

No.1 Feel the Lean

Start this drill with your hands against a wall or fence, with your body leaning from your non power leg ankle at a 45 degree angle. Your power knee is raised with your thigh parallel to the ground *(SEE FIGURE 123)*. Now hold that position for five seconds while straightening up then trying to feel a "straight line" from your head through your shoulders, hips, knees and down to your feet. Rest a minute in between then do this at least three times at a practice session.

No.2 Moving While in Place

From the same position leaning against the wall, take three to five steps in place. Do it first walking, then marching and last running. Focus on making sure your feet land in the same position that they start in. Have mom or dad watch, observe and remind you to keep that same straight line from your head to your toes.

No.3 Moving to Upright

Repeat drill No.2, except this time gradually work your way forward, getting more upright with each three to five steps of walking, marching, and running foot contact with the floor or ground. Do this drill two times through, with each of the three methods at a practice session.

The Partner Series

No.1 Feel the Lean With a Partner

Repeat drill No.1 in the regular series, except this time you are supported at your shoulders by a partner's hands. Do this three times at a practice session.

No.2 Full Effort Push Start

With your partner still supporting, do a five step marching lean, then progressing to a run with a full effort push for five steps.

No.3 Full Effort Start With a Release

With your partner still supporting repeat drill No.2. But this time when you get to the end of the five steps running, then your partner steps out of the way and lets you continue to accelerate for four yards straight ahead. Then stop. Do this sequence at least two times at a practice session.

No.4 Full Effort Run With Start Support

Get into your lean with partner supporting, knee is up and you are looking straight ahead. Have your partner say, "Go," then quickly step out of the way, release you, then let you accelerate straight ahead for ten yards on your own. Do this drill at least three times at a practice session.

Drill No. 54- Velocity Dynamics
The Basics are

This is the dynamics of long jumping. Your resultant velocity (Vo) to get you way out in the sand pit is determined by your horizontal (Vh) and vertical (Vv) velocities *(SEE FIGURE 124)*. This means that your flight curve will become steeper or flatter according to the horizontal and vertical velocity components (Vh and Vv). Your horizontal jump component (Vh) needs to be three times larger than your vertical component (Vv).

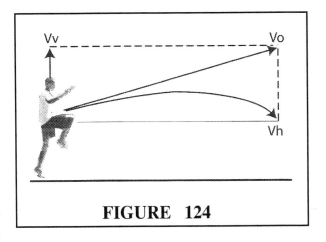

FIGURE 124

Your horizontal component will depend on your run-up speed. Your vertical component depends on your takeoff push up force. You can change your horizontal component by learning how to run faster (not that hard). But you can only increase your vertical component by learning how to make a more efficient takeoff (more difficult). As you look at the illustration you can see that if you are very fast at running, but your vertical takeoff is weak, you are going out more flat without much height. And you need more height to get out there farther.

Check *TABLE 5* to see some comparison jumping distances for you to achieve in order to be competitive. The main records are *"American outdoor"* youth track & field records, but we have also added the local *"CYC"* and national *"CYO"* records for a comparison.

COMPARISON PERFORMANCE DISTANCES - LONG JUMP				
BOYS		DISTANCE		
Age Division		Standing (Feet)	Record- Standing	Running (Feet)	Record-Running
6 - 8 (Primary)	Satisfactory	1.57m (5'-2")		3.50m (11'-6")	
	Good	1.78m (5'-10")	*□ 1.76m (5'-9.25")	3.81m (12'-6")	$□ 3.75m (12'-3.75")
	Excellent	1.96m (6'-5")	*△ 2.04m (6'-8.5")	4.11m (13'-6")	△ 4.24m (13'-11")
9-10 (Bantam) (Roadrunner)	Satisfactory	1.98m (6'-6")		4.11m (13'-6")	#4.33m (14'-2.5")
	Good	2.06m (6'-9")		4.42m (14'-6")	Sub=4.66m (15'-3.5")
	Excellent	2.13m (7'-0")	*2.28m (7'-5.88")	4.88m (16'-0")	5.15m (16'-10.75")
11-12 (Midget) (Cub)	Satisfactory			5.03m (16'-6")	#5.41m (17'-9")
	Good			5.33m (17'-6")	*5.38m (17'-8")
	Excellent		N/A	5.64m (18'-6")	5.92m (19'-5.25")
13-14 (Youth) (Cadet)	Satisfactory			5.33m (17'-6")	#5.75m (18'-10.5")
	Good			5.64m (18'-6")	*5.71m (18'-9")
	Excellent		N/A	6.10m (20'-0")	7.02m (23'-0.5")
GIRLS		DISTANCE			
Age Division		Standing (Feet)	Record- Standing	Running (Feet)	Record-Running
6 - 8 (Primary)	Satisfactory	1.52m (5'-0")		3.35m (11'-0")	
	Good	1.68m (5'-6")	*□ 1.70m (5'-7")	3.50m (11'-6")	$□ 3.87m (12'-8.25")
	Excellent	1.83m (6'-0")	*△ 1.98m (6'-6")	3.58m (11'-9")	△ 3.64m (11'-11.25")
9-10 (Bantam) (Roadrunner)	Satisfactory	1.91m (6'-3")		3.96m (13'-0")	#4.33m (14'-2.5")
	Good	1.98m (6'-6")		4.27m (14'-0")	Sub=4.32m (14'-2")
	Excellent	2.06m (6'-9")	*2.37m (7'-9.25")	4.65m (15'-3")	4.78m (15'-8.25")
11-12 (Midget) (Cub)	Satisfactory			4.42m (14'-6")	#4.65m (15'-3")
	Good			4.88m (16'-0")	*4.54m (14'-11")
	Excellent		N/A	5.33m (17'-6")	5.58m (18'-3.75")
13-14 (Youth) (Cadet)	Satisfactory			4.72m (15'-6")	#5.17m (16'-11.5")
	Good			5.33m (17'-6")	*4.81m (15'-9.5")
	Excellent		N/A	5.64m (18'-6")	6.07m (19'-11")

N/A = Not applicable in this age group.
All distances are measured in meters or feet and inches.
Unless otherwise noted all records are "American AAU/ USATF National Outdoor" youth (2002-2007).
* = A "CYC" (Catholic Youth Council, St. Louis, MO.) record or performance distance (2007).
# = A "CYO" (Catholic Youth Organization) National record or performance distance (2007).
$ = AAU/ USATF Regional private track club record.
□ = Record for 6 year olds. △ = Record for 7-8 year olds.

TABLE 5

Shot Putting

Explanation

The shot put is a field event. Where the other events are about running and jumping, the shot put is about power and strength. The O'Brien "glide" technique which most amateur shot putters use was developed by Perry O'Brien in the 1950s. In this technique you face the rear of the ring, then turn back towards the front as you kind of glide across the ring for the put. A newer technique called the "rotary" technique is growing in popularity though. World records are achieved using this technique. So why would you use the "glide" technique instead of the "rotary" technique. For you young kids the glide technique is easier to learn and more consistant in the results you get. In the "rotary" (spin) technique you start at the rear of the ring, whirl or spin around in several rotations like a discus thrower, then make your put.

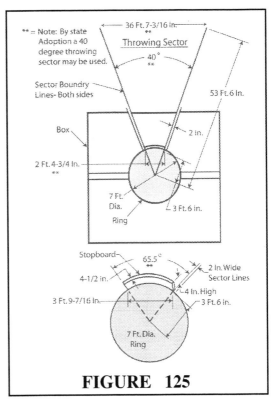

FIGURE 125

The "ring," by the way, is a small confined area which the shot putter must stay in. The shot put ring is smaller than the discus ring. The ring is a circular area with an inside diameter of 7 feet *(SEE FIGURE 125)*. And this makes it very difficult to do all these rotations using the "rotary" technique. World class shot putters have achieved long distances using both of these techniques. We will show both of these techniques in this book. I recommend you young kids starting with the "glide."

In both of these techniques the shot must stay in contact with your neck until the final put (push off) occurs. After the put the shot putter must not fall out of the ring area, or touch the top of the stopboard (toeboard) before the distance has been marked. Otherwise a foul is called. Also, after stepping in the ring, the shot putter must pause before making the put, or a foul is called. We will go into the techniques first, then go into the lead-ins (miscellaneous training) for the put.

For Practicing

For all training and practicing it's best to go down to your local high school track to work on your technique. The reason is their ring will have the markings and a stopboard. You could set up a ring in your back yard by marking a 7 foot diameter circle, then marking where the stopboard should be. Or you could buy one (with a stopboard), except they are very expensive. But sooner or later you need to get the feel of the stopboard (toeboard), and where the throwing sector is located. All our examples will refer to a right handed shot putter unless otherwise stated.

Drill No. 55- Holding the Shot (ball)

The Basics are

First you need to learn how to do is hold the shot. Put the shot in the palm of your hand *(SEE FIGURE 126-A)*, then roll it out on your finger tips so that it is resting between your little finger and your thumb *(SEE FIGURE 126-B)*. Don't let the shot drop down into the palm of your hand. This is called "palming" the shot. If you can not hold it out on your fingers away from the

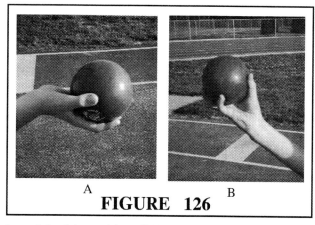

back of your palm, it's probably too heavy for you. This is why it is important you have a correct size shot for your age group, which you can handle. As an example if you are five years old, DO NOT pick up a 12 pound shot and attempt to throw it. It's way too heavy for you.

Five year olds should be using a six pound shot. Now that you are holding it properly, bring it down so that it is resting next to your right cheek and shoulder *(SEE FIGURE 127)*. *"TIP."* You must keep it in this position all the way up to your put (throw), or it's a foul and the attempt does not count. For left hand putters this is just the opposite. You would hold the shot next to your left cheek and shoulder. It stays in this position until you push it out for the throw.

FIGURE 126

Practice

Hold it correctly, then put the shot in the rest position next to your cheek and shoulder. Now raise the shot straight up extending your arm, then bring it back down. This is to help you get the feel of how the shot rests on your cheek and shoulder, and how it feels being held out and supported by your fingers. Do this about three times at the start of every practice session. Then you will get used to holding it correctly and placing it correctly next to your cheek and shoulder.

FIGURE 127

Drill No. 56- The Glide
The Basics are

There are three phases to the "glide" technique. They are the "angle of release," "the height of release," and "the velocity of release." We will cover different *core training* and *muscle memory* drills for you to use to sharpen and improve your shot putting skills. The shot can be put (thrown) with either the left or right hand. Since most shot putters will be right handed, our descriptions will be for a right handed shot putter. For left handed shot putters everything will be flip flopped or just the opposite. To start the shot putter stands at the very rear of the ring, facing to the rear with your back to the stopboard (front of the ring). The shot is in your right hand and craddled under your chin. Then you glide up to the front of the ring, use the stopboard to keep from falling out of the ring, then make your put (throw).

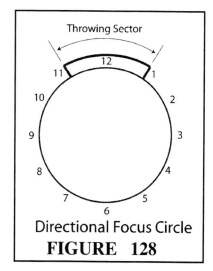

Directional Focus Circle
FIGURE 128

112

The Starting Position

The shot is in your right hand craddled under your chin. Your left arm is extended or hanging down and facing the rear of the ring at 6 o'clock *(SEE FIG.128 DIR. CIRCLE)*. All your weight is on your right leg which is bent and flexed. Your upper body is then lowered to where your hanging left arm is almost touching the ground *(SEE FIGURE 129)* or it is horizontal . Your eyes are focused on a point outside of thr ring. You are bent down, and your back and neck are in the same plane or straight line. Next is the pushing off with your support (right) leg in a backward glide across the ring to the front stopboard.

FIGURE 129

The Glide Technique

As you start to glide up to the front there are several positions in getting to the stopboard. The main position is the "power position." To get to the power position there are two techniques to consider. There is the long/short glide and the short/ long glide moves. This is about your first and second glide steps or foot slides towards the front. When determining which one of these techniques you should use, consider your "speed," "strength," "agility" and "height." If you are a smaller more athletic person, you will probably be more successful with the long/short technique. If you are a larger, taller person, you will probably be more successful with the short/long technique.

During the first part of your glide to the front you remain facing the 6 o'clock position *SEE FIGURE 130-A-E)*. To start the glide your left leg is thrust or kicked toward the front of the ring, and at the same time the right leg starts a push glide towards the stopboard using the long or short step *SEE FIGURE 130-C)*. By the end of the second step or glide, your left foot toe should be up to the edge of the stopboard. Your body is still in the 6'oclock position *SEE FIGURE 130-D-E)*. All through the glide your upper body stays in a bent over position or a slightly lowered position. At the end of the glide you should still be facing back at 6'oclock, your left hand has swung around facing towards 3'oclock. You are partially squatted with your weight on your right foot and center of gravity close to being over yor right (back) foot. This is your "power position." *(SEE FIGURE 130-E)*.

A   B   C   D

FIGURE 130   (Continued)

The Delivery Technique

Your delivery starts from the "power position" with your left arm swinging from 3 o'clock to

SHOT SIZE TABLE			
BOYS		**GIRLS**	
AGE DIV.	WEIGHT (Lbs.)	AGE DIV.	WEIGHT (Lbs.)
6 Only Primary	4	6 Only Primary	4
7 - 8 (Sub Bantam)	6	7 - 8 (Sub Bantam)	6
9 - 10 (Bantam) (Roadrunner)	6	9 - 10 (Bantam) (Roadrunner)	6
11 - 12 (Midget) (Cub)	6	11 - 12 (Midget) (Cub)	6
13 - 14 (Youth) (Cadet)	*8 or 8.82 (4 Kg)	13 - 14 (Youth) (Cadet)	*8 or 6

All weights are per USATF & AAU rules unless otherwise noted (2007).

*= CYC weight (Catholic Youth Council, St. Louis, MO.) 2007

TABLE 6

12 o'clock. At that same time you start to push the shot from your neck and cheek *SEE FIGURE 130-F)*. Your lead left leg begins to straighten, your right arm is fully extended, and you push the shot off the end of your fingers while keeping your thumb pointng down *SEE FIGURE 130-G)*. Your head is up and your eyes are focused on the trajectory of the throw. The finish of the throw has two methods that are used.

The first is the "reverse." Basically this is exchanging positions of the left and right foot. Your linear motion forward is stopped when your right foot swings around to block on the stopboard. Your right arm is then extended to 9 o'clock, and your left arm swings around to 6 o'clock and is parallel to the ground *(SEE FIGURE 130-G.-H)*. You land flat footed and end up facing 9 o'clock. The second method is the nonreverse position. Basically your feet remain in the power position as you release the shot. Your right foot moves forward about another 8 inches after your release, toe pointing toward the stopboard. Current biomechanical research is indicating that the nonreverse method is more efficient because it lets you use more force when compared to the longer reverse during delivery. The europeans throwers have been very successful using this method.

Practice

To practice the technique the first thing you need to do is get the correct weight shot for your size and age. To do this check **TABLE 6.** Many track coaches say the best way for young shot putters to properly learn the "glide" shot put technique is by first starting up at the front near the stopboard, learn the power throw, then work your way to the back part of the ring.

This is learning the "standing" shot put from the power position *(SEE FIGURE 130-E THROUGH- H.* You can work on this right out in your back yard. There are a series of training drills to go through before you make the put itself. We will go through them sequentially.

E	F	G	H
(Continued)	**FIGURE 130**		

Some Rules to Follow

Before you start any putting (throwing), make sure you are properly warmed up. And make

114

sure you go through all the upper body stretching exercises, from your neck down to your waist and hips. If your wrist is weak it is legal to have it taped to give you support. However, taping any part of your hands and fingers is NOT permitted unless there is an open wound that must be protected by the tape. Gloves can NOT be worn, but you CAN use a support belt around your waist.

All legal shot puts have to be made from the shoulder with one hand only so that during the attempt the shot does not drop behind or below your shoulder. Also you must pause before you make your shot put. Wait for your to be measured, then only exit the ring form the back of the circle. A word of *caution* if you are practicing out in the back yard, for safety reasons make sure you keep everyone out of your way, especially small children and pets. If a flying shot hits them they could be seriously hurt.

Standing Straight Ahead Position

In this position you will put the shot facing straight ahead, without the "glide". This just a simple position for beginners. First get in the "power position" *(SEE FIGURE 131-A)*, but only at about six to eight inches away from the front stopboard. Next from a standing still "power position," your head is looking straight ahead and you are slightly squatted down. Put the shot in the correct position cradled on your cheek and right shoulder. Then lean back just a litle bit and extend your left arm straight out to12 o'clock for balance *(SEE FIGURE 131-A)*.

Next take a little hop step out with your left foot bringing your toe up against the stop board. At the same time swing your left arm from 12 o'clock to the 10 o'clock position *(SEE FIGURE 131-B)*. Also at the same time you push up with your legs, then twist your hips from

FIGURE   131

facing 3 o'clock to facing 1 o'clock. Next.with all your power push the shot out, up, and straight ahead at about a 45 degree angle off your finger tips. Make three of these throws at a practice session.

Standing 90 Degrees Rotated Position

Now that you have worked on the "straight ahead position," we move to the next step which is the 90 degree rotated position. In this drill you will put the shot slightly squatted in a 90 degrees rotated positon facing towards 3 o'clock, without the "glide". First get in the "power position" *(SEE FIGURE 130-E),* only at about six to eight inches away from the front stopboard. Next from the standing still "power position," put the shot in the correct position cradled on your cheek and right shoulder. Then lean back in a half squatted position, and extend your left arm out to 3 o'clock for balance *(SEE FIGURE 130-E)*. Next do a little hop step out with your left foot bringing your toe up against the stop board, at the same time swinging your left arm from 3 o'clock to 12 o'clock position *(SEE FIGURE 130-F)*.

Now push up with your legs, twist your hips from facing 3 o'clock to facing 12 o'clock, then with all your power push the shot out, up, and straight ahead at about a 45 degree angle off your finger tips. *JUST FOR THIS DRILL* make sure you keep your elbow on your putting arm up high instead of dipping your body down to get more power for the pushing action. As you move forward the six to eight inches to the stopboard don't forget to rotate your hips forward, and keep your chest up high and squared up facing the front. If your chest turns to the side on this drill it will cause the put to go off to the side. The shot should leave your hand just above head level so that your throw goes up and out and not down. Basically this is form and strength training. This is where those dumbbell and push-up strengthening exercises come in handy. Make three of these throws at a practice session.

Standing 180 Degrees to the Rear

Now that you have worked on the 90 degrees rotated position, we move to the next step which is the 180 degree rotated position. This is the last part of the training action for the basic "glide" put. Except without the glide up to the front of the ring. There seems to be several ways to start the rotation to the front, in an attempt to get more momentum. And remember this is still basically a standing practice put (throw) from six to eight inches away from the front stopboard.

One, face the direction of the throw towards the front, left hand extended to 12 o'clock, and feet shoulder width apart. Then you step out one pace forward with your left leg (*SEE FIGURE 132-A*). Next you twist and pivot around to your right on the balls of both feet so that you are facing to the rear at 6 o'clock (*SEE FIGURE 132-B*). Then you dip down, bend your knees a little, drop your left hand down, and get ready for the whirl around and throw (*SEE FIGURE 132-C*). Last you whirl around to their left 180 degrees and make your throw (*SEE FIGURE 132-D & E*). All the previous drills work up into this put (throw).

Two, start by standing with your back toward the direction of the throw facing toward 3 o'clock, your left arm extended, and your right leg slightly bent (*SEE FIGURE 132-B*). Next you dip down the left shoulder and knee while still facing the rear (*SEE FIGURE 132-C*). Last you kick out with your left foot (*SEE FIGURE 133*), turn and whirl around to face the front at 12 o'clock, then make your throw just like in the previous two training exercises (*SEE FIGURE 132-D & E*). The second way may be the best for you younger kids because it puts you right in the position you need to be in to start with. Make three of these throws at each practice session.

A   B   C   D   E

FIGURE 132

Drill No. 57- The Glide Technique

The Basics are

This is working on the movement from the back of the ring to the front of the ring. It's kind of a little skipping hopping backward move with your right leg, keeping your foot close to the ground. Or another way to look at it is think of it as a series of backward pulls with your left leg, and pushes with your right leg. Keep the upper body low all the way through your "glide". Extend and flex the right leg so it is pulled in

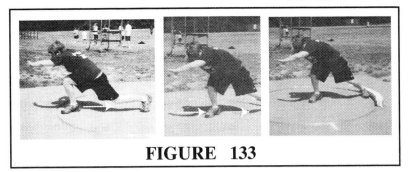

FIGURE 133

under your upper body at the end of the "glide."

Thrust and kick out with your left leg out to it's position in the putting mode, at the same time you push with the right leg *(SEE FIGURE 133)*. This move gets you to the front of the ring and ready to make the put (throw). Whether you use a first step long-short or a short-long "glide" will depend on which way works best for you, or which one your coach wants you to use. As you get close to the front, and are coming out of your glide, start thinking about turning and exploding upward using your legs, then hips, then chest, and last the arm (exactly in that order).

Practice

To practice your "glide" you younger kids use the second method because it will be easier for you to get into the correct starting position. Have mom or dad come out and walk you through several glides in slow motion until you learn the technique, then you can speed it up little by little. This may be hard for you younger kids to learn, so have mom or dad watch every glide step you make, to make sure you are doing it right. You can eventually learn how to do the "glide" if you start when you are six years old. Walk through at least three of these at every practice session.

Training with a Partners Assistance

This is another way to help beginners learn the "glide" to the front. You will need to get mom, dad, or a friend to come out and help you with this. Have the helper hold your hands for this practice drill. By having the helper hold your hands *(SEE FIGURE 134),* they can help you make sure to stay low, and keep your balance as you hop glide backwards. Make sure your shoulders remain in the horizontal position while you glide backwards. The helper can help you make sure to keep facing the rear of the ring all the way through the technique, and don't get turned to the side.

While you are learning this technique you need to focus on several things all of which have to happen simultaneously. First you need to make sure your left leg is thrust backwards with your foot just skimming the ground. Next your left foot has to land every time slightly offset and still facing the rear. Your right leg needs to extend every step and push you backwards towards the front of the

ring. Each step your right leg is flexed and pulled in under your body.

On the last glide step your right foot and knee rotate about 45 degrees to your left, towards the direction of

FIGURE 134

117

the throw at 12 o,clock. The hardest thing for you to learn is going to be both of your legs have to perform thier separate actions simultaneously. And the helper has to apply resistance, to try and hold you back. But every time you step the helper needs to move right with you to keep you balanced *(SEE FIGURE 134 SEQUENCE)*. For a left handed putter everything is just flip flopped and opposite. You should learn to make a short "glide" and a long "glide" across the seven foot ring length. A short glide may be better and easier for you younger five year old beginners, with a long glide working better for ten year olds and up. Do three of these at every session so that it becomes *muscle memory*.

Drill No. 58- The Glide Delivery

The Basics are

This is the technique that gets your arm up to the release point. The delivery phase starts with the arm swing or "strike" as it is sometimes referred to, and the shot being pushed from your neck *(SEE FIGURE 130-F,G)*. Next your lead leg begins to straighten and goes into a blocking type move which stops your left side body movement. At the same time the right side of your body accelerates your arm movement to your release point. To work right your body needs a coordinated effort on this part of the phase. Your head needs to be up, and eyes focused on the trajectory or flight of the shot.

Practice

The best way to pracice this phase ot the technique is stand right up against the stopboard with your upper body facing 3 o'clock, your lead foot up against the stopboard, toe pointed straight ahead at 12 oclock. Your right leg is behind you, slightly bent, and toe down. Your left arm is extended and pointing slightly up at the 12 o'clock position *(SEE FIGURE 130-G)*. The shot is craddled agaist your cheek with your thumb pointing up. Then in one motion you PUSH the shot out at an upward 45 degree angle, with your left arm swinging around (striking) to your left, with your forarm ending up nearly parallel to the ground *(SEE FIGURE 130-G)*. Just as you start to push the shot away from your cheek, pretend you are pushing up a barbell or dumbbell with your right arm. Just say to youeself, "Push up the barbbell." Do at least three of these at every training session so that it becomes *muscle memory*.

FIGURE 135

Drill No. 59- The Glide Release

The Basics are

This is the technique that shoots the shot out of your hand at the end of your delivery. This is very important because at the end of the delivery with your arm extended straight out if you just open up your hand then the shot kind of just falls out and drops. This results in a low trajectory and no distance to the shot flight. I see this a lot with you young beginners. What you need to learn how to do is flick the shot away out of your hand with a lot of wrist action while keeping the thumb and little finger pointing down *(SEE FIGURE 135)*. And remember it's a push not a throw.

Practice

The best way to practice this phase of the technique is find a softball, then start in the same position for starting the "delivery" practice. Then use the softball first until you get the feel of the flicking action. Then switch to your shot. If it's not working for you with the shot, then go back and work on flicking the softball until you get the technique mastered.

Drill No. 60- The Reverse at the End of the Shot Put

The Basics are

This is a technique to keep you from loosing your balance and falling out of the ring. It's a little tricky for little kids, but you can learn how to do it if you start when you are six years old. The reverse has to happen just after your left foot hits the stopboard, and the shot has left your hand. Then with a quick shifting of your feet your right leg swings around, dips, bends, and goes up against the stopboard (toeboard), toe first, to help you keep your balance *(SEE FIGURE 136)*.

Practice

To practice the "reverse" you will need to work where their is a ring with a stopboard. You don't need to go through a glide to practice the "reverse." Stand feet apart with your left foot about 12 inches back of the stopboard. Then get into your putting stance, and dip down with your right leg. Next take a short step with your left foot to get a little momentum up against the stopboard, then make a throw *(SEE FIGURE 136-A)*. For practicing the reverse you don't need to use the shot you can just pretend to have it in your hand. Just after the shot leaves your hand you kick your left foot back keeping your balance, then swing your right foot around with the toe up against the stopboard *(SEE FIGURE 136-B)*.

Some *TIPS* are:
1.) Make sure your chest and hips are forward and slightly beyond your left foot before you start the "reverse." 2.) Don't start

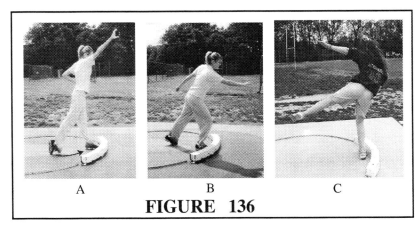

FIGURE 136

your "reverse" before your legs are extended, and your body has driven forward for the throw (put). 3.) Look at *FIGURE 136-C*. If you turn your foot sideways up against the stopboard, your momentum going forward may cause you to lose your balance, and possibly fall out of the ring for a foul. If you got a great throw off this would cancel it. 4.) Make sure to always keep your toes pointing forward through your "glide" and "reverse." Work on at least three of these reverses at practice session.

Drill No. 61- The Rotary (Spin) Technique

The Basics are

This is a drill for you to learn the "rotary" (spin) technique for shot putting. This technique is very similar to the discus throwing technique. Some world class shot putters have made very long throws using this technique. However, not only can this technique be difficult to learn for you young kids, but it can be dangerous also. The putter (you) could accidentally loose their grip on the shot due to the centrifugal outward force, sending it out to the side where a by-stander could get hurt. So for this reason I am *NOT* recommending that you six through eleven year olds use this technique. Wait until you are 12 years old, or older, and you have been shot putting for several years already. The shot can be put (thrown) with either your left or right hand. It is held the same as in the "glide" technique *(SEE FIGURE 126)*. The main difference between the "spin" and the "glide" technique is the spin action across the ring instead of a forward "glide" type of move. Since most shot putters will be right handed, our descriptions will be for a right handed shot putter. For left handed shot putters everything will be flip flopped or just the opposite.

   To start you stand at the very rear of the ring, with your back to the stopboard (front of the ring) facing towards 6 o'clock *(SEE FIGURE 137-A)* . The shot is in your right hand and cradled under your chin. Your left arm is down at your side. Then you pivot, turn to your left, and do series of whirling around rotations continually going to your left. You end up facing the front at the 12 o'clock in position, ready to push up and make your throw *(SEE FIGURE 137-E)*. The shot put, the release, and the reverse are basically all the same as in the "glide" technique.

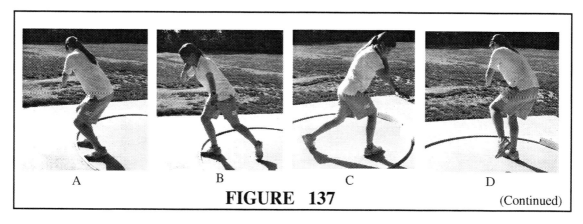

A   B   C   D

FIGURE 137   (Continued)

Practice

   To practice the technique you will need to get a correct weight shot for your size and age. To do this check **TABLE 6**. Many track coaches say the best way for you young shot putters to properly learn the "rotary spin" technique is learn how to do the spinning first. If you can't master the rotations you better just stick with the "glide" technique. If you are 12 years old or more it's OK if you want to try to learn this technique. Just to see if you can increase your distances on your throws. Some discus practice methods are very good for training the rotating spin turns process (see the section on Discus). In order to understand the technique better as well as your coach, you need to develop the common vocabulary that is used in rotary spin practicing and training. Some common terms used that relate to the body position are:

- **The Power Position**- This is the position where your left leg has touched down in the front part of the circle while your right leg is near the center of the ring. Your shoulders are facing at 6 o'clock while your hips are facing at 3 o'clock.
- **Wrap**- This is the relationship of your left arm to your right leg at the power position. It refers to your left arm position which is across your body at the moment you reach the power position. This is what keeps your shoulders from opening up too soon.

120

- **Cowboy**- This is a bowlegged starting position at the back of the circle.
- **Separation**- This is the relationship between your upper and lower body during your spin. This means your lower body is always moving ahead of your upper body so that it drags your upper body along.
- **Torque**- This is the muscular tension between the abdominal oblique muscles and the trunk of your body which is the result of separation.

Another communication concept between you and your coach is two words. They are "key and "cue." These are words or short phrases that help you to focus on a specific part of the technique you are working on. These are very helpful during competition when you need a limited number of thigs to think about when direct contact with your coach is limited. Because of the shot put's technical nature there is a lot of frustration. So you and your coach need to be patient. Improvement is not always steady, but comes in spurts as you are training.

The Hoop Throw Technique Drill

To practice your spinning using this drill you will need to get a rubber or plastic ring to use.

E   F   G   H

(Continued)   **FIGURE 137**

Or you can use a larger hoop. Hoops help in learning the process, and they are a little less dangerous than throwing a shot. The smaller rubber ring is best for you younger kids. Let me point out that for you young kids it is going to take about 1-1/2 to 2-1/2 rotations to get to the shot putting position in the front of the ring. Start out by putting the ring or hoop in the same hand which you would use to hold the shot. The trick or advantage to this technique is getting a lot of speed and momentum going to help you make a powerful throw. The hardest part to learn is going to be coming out of the spins just in the right position to make the put (throw).

Other disadvantages are: 1.) Whirling around real fast and over rotating. 2.) Not being able to stop the spins. 3.) Out of position to do your reverse. 4.) Not being able to stop from falling out of the ring. As you can see, you will need to be very coordinated to use this technique. This is where working on those "coordination and agility" drills is going to come in handy.

To start go to the back of the ring and face to the rear at the 6 o'clock position *SEE FIGURE 137-A)* away from the stopboard (toeboard). Put the rubber ring in your throwing hand. Next you pivot and turn to the left on your right foot, simultaneously you swing your left foot around as far as you can to the left *SEE FIGURE 137-B,C)*. Then you bring your right foot up towards the front making half a turn or rotation *SEE FIGURE 137-D,E)*. Then if you need to

FIGURE 138

you repeat the half turn process two more times to end up facing the front *(SEE FIGURE 138)*. This is if you take fairly small steps. For you younger kids taking smaller steps, you may need to make two more half turns to get to the front of the shot put ring where you are in position to make the throw.

You will need to try this out a number of times through trial and error, to see which works best for you. It is best to have mom or dad come out and help walk you through the footwork several times slowly to get the feel of the technique. Then speed it up little by little until you can master the movements. After you can perform the "rotary" technique correctly with the hoop-ring, then you can substitute a shot and practice the technique. Work on at least three of these rotation sets at each practice session.

There are 2 other ways to start the rotating technique practice drill. One is, face the front at 12

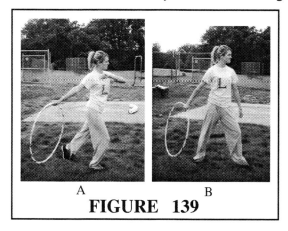

A   B
FIGURE 139

o'clock *(SEE FIGURE 139-A)*, the other is face the side *(SEE FIGURE 139-B)* at 3 o'clock. Try all three ways to see which way will best for you. There still is one more way to practice for spinning. You don't use a shot or a hoop ring in your hand. You just put your throwing hand under your chin against your shoulder, then pretend you have a shot in your hand. If you don't have a hoop ring this may work out better for you younger kids and beginners. Work on one of these rotation sets at least three times at each practice session.

Drill No. 62- The Rotary Delivery and Release

The Basics are

The "rotary" delivery and release is a little different than the "glide." When you have been spinning you need to develop the ability to come out of the spin just right, then push out and make your release. When you come out of your spin in the center of the circle, and your left leg is touching down, you have to be in the "wrap" position *(SEE FIGURE 137-D)*. Your hips and right foot continue to turn, the shot is kept back under your chin and behind your right hip as it turns to the center of the circle *(SEE FIGURE 137-E)*. Your left arm should be extended, then brought up and over to 9 o'clock at release *(SEE FIGURE 137-E THRU G)*. *"TIP"*- To help with this whole move try to imagine you are squeezing an orange underneath your left armpit. Next your hips then accelerate up with a strong block against the stopboard, your left toe pointing straight ahead *(SEE FIGURE 137-F THRU G)*. Then you release the shot up high off your finger tips *(SEE FIGURE 135 & 137-G)*. The higher your release point, the longer the distance.

There are two different ways to finish after your release. One, you keep your left leg aggressively straightened, toe facing straight ahead against the stopboard, with no bend in your left leg. Your right leg bends a little and your body leans back to help your balance, and keep you from going over the stopboard and fouling. The follow through is your hips keep turning to your left after the release. Two, you can use a standard reverse *(SEE FIGURE 136-A,B & 137-H)*. The rotary spin style has a lot of turning and twisting, so you will need to find which release-follow through works best for you by using trial and error methods.

Practice

Practice the delivery and release technique from the power position *(SEE FIGURE 137-E)*. To make it easier use a softball. It's lighter in weight for you younger kids, and will let you focus more on your technique. Try different follow throughs, either the simple left foot against the stopboard or a standard reverse. Have mom or dad watch your technique to make sure you don't fall out of the ring. When you have the technique mastered, then you can use the shot. Make sure that the softball or shot is coming off your fingers correctly *(SEE FIGURE 135)*. Work on this technique at least three times at each practice session.

Drill No. 63- Rotary Trouble Shooting
The Basics are

The following are a few trouble shooting USA Track & Field coaching manual *TIPS*:

Testing Balance

In the rotary spin technique your balance is very important. If you don't have good balance, then DO NOT use this technique. Here are some ways to see, detect, or indicate poor balance. You may have trouble staying in the circle; your throws are going out of the sector. Your shoulders are tilted or you may appear to be falling into the middle of the circle. You are having trouble completing a full turn on the 360 degree drill. These are all control and balance problems. You need to be in control of your body during the entire throw and follow through.

A good way for mom or dad or your coach to test your balance is ask you to stop in different phases of your throw. If you can stop and hold the correct position at any part of the spin, then it's a good indication that you are well balanced.

Checking the Position of the Shot During Your Throws

Another very important part of the rotary spin technique is the position of the shot relative to your right hip during your throw. When you start by setting up in the back of the circle (the cowboy position) you need to position yourself so that the shot is behind your right hip. When you run through the full technique, or just from the power position, focus on keeping the shot behind your right hip all the way through to the release. If you let the shot get ahead of your right hip anywhere in the spin, then you will *NOT* be able to regain the proper relationship for your rrelease.

Videotaping Competitions and Practices

If your coach, mom, or dad has a video camera, then have them videotape some events or practices so that you can both go back over them and look for errors, flaws or successful throws. It's hard to visually remember what you did or didn't do. Once you have a video of your shot put you could send a copy long distance to an expert coach for an analysis if you wished. Almost all the concepts for the discus spin throw are the same for the rotary spin shot put. Try to be a student of the sport. Study the technique. Balance is the real key. Without it you will *NOT* be very successful.

Miscellaneous Lead In Training

Explanation

These are a series of drills to help with your *core training* and *muscle memory*. They are all designed to help you improve the different phases of your shot putting. It's best to go down to your local high school shot put ring for these drills. Have mom or dad come down with you for another set of eyes. They can notice things you don't while you are shot putting. Lead ins are specifically designed help you with your *core training* and *muscle memory*.

Drill No. 64- Push Throw in Pairs

The Basics are

This is a drill for building up your arm and finger pushing skills. You will need to get one of your friends to come over and help out on this drill. Basically you push pass a medicine ball back and forth using a one or two handed throw over a marked distance course. You younger kids will need a six to ten pound medicine ball for this drill, depending on your age. They are much heavier than a regular ball. The better medicine balls are all rubber.

If you are serious about training for the shot put, I recommend you buy a medicine ball or have mom or dad get you one for christmas or your birthday. You can use them for strength training in other sports also. They are not terribly expensive, you can get them at some athletic equipment stores for around $40 to $60. And you can also find used medicine balls on the InterNet at amazon.com for much less. If not maybe you can find someone to borrrow one from.

FIGURE 140

Practice

To practice this drill have one of your friends come over, then both of you get about three or four yards apart and face each other. This distance may have to be a little shorter for you younger kids, or farther for bigger kids. Next you push pass the ball back and forth using a one or two handed throw *(SEE FIGURE 140)*. This might be more fun for you little kids than throwing all by yourself. Do at least ten of these at a practice session.

As an alternative drill, you can put (throw) the medicine ball for distance *(SEE FIGURE 141)*. You can do this drill out in the back yard. It will also be more fun if a friend throws with you on this drill. And you can use the old plastic one gallon milk bottles to mark the edges of a short course *(SEE DRILL NO. 19)*. Make your throw (put), then measure the distance with a tape. Keep a record of how far you are throwing. Then remember how far you throw each time, it helps their mind stay focused

FIGURE 141

and competitive during a practice session. Make at least five throws at a practice session. Use the farthest distance for the session to keep a record of your throws. This way you can see if you are progressing or not

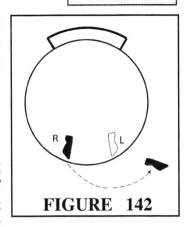

Shot Put

FIGURE 142

Drill No. 65- 360 Degree Spin Drill
The Basics are
This is a drill for helping you with your balance while spinning around. Start by going to the back of the circle *(SEE FIGURE 137-A)*. Face the back of the circle in the "cowboy" position. What you are going to do is attempt to spin around with your right foot leading, 360 degrees, and end up in the same spot you started in. Your right foot is swung around to your left 180 degrees for starting your turn or spin *(SEE FIGURE 142)*. Then pivot and swing all the way around to where you started, facing at 6 o'clock. Make sure your left arm never gets ahead of your left thigh and knee. Your movement is like a door swinging open. Your left side is the hinge and you, like a door, swing around your left side as if it's a post.

Practice
Practicing this 360 degree drill many times is one of the keys to becoming a good rotary spin shot putter. Think of yourself as spinning right over your left foot, a lot like an iceskater does. Do at least five of the 360s at a practice session.

Check *TABLE 7* to see some comparison throwing distances for you to achieve in order to be competitive. The main records are *"American outdoor"* youth track & field records, but we have also added the local *"CYC"* and national *"CYO"* records for a comparison.

COMPARISON PERFORMANCE DISTANCES - SHOT PUT

BOYS		DISTANCE		
Age Division		Weight (Kg.)	Meters (Feet - Inches)	Record - (Feet - Inches)
6 - 8 (Primary)	Satisfactory		5.49m (18 Ft.- 0 In.)	$ 5.55m (18 Ft.- 2.5 In.)
	Good		7.01m (28 Ft.- 0 In.)	$ 7.65m (25 Ft.- 1.25 In.)
	Excellent	4 Lb. (1.81)	8.53m (28 Ft.- 0 In.)	9.13m (29 Ft.- 11.5 In.)
9 -10 (Bantam) (Roadrunner)	Satisfactory		7.62m (25 Ft.- 0 In.)	# 8.17m (26 Ft.- 9.5 In.)
	Good		9.14m (30 Ft.- 0 In.)	* 9.75m (32 Ft.- 0 In.)
	Excellent	6 Lb. (2.72)	10.67m (35 Ft.- 0 In.)	12.44m (40 Ft.- 9.75 In.)
11 -12 (Midget) (Cub)	Satisfactory		12.80m (42 Ft.- 0 In.)	# 13.41m (44 Ft.- 0 In.)
	Good		14.02m (46 Ft.- 0 In.)	* 13.21m (43 Ft.- 4 In.)
	Excellent	6 Lb. (2.72)	15.24m (50 Ft.- 0 In.)	16.15m (53 Ft.- 0 In.)
13 - 14 (Youth) (Cadet)	Satisfactory		☆ 13.11m (43 Ft.- 0 In.)	# ☆14.76m (48 Ft.- 5 In.)
	Good		☆ 15.85m (52 Ft.- 0 In.)	* □13.23m (44 Ft.- 9.5 In.)
	Excellent	*8 or 8.82 Lb. (4)	☆ 18.29m (60 Ft.- 0 In.)	☆ 19.29m (63 Ft.- 3.5 In.)
GIRLS		**DISTANCE**		
Age Division		Weight (Kg.)	Meters (Feet - Inches)	Record - (Feet - Inches)
6 - 8 (Primary)	Satisfactory		3.66m (12 Ft.- 0 In.)	$ 3.96m (13 Ft.- 0 In.)
	Good		4.57m (15 Ft.- 0 In.)	$ 5.19m (17 Ft.- .25 In.)
	Excellent	4 Lb. (1.81)	5.49m (18 Ft.- 0 In.)	6.26m (20 Ft.- 6.5 In.)
9 -10 (Bantam) (Roadrunner)	Satisfactory		6.71m (22 Ft.- 0 In.)	# 7.42m (24 Ft.- 4 In.)
	Good		8.23m (27 Ft.- 0 In.)	* 8.47m (27 Ft.- 9.5 In.)
	Excellent	6 Lb. (2.72)	9.75m (32 Ft.- 0 In.)	10.46m (34 Ft.- 4 In.)
11 -12 (Midget) (Cub)	Satisfactory		8.53m (28 Ft.- 0 In.)	# 11.13m (36 Ft.- 6 In.)
	Good		10.36m (34 Ft.- 0 In.)	* 9.07m (29 Ft.- 9 In.)
	Excellent	6 Lb. (2.72)	12.19m (40 Ft.- 0 In.)	13.9m (45 Ft.- 7.25 In.)
13 - 14 (Youth) (Cadet)	Satisfactory		△ 11.58m (38 Ft.- 0 In.)	#△12.29m (40 Ft.- 4 In.)
	Good		△ 13.41m (44 Ft.- 0 In.)	*□ 10.71m (35 Ft.- 1.5 In.)
	Excellent	*8 or 6 Lb. (2.72)	△ 15.24m (50 Ft.- 0 In.)	△ 15.88m (52 Ft.- 1.25 In.)

Unless otherwise noted all records are "American AAU/ USATF National Outdoor" youth (2002-2007).

$ = AAU/ USATF Private track club record.

= A "CYO" (Catholic Youth Organization) national record performance distance (2007).

* = A "CYC" (Catholic Youth Council, St. Louis, MO.) record performance distance (2007).

△ = Using a 6 Lb. shot.   □ = Using a 8 Lb. shot.   ☆ = Using a 8.82 Lb. shot.

TABLE 7

Race Walking

Explanation

Race walking takes a very special skill. Not too many young kids can do it. Because of that you don't have as much competition when you get to your first team or club. If you can naturally catch on to this technique at an early age you could become a champion by the time you get to high school or college. In other words this is an opportunity for you if you can master the technique. Race walking in youth track & field really means the 1500m, and 3000m race events. Race walkers must be truly walking and not running. Some simple rules have been set up to control the walkers, to make sure they are walking and not running. The rules say the walker must be taking a progression of steps that are taken in such a way so that to the trained eye of the officials watching their feet are always in contact with the ground.

An additional rule states that the race walkers leg as it is swung forward for each step can *NOT* be flexed at the knee, from the moment the foot contacts the ground. In other words, your leg must stay locked or straight until it has reached a vertical position below your body. This repetitive straight legged motion along with the forward and downward rotation of your hips, is what gives race walkers that flowing style as they move forward down the track. Do not confuse race walking with "power walking" that many people are doing for exercise these days. They are two entirely different styles of walking. Power walking is not an event in track and field meets, at least at this point in the sport. We will go into the basic technique of race walking first, then the lead- ins or lead-ups you need to build up and improve your skills for this event.

NOTE:

You can practice race walking just about anywhere. Go to the nearest high school track, the street, the sidewalk, or even in a large back yard if it's nice and flat (not the best). For all practice in this section I would suggest you use your nearest high school track for better results. Even though this is walking and not running, make sure you are lightly stretched out, and warmed up properly with a little calisthenics before starting the session. Have the right clothing on for the weather, use good shoes. For the best results get mom or dad to come out and observr or help.

Drill No. 66- The Race Walk Technique

The Basics are

This is a drill for you to learn the race walking technique. It's hard to imagine, but world

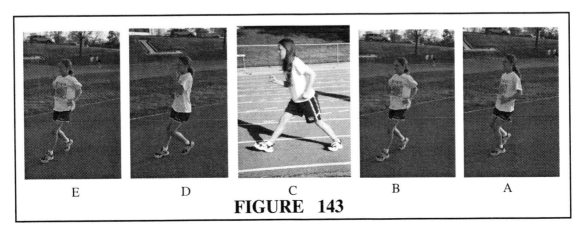

| E | D | C | B | A |

FIGURE 143

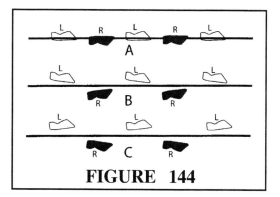

FIGURE 144

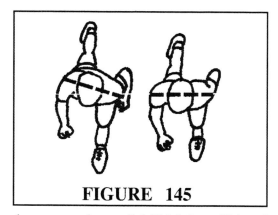

FIGURE 145

class race walkers can get up to a speed of 9.3 miles per hour (15 KPH). The key to this technique in great focus and concentration. The technique can be broken down into 3 phases. The first is the double support phase *(SEE FIGURE 143-A)*, the second is the traction phase *(SEE FIGURE 143-B)*, the third is forward drive or thrust phase *(SEE FIGURE 143-C)*. You should be walking in as straight a line as possible *(SEE FIGURE 144-A)*. Correct hip action is what leads to a longer stride length *(SEE FIGURE 145)*. This also leads to the correct foot placement along a straight line. Insufficient rotation of your hips or limited flexibility in your pelvis can lead to foot placement on either side of a straight line *(SEE FIGURE 144-B,C)*.

While the ideal foot placement is in a straight line, some people's foot placement will naturally point in or out just because of the way you are built *(SEE FIGURE 144-B,C)*. DO NOT try to change your foot placement. If you use your hips properly your footstrikes will hit in a straight enough line, but they may not be parallel. This is less efficient, but forcing the straightening of your foot placement can cause stress on your feet, legs, knees. There are other basics also involved like posture, feet position, hip motion, stride length, knee action, arm action, rhythm and type of shoes to use.

The Double Support Phase Basics

This is a short phase. This starts when both of the your feet are in touch with the ground . The double support starts just after the you have pushed forward with the back leg, and the front foot has just contacted the ground *(SEE FIGURE 143-A)*. At this point your center of gravity is between your feet, and a little to the rear of the front foot *(SEE FIGURE 143-B)*. The front leg should be straight as it hits the ground *(SEE FIGURE 143-C)*.

The Traction Phase Basics

The traction phase starts when your leading leg has been brought forward and your foot has made contact with the ground. Your leading leg stays straight with no flex or bend at the knee as your front foot lands. At this point your center of gravity is almost over the leading leg *(SEE FIGURE 143-C)*. Your toes then grab, or claw, at the ground and pull the ground backwards. This thrusts you forward. Your center of gravity then passes smoothly over your leading leg, without moving up or down. The shrinking action of your hamstring and gluteal (buttocks) muscles, along with your forward momentun that has been built up with each stride, are both contributing factors in the traction process *(SEE FIGURE 143-D & E)*.

The Drive or Thrust Phase Basics

The drive or thrust phase happens at the same time as the ground is being pulled backwards in the traction phase. When either leg is ahead of your body, the other rear leg is simultaneously thrusting or pushing you forward. Once the push from the rear leg is complete, the leg is then flexed at the knee and brought forwad for the next step *(SEE FIGURE 143-D & E)*. Do not swing or kick your heel upward off the ground while the knee is flexed *(SEE FIGURE 143-D & E)*.

Your Posture

The principal of race walk posture is simple. You body should be as straight up and down and relaxed as possible through each stride you take. Try to keep your pelvis from tilting forward or backward. Bending forward at the waist strains your lower back, and limits your hip movement. It may be due to muscle weakness or an imbalance in your torso muscles. So keep your torso and stomach muscles toned up. Leaning backward or swayback limits your hip motion and moves your center of gravity backwards. It aso shortens your stride and can lead to an illegal stride. It may be due to a tightness or weakness in your lower back or abdominal muscles. All the more reason to work on those "abs."

To maintain good posture your head should be in a neutral position looking forward and down the track. If your head seems to point down a lot, it's usually caused by a lack of concentration or weak neck muscles, which can lead to cramps in your neck and shoulders.

Your Hip Motion

Your hip movement is your primary or main *(most important)* source of locomotion provided by your body. When your rotate your hips forward in a plane that is parallel to the ground, your rear leg is pulled off the ground. Your hips act like a motor, accelerating your knee and foot forward. In the later movements of the swinging phase your knee will reach a position forward of your hip. At ground contact your heel is slightly forward of your knee.

Watch out for excessive hip drop. Modern race walking stresses hip rotation without much vertical movement of your hip joint. Also watch out for excessive lateral hip movement. If your hips move from side to side too much your body's center of gravity will move with your hips. This slows your forward movement and will waste or drain your energy.

Your Stride Length

If you are using the correct hip movement it will lead to an increase in stride length *(SEE FIGURE 145)*. Correct hip movement will also lead to the correct foot placement along a straight line *(SEE FIGURE 144-A)*. Insufficient hip rotation or limited flexibility in your pelvis could lead to foot placement on either side of a straight line *(SEE FIGURE 144-B,C)*. You should NOT try to increase your stride length by reaching too far out in front of your body with your foot because this will cause overstriding. You need to learn to visualize and focus your hips to lead your legs and feet. Increasing the speed your hips move will directly increase the speed of your legs.

Don't try this just to see if you can do it unless you are seriously training as a race walker. Foot placement without the proper hip motion will place an unneeded stress across your knees.

Your Knee Action

Knee action is also very important. Your knee must be straight from the moment your heel contacts until your support leg is in the vertical position. Your knee should be flexed in the recovery swing because short pendulum swings are faster. The point at which your rear leg starts to bend at your knee will vary from race walker to race walker *(SEE FIGURE 143)*. The optimum point for it to bend depends on your body structure, strength and flexibility. Watch out for your lead knee swinging through to the forward position too high. This is usually due to habits carried over from running. It will waste your energy and can lead to illegal strides. A bent knee on heel contact is illegal. Causes for this are overstriding in front of your body, inadequate strength in your quadriceps, and tight or weak hamstring muscles. Watch out for your lead knee bending before your other leg is vertically upright *(SEE FIGURE 143-E)*. This is also illegal. This may be caused by you trying to walk faster than your fitness level is capable of.

Your Foot Action

You heel should strike the ground first with your toes pointing up, NOT flat footed. Then once your foot has made contact you roll it forward, keeping your toes off the ground until your leg is supporting your body's weight. The strength of your chin determines how long you can hold your toes off the ground. You do a push off with your calf which causes your foot to roll to vertical before it leaves the ground. Then the other foot (your swing leg) is brought forward close, but not brushing, the ground. Watch out for landing either foot flat footed, or with your foot slapping too soon. When this happens there is a braking effect that wastes your energy, shortens your stride, and may cause your knee to bend early. This may be caused by weak chin strength, not much flexibility, or lack of mobility in your hips.

Arm and Hand Action

Your arms are also important in race walking. They should be flexed at the elbows. The angle of the elbows should be between 90 and 45 degrees. The elbow angle must stay fixed throughout your arm swing, but with your muscles relaxed (you must stay focused). You swing your arms so that they go forward and backwards in a piston pendulum like action. This way the arms swing more quickly than if they are held straight. Your swing should be in a plane straight ahead, and not across your chest. The hands should trace an arc shape as they move from just behind the hip at waistband level to the sternum. Basically the arm swing is to help the walker move forward in an efficient manor and to give you momentum. The arm movement is low and relaxed.

The shoulders should be relaxed, *NOT* hunched up and tight causing your hands to brush against your hips as they swing backward and forward. The lower position of your hands during your arm swing is acheived by relaxing your shoulders and by the way your shoulders are carried without as much turning, twisting, hunching or lift at the front and rear of your arm swing. Your wrist should be straight while your hands should be held in a loose fist with your fingertips facing your hips as your arms swing past. If you are having trouble holding your hands in a relaxed position make a fist, hold it loosely, then place your thumb between your index finger and middle finger.

Watch out for too much side-to-side arm swing, which causes side-to-side motion of your center of gravity and drains your energy. This is caused by incorrect motor skills learning. Watch out for an elbow angle that is too tight or less then 45 degrees. This can lead to a shortened stride and a bouncing motion that wastes energy. As you get more fatigued this angle tends to increase. It is caused by losss of concentration and incorrect motor learning. Watch out for your elbow angle getting too large, which will lead to a slower stride rate. This is caused by incorrect motor learning.

Rhythm of Movement

The motion of your body, arms and legs should be smooth almost gliding along the ground. Your speed has to be same, not speeding up and slowing down. In other words a steady rhythm or flow. A fluid motion to your walking pattern and speed must be developed. Again this takes concentration and focus. There is a rotary motion with your hips going up and down that should be a fluid rolling type of motion, with a tempo to it. A walker should develop a cadence or tempo to their walking speed. Your center of gravity should be in a straight line flow as you move along. The stride length has to be just right for the size of the walker. Too long of a stride will cause you to bounce just a little bit. Thats no good in race walking. If you look straight ahead and focus on a point with your eyes, then you can tell if you are bouncing or not.

Footware

The type of shoes you wear can effect your race walking. If you are serious about race walking and want to compete as opposed to just walking, then you need shoes that are more flexible and have less padding than a normal walking shoe. Lots of race walkers train and compete using light weight shoes that are designed for distance running. These shoes go by the name of "racing flats."

Practice

Just to see where you are on understanding race walking, measure out about 50 yards, use no instructions other than you can't run, then go "race walk" as fast as you can for the distance. Have mom or dad or someone else that understands the technique observe your style, then when you come back to the starting point let them tell you how you looked and how you should have done it.

If you can get a group of your friends together it will be more fun, then have them all "race walk" for the 50 yards with you. To start actual practice, work on the race walk technique by going over the fundamentals with mom or dad first then a slow walk through. This is not easy to learn for you younger kids. It's going to take some time and patience on your part, along with mom or dad helping. Four eyes are better than two. This is because you can't see if you are doing it correctly while actually race walking. Probably the hardest thing for you to learn is going to be the rolling up and down motion of your hips.

One way for you to start learning is stand straight up, feet side by side about 6 inches apart, with one leg straight and flexed or stiff. The other leg is bent with the toe lifted (*SEE FIGURE 143-D*). Then slowly you push your bent leg down flat on the ground while simultaneously lifting the other leg to the bent position with your heel lifted. Then speed it up little by little by snapping the feet up and down in unison. Sort of like marching in place, except as you do this you can feel your hips pumping and rolling up and down. Do this faster and faster without either toe leaving the ground. You should do this for about three or four minutes at a session, speeding up for awhile then slowing down for awhile. All of this is to get you into the habit and feel of rolling and pumping the hips up and down.

Once you have mastered the rolling and pumping of your hips, then the next step is to put forward motion to it. Go out to a high school track for this training if you can because they have lane lines to use as a guide. Start pumping your feet up and down in place for a minute or two then say, "GO," or have mom or dad say it, then you step out and start race walking straight ahead. Take short steps and go slow at first, concentrate on your toes and feet not lifting up and leaving the ground. While doing this you need to keep your hips rolling and pumping up and down. Stick with it. After a while you will get the feel of it. Then you can speed it up little by little as you begin to get a rhythm going, and settle into a rhythm that suits your size and age. One time around the a quarter mile rack at a session should be enough for you younger kids.

Now we will get into the lead-ins and lead-ups which will help you improve on your basic skills (*core training*) which are needed to perform the race walk technique. These drills are preparatory.

Drill No. 67- Easy Walking mixed with High Tempo Walking
The Basics are

This is a really a drill to let you get the experience of high tempo walking. In this drill you will mix easy walking with high tempo walking. You will be working in segments. Easy walking is just normal walking at a slow to moderate pace. High tempo walking is just walking with shorter step, but at a fast speed.

Practice

Start out easy walking around the track at a moderate speed and stride length. Keep your head up and still and don't look down. After you have walked about 30 or 40 yards, have mom or dad blow a whistle or say, "GO," then you reduce your stride length to 3/4 of what it was. Now you pick up the speed and cadence of your walking. This is called high tempo walking. Each step will be taken faster. Swing your arms forward and backward very vigorously with your elbows bent. This is kind of like short step power walking. Do this for about 20 yards, then have mom or dad blow the whistle again, then you go back to your moderate speed easy walking, relaxing and resting as you go. After another 30 or 40 yards mom or dad blows the whistle again, then you switch back to your high tempo walking. You keep repeating this process all the way around the track (440 yards or 400 meters). Tell mom or dad to watch you closely and as they see you getting tired and slowing down, then change the segment of high tempo walking to 15 yards, then down to 10 yards. As you get better conditioned for this you can go back to the 20 yard segments. Once around a 440 yard (or 400 meter) track at a session should be enough for you younger kids. A fun alternative for this drill is have a friend come over to walk with you, side by side, around the track. It's a lot more fun and less boring this way.

Drill No. 68- Arms, Hands, and Body Position Movement
The Basics are

This is a drill to work on your arm and hand action along with your body movement. Concentrate on flexing your arms at the elbows while you swing them back and forth in cadence with your legs. Focus on keeping your forearms parallel to the ground and in line with the direction you are going as you go in and out *(SEE FIGURE 143-B)*. Your shoulders need to keep straight, no twisting side to side. Your arm swing starts from your shoulders and the movement has to be straight forward and backward, not across your chest. Make sure your elbows swing backward only far enough that your hands reach the middle of your body. Shortening the length of each stride will make your normal stride quicker. A quicker stride rhythm helps generate more push to move you forward. Always look directly forward and keep the torso of your body in an upright position as much as possible

Practice

For this practice you will be going about 50 yards distance per segment while working on the drill. Have mom or dad blow a whistle or say, "GO," then you start walking down the track ata moderate speed swinging your arms and hands properly. Have mom or dad watch you and make sure your body stays upright. When you have gone about 50 yards, have them blow the whistle again and you walk slowly back to the starting point, resting as you walk. The next time down the track try to concentrate on your stride length, making it shorter and speeding up your tempo from the first time down. For beginners and most of you younger kids two segments of down and back on this drill should be enough at a practice session.

Drill No. 69- Straightening the Lead Leg

The Basics are

This is a drill to work on straightening your leading leg just as it hits the ground. As you get better at race walking you will automatically stiffen and flex your leg just prior to it's contact with the ground (*SEE FIGURE 143-C*). Figure "C" is exagerrated just to show the straightened leg better. Your actual stride would be much shorter. This comes with lots of practice and training. Pulling backward on your leg by tightening your thigh muscles helps in straightening your leg.

Practice

For this practice you will be going about 50 yards distance per segment just like in *Drill 68.* Have mom or dad blow a whistle or say, "GO," then you start walking down the track at a moderate speed. Then every time your right leg is leading, you straighten it. Concentrate and do only the right leg for the whole segment (50 yards). Easy walk back, then on the next segment down you straighten only your left leg. Have mom or dad walk right along side of you and observe, to see that you are correctly straightening your leg. For beginners and most of you younger kids two segments of down and back on this drill should be enough at a practice session.

Drill No. 70- Pushing and Thrusting with the Rear Leg

The Basics are

This is a drill to work on getting thrust by pushing and thrusting with your rear leg. You push and drive forward with your favored leg (strongest) when it is to the rear. The push has to be forward, not upward. Concentrate on not kicking your rear heel up in the air when the leg is flexed and brought forward. Your toes are lifted up toward your shin as your leg comes forward, making a 90 degree angle between the top of your foot and your shin. Your other leg is flexed just enough so that it kind of skims the ground as it comes forward (*SEE FIGURE 143-B, D*).

Practice

You will be walking about 10 yards down the track at a segment for this training practice. Start out by pushing with your right leg (usually your power leg) only for the first 10 yards. Then you switch and push only with your left leg for the next 10 yards. Have mom or dad walk right along side of you and observe to see that you are correctly pushing and thrusting with your power leg. After about 20 yards you turn around and "easy walk" back to the starting point. For beginners and most of you younger kids two segments of down and back on this drill should be enough at a practice session.

Drill No. 71- Lift and Shift the Hips

The Basics are

This is a drill to work on developing your hip movement. This is a drill you can work on inside the house in the winter pre season when it's too cold and wet to go outside. You sit on the floor or the ground outside, your legs are together straight out in front. The hip is lifted and shifted forward, first one hip then the other. This is kind of like race walking across the floor on your hips. It's one of the best drills for learning hip movement.

FIGURE 146

Practice

Sit on the floor or ground with both legs together and out in front of you. Your arms are extended out to your sides, elbows bent, but DON'T let your arms touch the floor or ground after you start *(SEE FIGURE 146)*. You move forward by lifting and shifting your right hip (buttock) forward. Then lift and shift your left hip forward. Concentrate, focus on the movements, and say to yourself, "Lift," "shift," "lower," "lift," "shift," "lower," and so on. Do about ten of these shifts with each hip across the floor or ground. Rest for a few minutes, then do ten more with each hip. At least two sets of ten each should be enough each practice session for you younger kids.

Drill No. 72- Thrusting the Hips

The Basics are

This is a drill to work on thrusting your hips. Start out by walking at a moderate speed. First your right hip is thrust forward, then 3 normal "easy walking" steps, then your left hip is thrust forward. Do not kick your lead leg too far out in front. When your leading leg foot contacts the ground it should already be moving backward. As soon as possible try to get your body weight over your lead foot. When you start to thrust your hip say to yourself, "Hip forward" rather than "Leg forward."

Practice

For this practice you will be going about 50 yards distance per segment just like in *Drill 68*. Have mom or dad blow a whistle or say, "GO," then you start walking down the track at a moderate speed. First you thrust your right hip forward for a step. Then you take 3 "easy walking" steps followed by 1 step thrusting your left hip forward. Then you keep repeating this down the track for a 50 yard segment. Next do an "easy walk" back to the starting point, resting as you go. Then you walk the whole 50 yard segment the same way again, except this time you speed up the tempo a bit. For beginners and most of you younger kids two segments of down and back on this drill should be enough at a practice session.

Drill No. 73- Technique and Rhythm Endurance

The Basics are

This is a drill to work on building up your endurance for either a 1500 meter or a 3000 meter race walk event. You need to walk at a speed that will let you concentrate on the "race walk" technique. And you need to start working on getting into a rhythm you are comfortable with. In this drill you will work on longer distances to build up their endurance. It's best to work on a track with lanes marked. This way you can walk correctly right next to a straight lane line and know you are going straight. Concentrate on things like pulling the ground back toward you when your lead foot hits the ground, straightening your legs, driving with your rear leg, thrusting your hips, moving your arms correctly and keeping your body posture upright.

Practice

Go to your local high school track for this training because they will have lane lines to use as a guide. Work on the straightaway where the line is straight. Start out down at one end of the straightaway, right next to a lane line. Have mom or dad blow a whistle or say, "GO," then you start walking down the track at a moderate, but even speed. You need to work on 70 yard segments for this drill. This is where you "race walk" for the 70 yards, then "easy walk" back to the starting point, resting while you walk. When you get back to the starting point you "race walk" back another 70 yards, then "easy walk" back again. You keep repeating this for six segments of down and back at a practice session (about a 440 yard distance). Have mom or dad watch you carefully, make sure you go at an even tempo and don't lift your feet incorrectly. When you start getting tired you are going to want to slow way down.

Before you start have mom or dad explain to you that they will blow the whistle at you when they see you are slowing way down. This means you can slow down a little bit, but only by shortening your stride length, then still keeping an even tempo or pace at the slower speed. What you DO NOT want to do is get into a habit of slowing way down, then start to speed up again when you get a little rested. It's going to be hard for you to learn to stay at a even tempo or pace. Don't give up though because you can learn how to do this. Keep encouraged by noticing your progress. If you take a stop watch with you each time, then you can record your progress as you move along in training.

Check *TABLE 8* to see some comparison times for you to achieve in order to be competitive. The main records are "*American outdoor*" youth track & field records, but we have also added the local "*CYC*" and national "*CYO*" records for a comparison.

COMPARISON PERFORMANCE DISTANCES -RACE WALKING					
BOYS		**DISTANCE**			
Age Division		1500 Meter	Record (Min- Sec)	3000 Meter	Record (Min- Sec)
6 - 8 (Primary)	Satisfactory	17:00.0			
	Good	15:30.0			
	Excellent	14:30.0	13:51.4		N/A
9 -10 (Bantam) (Roadrunner)	Satisfactory	11:00.0	△9:41.00		
	Good	9:00.0	Sub = 7:53.71		
	Excellent	8:00.0	7:13.01		N/A
11 -12 (Midget) (Cub)	Satisfactory	10: 00.0	△8:56.34		
	Good	8:30.0	Sub = 7:31.34		
	Excellent	7:30.0	6:44.1		N/A
13 - 14 (Youth) (Cadet)	Satisfactory			18:00.0	△16:56.15
	Good			16:00.0	Sub = 14:44.76
	Excellent		N/A	15:00.0	14:02.58
GIRLS		**DISTANCE**			
Age Division		1500 Meter	Record (Min- Sec)	3000 Meter	Record (Min- Sec)
6 - 8 (Primary)	Satisfactory	15:00.0			
	Good	13:00.0	□13:31.3		
	Excellent	12:00.0	11:33.2	11:33.2	N/A
9 -10 (Bantam) (Roadrunner)	Satisfactory	12:00.0	△9:37.27		
	Good	10:00.0	Sub = 9:08.56		
	Excellent	8:30.0	7:30.8		N/A
11 -12 (Midget) (Cub)	Satisfactory	11:30.0	△8:23.55		
	Good	9:30.0	Sub = 7:40.82		
	Excellent	8:00.0	6:53.7		N/A
13 - 14 (Youth) (Cadet)	Satisfactory	11:00.0		18:00.0	△17:01.53
	Good	9:00.0	□9:52.1	16:30.0	Sub = 16:44.36
	Excellent	7:45.0		15:30.0	14:46.46

N/A = Records not applicable or available in this age group.
All times are measured in minutes and seconds.
Unless otherwise noted all records are "American AAU/ USATF National Outdoor" youth (2002-2007).
△ = AAU/ USATF Private track club record.
□ = USATF- L1 Open championship record (2007).

TABLE 8

Javelin Throwing

Explanation

Javelin throwing is another field event that takes a very special skill. Not too many of you young kids can do it. Not necessarily because you don't have the ability, but because many youth track & field organizations don't offer it as an event. It has been around in modern Olympics since 1908. However, USA track & field does have "mini javelin," and they do have a "regular javelin (new & old)" event just for young kids 14 years old and younger. The "mini javelin" has been developed for you younger kids to start learning the javelin throw. The "mini javelin," or "turbojav" as it sometimes goes by, is thrown by up through 12 year old boys and girls. It was designed by Tom Petranoff a two time world record holder in the javelin throw. It looks sort like a two and a half to three foot long dart used in a dart game. A soft nose has been added for safety reasons. And so thanks to Tom, both you younger boys and girls have a javelin event in your track meets now in parts of the USA. Boys and girls 13 years old and up start to throw the "regular javelin."

We will cover "regular javelin" throwing in the book, and how it relates to you younger kids just starting out. The "regular javelin" is a long spear basically sharp on both ends. For safety reasons many precautions have to be taken. At one time their were attempts to use a rotary technique style of throwing. It is banned now. And we are back to the traditional technique style of throwing which we will cover in this book. The rules say when you start now you have to face the direction of the throw. First we will go over the "mini style" and then the "traditional style." Then we will cover the lead-ups and lead-ins you need, to build up and improve your skills for this event.

For Practicing

For all training and practicing it's best to go down to your local high school or college track to work on your technique. The reason is they will have the markings for the run-up lane and throwing sector lines .You could set it up in your back yard if it is big enough (probably not likely) by marking the lane lines and a scratch line arc. But sooner or later you need to get the feel of the real field markings and where the throwing sector is located. With the sector lines and a scratch arc you will know if your throw is a foul or not.

Drill No. 74- The Mini (Turbo) Javelin Throwing Technique

The Basics are

This is a drill for you to learn the technique of "mini (turbo) Jav" throwing. This is a small javelin especially designed for kids. There are 3 models of the original "Turb Jav" weighing from 300 to 500 Gr., 2 models of the "Long Tom" weighing from 600 to 800 Gr. and a Nordic "Junior Javelin" weighing about 270 Gr. Assembled, they are about 3 Ft. to 3 Ft.- 9 In. long. The Junior Javelin is the longest and lightest in weight. The Turbo Jav VII has a unique system to show you how to hold it properly. The mini javelin's are thrown overhand over your shoulder. They can be thrown standing still all the way up to a seven step or a full approach. The mini jav needs to be thrown in a way that lets it come down tip

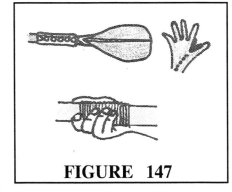

FIGURE   147

first. Where the tip hits registers your distance. The best way to throw it is with the tip pointed up. If you throw it with the tail section higher than the tip, you will have a bad throw without much distance.

How to Hold the Mini Jav

All the mini jav's have some kind of raised section on the shaft to indicate where you need to hold it in your hand. That area is it's balance point. If you hold it way back on the tail section or way towards the tip you will *NOT* be able to throw it correctly. On the turbo jav you will see a raised "V" towards the tail section and just above the grip. All the way down the grip there is series of raised dots. This is called the "Y" system. First you open your throwing hand, notice the crease, then place the grip with the dots face down into your hand. Now rest your thumb and index finger on the raised "V". Next bring your thumb and index finger down around the hip part of the grip *(SEE FIGURE 147)*. Now you are ready to throw.

How to Throw the Mini Jav

For a standing throw first face forward toward the direction you want to throw. Bring the turbo jav up to head height and parallel to the ground. It should be beside your eyes, just above and slightly behind your ear. Your other arm should be extended and pointing in the direction you are throwing *(SEE FIGURE 148-A)*. Next you extend your throwing arm back with the tip pointing forward. Your opposite arm is pointed in the direction of your throw *(SEE FIGURE 148-B)*. Now you start to pull your opposite arm into your rib cage, which starts your right shoulder to rotate as you start the throw. Next in a smooth continuous action, with the tip pointing more upward, you pull the turbo jav forward and throw over your shoulder *(SEE FIGURE 148-C, D)*.

A   B   C   D

FIGURE   148

The Run Up for the Mini Jav

Once you have learned the technique, you start with a on step approach, then work up to a three, five, seven and finally a full running approach. You always keep the tip pointing in the direction of the target. DO NOT wiggle wag the turb jav around as you hold it back. For the one step throw right handed throwers start with your right foot forward. Your right arm is back and your left arm is pointing in the direction of the throw. Keep both arms held high, just slightly above your shoulder level. Your first step is with your left foot, then throw. At the plant or block your left arm should pull into your rib cage area. This allows your right shoulder and hip to accelerate over your leg as you make the throw and follow through.

Always start with your right foot forward. For the three step move, your first step is with the left foot. The second step is with your right foot, moving it very quickly which lets your third step off your left plant leg to get down quickly for your throw. You always trace back your steps so that your starting point lets you throw without going over the foul line arc or scratch line. Your run-up must stay within the run-up lane lines. For the five step throw you just add two more steps, and for the the seven step throw add four more steps. For your full approach you start the same but then move into a run. Learn to run smoothly, then draw back the turbo jav using control to keep the tip always pointing forward as you run. Try to keep the tip parallel to the ground, not allowing it to move up or down too much as you start to apply the force for your throw. DO NOT stop too soon after your throw. Allow room for your body to follow through.

Practice

Before you start be sure to warm up with several minutes of jumping jacks or jogging. Follow that with stretching exercises for your legs, hips, torso, shoulders and arm to make sure you are loose because javelin throwing is very stressfull on all the parts of your body. For practice start with the one step throw. When you have mastered that then go to the three step, then the five step, then the seven step and last to a full run approach. It's probably a good idea to have mom or dad come out and watch you to make sure you are holding and throwing the turbo jav correctly. Make at least three throws at each of the run-up steps and at least three throws at a full run-up approach at a practice session.

Drill No. 75- The Traditional Javelin Throwing Technique

The Basics are

This technique is much different than throwing the turbo jav. If you are just beginning, then learn how to throw the turbo jav first before you even think about traditional javelin throwing. Wait until you are high school or college age. This is a drill for you to learn the technique of "regular" javelin throwing. For a typical sequence ***SEE FIGURE 149***. In this drill we will use instructions for a right hand javelin thrower. Left hand throwers are flip flopped or just the opposite. The javelin throwing technique can be broken down into five basic phases.

- Starting.
- Approach.
- Transition.
- Block and Release.
- Follow Through

Starting

Before you start make sure you are properly *warmed up* and *stretched* out. First you need to learn how to grip the javelin in the carry position. There are three basic javelin grips. The "index finger," *(SEE FIGURE 150-A)*, the "second finger,"*(SEE FIGURE 150-B)* and the "V" grip

A	B	C	D

FIGURE 149

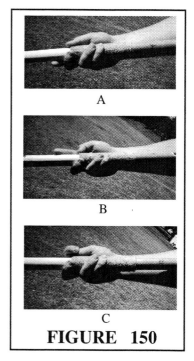

A

B

C

FIGURE 150

(SEE FIGURE 150-C).

For the *"STARTING"* phase your body has to be facing the direction of the throw. There are several schools of thought on how to place or hold the javelin when you start. **1)** The old school way of holding it raised above the head, tip up, is more for older athletes using a 5 stride or longer run-up *(SEE FIGURE 151-A).* They feel they get even more downward thrust from the arm in the higher position. **2)** One of the newer ways is more relaxed with the javelin held held right next to your ear and eyes, with your elbow bent *(SEE FIGURE 151-B).* The reasoning is better throw thrust from back to front. This method is probably going to be easier for you younger high school age beginners. It is held basically horizontal, but some like the front tip lowered just a little bit. **3)** One of the more modern ways is hold it over your head, lean back just a little with the arm slightly back, and the elbow held up higher *(SEE FIGURE 151-C).* For younger kids just beginning then it may depend on which way you are more comfortable with.

Your Approach

Next is the *"RUN-UP"* phase. The javelin is moved a full arms length back toward the rear, the tip slightly up and facing forward. While staying comfortabl, you accelerate quickly and run as

A

B

C

FIGURE 151

fast as you can up to the block and throw point. There are three stride, five stride, and 12 to 15 stride run-ups. In the run-up there are transition cross over steps. As with any of the run-up events you need to measure out your run-up starting point. This is so that your follow through does not carry you over the "foul arc." This is where the agility "crossover foot" drill practice comes in handy.

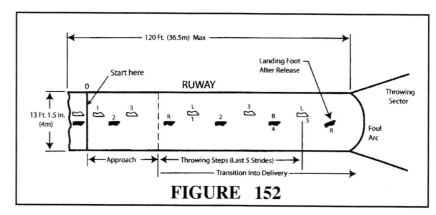

FIGURE 152

Your Transition

The third is the *"TRANSITION"* phase. In this phase you withdraw the javelin in preparation for the "whip-and-flail" action using your upper body. You lower your body and trunk for a quick explosive drive into your block and release. The transition phase is usually accomplished with a five step pattern *(SEE FIGURE 152)*. This phase starts when the left foot (L-1) lands. Your shoulders turn and your throwing arm is laid back slightly above your shoulders with your palm up. Your shoulders rotate as your arm comes back *(SEE FIGURE 154-A,B)*. This prepares your shoulder and arm for an automatic high "whip-flail" release."

Your left arm is swung long and low across your chest to aid in your balance through the running strides. Your left leg pulls and pushes your hips and body trunk forward. The next to last step (penultimate) should be a very vigorous forward push off your left leg. This pull-push action of your left leg aids in it's quick recovery, and places it in a fully extended position to block at foot contact. The throw begins at the end of the transition phase. On the last step (L-5) with your arm still all the way back to the rear, your arm is whipped forward and past your head. It's been described as "like pulling a rope past your ear." Your body is pushed forward off of a stiffened and flexed left leg.

The Block and Release

Your left leg is the block, just as if it came up against a stopblock Then the javelin is released just in front of yur head. In order to get a good throw off, maintain your speed through the approach and then the transition. Your hips and body trunk are thrust forward against a straight blocked left leg. Your right hip rotates around to face the direction of the throw. Your left arm which was initally extended in the throwing direction is brought down quickly against your left side as part of the blocking action. Keep your left shoulder forward and closed as much as possible. These actions cause a prestretch of your chest and body trunk muscles. This results in a reflex contraction of your body trunk, then finally the flail like action of your throwing arm. You finish with your eyes, head, shoulders, and hips all focused and facing forward in the throwing direction.

Your Follow Through

For your follow through, try to visualize driving on through your block (left leg) after release, not just up to your blocked left foot then stopping. This should force your body up on your left toe.The final single step is for stopping your forward momentum. The experts say allow seven to eight feet for your follow through so that you won't go over the "foul arc." If you get up too close and croud the foul arc line trying to get a little extra distace it will cause you have premature deceleration and a poor throw. Some coaches label the swinging your right foot around to the front as a "reverse." This move with your feet is to keep your body from being out of balance, causing you to fall over from too much forward momentum.

Practice

Before you start be sure to warm up with several minutes of jumping jacks or jogging. Follow that with stretching exercises for your legs, hips, torso, shoulders and arm to make sure you are loose because javelin throwing is very stressfull on all the parts of your body. You could practice in your back yard, but you will need a clear area at least 40 to 60 yards (36-55 meters) long. When practicing, make sure no one is in *front, back, or right next to you.* This is for safety reasons. It's probably a good idea to have mom or dad come out and watch you closely, just to make sure you are holding and throwing the javelin correctly. Start by working on your grips. Try all three.

The Index Finger Grip

Your "index" finger grips the javelin at the rear of the ribbed binding, with your palm facing up *(SEE FIGURE 150-A)*. When your arm is bent and brought up, then your hand is rotated to behind your head. On the "traditional" javelin the index finger can be on the end of the ribbed binding, away from you on the back side. The thumb lays along the side of the ribbed binding *(SEE FIGURE 150-A)*. The javelin is laying in the center of the palm now, the rest of your fingers gripping the ribbed binding. Practice gripping the javelin at least three times at a session this way so that you become familar with this grip, see if it works for you.

The Second Finger Grip

On this grip your "second" finger grips the javelin at the rear of the ribbed binding, with your palm facing up *(SEE FIGURE 150-B)*. When your arm is bent and brought up, then your hand is rotated to behind your head. The "second" finger can be on the end of the ribbed binding facing your back. Your thumb lays along the side of the ribbed binding *(SEE FIGURE 150-B)*. The javelin is laying in the center of your palm now, with your index finger laying along the shaft and facing the rear. The rest of your fingers are gripping the ribbed binding. Practice gripping the javelin at least three times at a session this way so that you become familar with this grip, see if it works for you.

The "V" Grip

On this grip your "index" and "second" fingers form a "V" as they grip the javelin at the rear of the ribbed binding facing away from you, with your palm facing up *(SEE FIGURE 150-C)*. When your arm is bent and brought up, your hand is rotated to behind your head. The "V" is on the end of the ribbed binding facing away from you. Your thumb lays along the side of the ribbed binding *(SEE FIGURE 150-C)*. The javelin is laying in the center of your palm now, the rest of your fingers gripping the ribbed binding. Practice gripping the javelin at least three times at a session this way so that you become familar with this grip, see if it works for you.

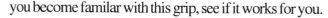

FIGURE 153

Of the grips, the "index" finger grip is the most popular now. It is probably the one you should start out using. The "second" finger grip has been called "the Finnish grip", and it is the second most popular. The "V" grip is the least used of the grips. Again try all the grips. You should use the grip that is most comfortable for you. There is a method that makes it easier to grab or secure your grip on the binding. You stick the javelin in the ground, slide your throwing hand down the shaft, then form your grip around the ribbed binding *(SEE FIGURE 153)*.

Backward Arm Extension

This is a drill to practice just extending your arm back at the start of your run-up. Walk through the footwork first, then go to a slow jog for several steps. Start out in the ready position. This is with the javelin resting on your right shoulder, pointing in the direction you are moving. The tip can be up just slightly. Keep your body square to the front, your shoulders should be relaxed

(SEE FIGURE 154-A). Next say to yourself, "GO," bring the javelin to the overhead position, then step out with your left foot *(SEE FIGURE 154-B)*. After that you walk or jog forward

A   B   C

FIGURE   154

starting with your right foot, at the same time you rotate your shoulder, and extend your right arm all the way to the rear *(SEE FIGURE 154-C)*. Keep the tip of the javelin at eye level through this move. Simultaneously you keep looking forward, keeping your hips square to the front, and take one more step with your arm back, then stop. Younger kids should do at least three of these short extensions walking, and 3 jogging, at a practice session.

The Run-Up Approach

Start practice with the one step throw. When you have mastered that then go to the three step, then the five step, then the seven step and last to a full run approach.   The run-up is to practice getting your momentum going to make a good throw. This is a progressive training drill. After the one step approach, start with the short 3 stride run-up first and work your way up in steps. To simplify things you can practice this drill using either a tennis ball or a baseball. We will use the right hand for throwing instructions. For a left hand thrower you would just be flip flopped or opposite. First walk through this several times before jogging through it. Grasp the ball in your extended to the rear right hand, palm up. Your left arm is extended in the direction of the throw.

For the three step approach you take one step forward with your left foot **(step 1)**. Following that your right foot crosses, and steps in front and ahead of your left foot **(step 2).** At this point your body tilts back a little. Next your left foot steps forward, goes into the throwing position, and comes down on your heel **(step 3).**

Your body then starts to shift forward. Your chest and hips rotate forward as your right hand starts to make the throw. Your right hand is pulled, or thrust forward, above the shoulder and past yor right ear. This is called "block and thrust through" **(step 4).** The right side of your body then rotates around to the left as your arm comes through. The ball is then released in front of, and above, your head *(SEE FIGURE 155)*.

FIGURE   155

Through the whole throw you should try to stay relaxed, not bend the elbow of your throwing arm as it comes through for the release. You should do at least three of these short extensions walking, and three jogging, at each practice session.

Just at the throw start here is an alternative drill, just to make it a little more fun and do something different once in awhile. What you do is to place a box top, or stand, behind you with

FIGURE   156

several balls on it. Place the box far enough back that you have to reach way back with your arm extended to grab the ball. Stand in a wide stance. Then reach back, grab a ball, turn and throw *(SEE FIGURE 156)*. The illustation is showing a "left hand" thrower. A right hand thrower is just flip-flopped or opposite.

As you start the throw you turn and pivot your left knee hard towards the front. Your left leg should be partially flexed. Rotate your hips around to the front also. The hips will then pull the chest and the arm around to the front with them. Your elbow has to lead your hand in the throwing action. To do all of this, remember to concentrate and focus before you start your throw. The ball should be released ahead of you, and above your shoulder level. Don't worry about cross stepping over with your left foot, or doing a reverse. This drill is just for the arm back and shoulder practice. You should practice by going through four or five balls, at least two times at a training session.

The 5, 7, 9-11 Stride Approaches

This is the the next step in the progression. The five stride (steps) approach is the same as the three stride run-up, except you just add two strides to the beginning of your run-up. The 9-11 stride approach is also the same except you add the appropriate number of steps to your start. Walk through each approach several times before jogging through it. Start by stepping out with your left foot first, just the same as the three stride run-up. My suggestion is count out loud, every step you take while walking through the run-up. Make sure that all the way through the run-up you keep your arm way back and pointed to the front. During the run-up your shoulders should always be squared to the front until the last step for the throw.

The cross step is on the fourth stride of the five stride approach. Or after the sixth, eighth or tenth stride on the other approaches. By counting out loud you will know for sure when you get to the cross over step. The throw is made after the fifth stide has been made on the five stride approach. The more steps in the run-up, the harder it will be for you younger kids to get it right. So concentrate and keep focused because you can learn how to do it. Here is another incentive. There are not nearly as many kids out for the "mini jav" in youth track, or the "traditional javelin" throw in college. This means you have a better chance in competing for the event. Do at least three walking, and three jogging for each of the different approaches at a training session.

The 9 to 11 Stride Run-Up Approach

This is the the last step in the run-up approach progression. Many track coaches recommend the 9 to 11 stride run-up for you younger kids, and beginners. World class javelin throwers will

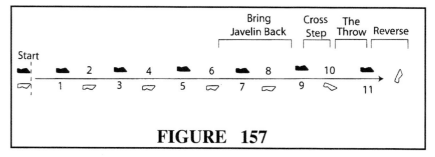

FIGURE   157

typically use a 10 to 15 stride run-up. Many also use check marks to let you know where to extend your arm, and where to start your throwing plant. Practice this drill with a ball, and

144

not the javelin because it will be easier for you and not as dangerous. It is the same as the 5 stride run-up, except you just add four or six strides to the beginning of your run-up. At first walk through these run-ups several times before jogging through them. Start by stepping out with your left foot first, just the same as the three, five and seven stride run-up. For the foot steps in a typical 11 stride run-up *SEE FIGURE 157.* The cross over step always occurs just before the last step, which is your throwing step. You should do at least 3 of these walking, and 3 jogging, at a training session.

The Throw

Use a ball to practice your throwing. It's easier. A three stride run-up will be enough to work on your "throw". The throw has been covered at the end of the three step run-up *(SEE PAGE 143)*. As your right knee swings around to the front, it pulls your hips and the arm with it. Walk through this at first until you learn the movements. Then increase your speed until the whip and flail part of the move is explosive and powerful. Step out long and low using your left foot the heel to plant for the throw. Then your body rises up, goes forward, and over your extended left leg. The ball should be released ahead of your body at about an angle of 30 to 40 degrees up from the ground. Some coaches say, "Think of your body as the handle of a whip, with the javelin as the tip of the whip. Then you move forward with the handle and crack the whip." To be a good thrower you need good strong flexible shoulders. Lifting weights for the older kids or push ups for the younger kids builds up the shoulders. You should do at least three of these throws walking, three jogging, and three at full speed, at each training session.

The Reverse

The "reverse" is one method to get you stopped and come under control after your throw has been made. This is where your right foot swings around slightly to the left in front of your body, to keep you from falling over from the momentum or fouling after your release. It's basically the same as in the "shot put" *(SEE FIGURE 137)*. The only difference is the right arm ends up down and across the front of the body in the follow through, with your right shoulder dipped down while you stay balanced. You can practice the "reverse" the same as with the shot put. You can also use a ball in your hand to practice the "reverse" if you like. Except don't throw it, keep it in your hand to get the feel of the end of the throw. Make at least three reverses at a jog first, then three at a full run-up approach at each practice session.

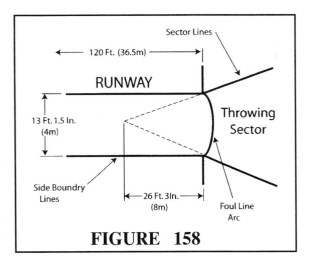

FIGURE 158

The Foul Line

After you make your throw and do your reverse to stop, then you need to make sure you *DO NOT* touch or go over the runway side boundary lines or the foul line arc. The runway is usually 120 feet (36.5 meters) long at a college. It will have a width of 13 feet 1.5 inches (4 meters). The lines are usually 2.75 inches (7 cm) wide and white in color. The foul line arc may be painted, made of metal, plastic, or wood, and it is level with the surface. Your javelin must land in the throwing sector, which extends out on both sides from the intersection of the foul line arc and end of the runway lines *(SEE FIGURE 158)*. Try to learn how to make your throw so that the tip of the javelin lands sticking in the ground.

Now we will get into the lead-ins and lead-ups to will help you improve on your basic skills, which are needed to perform the javelin throw. These are preparatory in nature for "core training" and "muscle memory."

Drill No. 76- Throwing for Accuracy

The Basics are

This is a drill to help you build up your accuracy for throwing. If you get a friend to come over, you can have a little competitive fun with this drill. What you do is throw tennis balls at a basketball, trying to knock it off of a box or stand.

FIGURE 159

Practice

To practice this drill get a box or stand of some kind, and put a basketball on the top of it. Then mark off using cones or something, an appropriate distance away for your age and size *(SEE FIGURE 159)*. Next take turns, and try to hit the basketball with the tennis ball and knock it off of the box. Then you can have mom or dad come out and keep score. They can make a list, and keep track of how many times you knock off the basketball, and how many times you miss. Try to remember yourself how many knock off's and how many misses you have at each session. Then remind mom or dad to ask you at the end of a training session how many times you made a hit or a miss. It is good training for you to remember. Make at least ten throws at a training session.

Drill No. 77- Two Handed Ball Throw

The Basics are

This is a drill to help you experience the stretch and pull action of your chest and shoulder muscles, and to build up these same muscles which are used in the javelin throwing process. You will need a volleyball, then a basketball, and last a light weight medicine ball, for this drill. This is a

A   B   C   D

FIGURE   160

146

progressive drill. From the sitting position, to the kneeling position, to the standing position, and last to the standing run-up position *(SEE FIGURE 160)*. Also the size and weight of the ball you use is progressive. Starting with a "volleyball", then as you get stronger going to a "basketball", and last a light weight "medicine ball". Younger kids and beginners should start with the ball over your head and push it. Each time you push it, you jump up a little. Then move the ball progressively farther back a little, and jump a little higher, to where you are pulling it forward.

Practice

First start in the "sitting" position to practice this drill, with a volleyball directly over the front of your head. Have mom or dad come out and help you, they can go out several yards or an appropriate distance in front of you to catch the ball, and then roll it back to you. Make several throws, then move the ball a little farther behind your head each time with your arms extended *(SEE FIGURE 160-A)*. You can do this about six or eight times, then go to the "kneeling" position and do the same thing *(SEE FIGURE 160-B)*. Followed by the "standing" position *(SEE FIGURE 160-C)*, then the "standing run- up" position *(SEE FIGURE 160-D)*. Maybe after a few practice sessions try a basketball. Then after a several weeks go by try a medicine ball. Pull in your stomach muscles just before you throw, to help pull your chest forward. About six or eight times in each position should be enough for younger kids or beginners at a training session.

Javelin Biomechanics

I think it is important for younger kids and beginners to understand the biomechanics of javelin throwing. If you are going to be serious about javelin throwing you need to learn some of the terms that your coaches will be using. These factors determine the the flight characteristics of the javeline and the distance you can achieve.

Modern biomechanics are carried out using three dimensional methods. These methods may give different values and informatio

FIGURE 161

than the older two dimensional reports *(SEE FIGURE 161)*. Some of the terminology used is:

- **Release Velosity**
  This is usually reported in meters per second (m/s). For elite world class males these values are 28-30 m/s, for females these values are 25-26 m/s.
- **Attitude Angle**
  This is the angle of the javelin in relation to the horizontal.
- **Angle of Release**
  This is the angle at which force is applied to the grip of the javelin at release, and which follows closely the path of the hand.

■ **Angle of Attack**

This is the difference between the attitude angle and release angle. This should be as close to 0 as possible, indicating that the athlete is "throwing through the point."

■ **Tumbling Angular Velocity**

This is a measure of the rotational forces applied to the shaft of the javelin, which cause it to oscillate (vibrate) and rotate forward (tumble).

Check ***TABLE 9*** to see some comparison distances for you to achieve in order to be competitive. The main records are "***American outdoor***" youth track & field records, but we have also added the national "***CYO***" records for a comparison.

COMPARISON PERFORMANCE DISTANCES - JAVELIN

BOYS		DISTANCE		
Age Division		Weight (Grams)	Meters (Feet - Inches)	Record - (Feet - Inches)
6 - 8 (Primary)	Satisfactory		9.14m (30 Ft.- 0 In.)	
	Good		10.67m (35 Ft.- 0 In.)	△ 13.92m (45 Ft.- 8 In.)
	Excellent	□500 (Mini)	12.19m (40 Ft.- 0 In.)	
9 -10 (Bantam) (Roadrunner)	Satisfactory		□21.34m (70 Ft.- 0 In.)	□△Sub = 22.56m (74 Ft.- 5 In.)
	Good	□500 (Mini)	30.48m (100 Ft.- 0 In.)	□# 32.84m (107 Ft.- 9 In.)
	Excellent	300 (Mini)	39.62m (130 Ft.- 0 In.)	41.16m (135 Ft.- 0 In.)
11 -12 (Midget) (Cub)	Satisfactory		□33.53m (110 Ft.- 0 In.)	
	Good	□500 (Mini)	38.10m (125 Ft.- 0 In.)	□# 38.53m (126 Ft.- 5 In.)
	Excellent	300 (Mini)	53.74m (175 Ft.- 0 In.)	54.53m (178 Ft.- 11 In.)
13 - 14 (Youth) (Cadet)	Satisfactory		□ 39.62m (130 Ft.- 0 In.)	□△Sub = 41.22m (135 Ft.- 3 In.)
	Good	□500 (Mini)	48.77m (160 Ft.- 0 In.)	□# 50.57m (165 Ft.- 11 In.)
	Excellent	600 (Mini)	56.39m (185 Ft.- 0 In.)	57.77m (189 Ft.- 6 In.)

GIRLS		DISTANCE		
Age Division		Weight (Grams)	Meters (Feet - Inches)	Record - (Feet - Inches)
6 - 8 (Primary)	Satisfactory		10.06m (33 Ft.- 0 In.)	
	Good		11.58m (38 Ft.- 0 In.)	△ 14.78m (48 Ft.-6 In.)
	Excellent	□500 (Mini)	13.11m (43 Ft.- 0 In.)	
9 -10 (Bantam) (Roadrunner)	Satisfactory		□12.19m (40 Ft.- 0 In.)	□△Sub = 22.56m (40 Ft.- 1.25 In.)
	Good	□500 (Mini)	24.38m (80 Ft.- 0 In.)	□# 24.0m (78 Ft.- 9 In.)
	Excellent	300 (Mini)	35.36m (116 Ft.- 0 In.)	37.15m (121 Ft.- 10 In.)
11 -12 (Midget) (Cub)	Satisfactory		□20.42m (67 Ft.- 0 In.)	□△Sub = 22.45m (67 Ft.- 1 In.)
	Good	□500 (Mini)	36.58m (120 Ft.- 0 In.)	□# 30.63m (100 Ft.- 6 In.)
	Excellent	300 (Mini)	44.2m (145 Ft.- 0 In.)	45.84m (150 Ft.- 4 In.)
13 - 14 (Youth) (Cadet)	Satisfactory		□33.53m (110 Ft.- 0 In.)	□△Sub = 34.26m (112 Ft.- 5 In.)
	Good	□500 (Mini)	47.85m (157 Ft.- 0 In.)	□# 40.72m (133Ft.- 7 In.)
	Excellent	600 (Mini)	51.21m (168 Ft.- 0 In.)	52.9m (173 Ft.- 6 In.)

All distances are measured in meters or feet and inches.
Unless otherwise noted all records are "American AAU/ USATF National Outdoor" youth (2002-2007).
△ = AAU/ USATF Private track club record (2007).
□ = AAU weight.
= A "CYO" (Catholic Youth Organization) national record performance distance (2007).

TABLE 9

Discus Throwing

Explanation

This was a gymnastic exercise in ancient Greek times. It has been revived in modern Olympics, for quite a number of years now. USA track & field does have a discus throwing event for young kids 11 years old and up. The discus is a disk, similar to the "Frisby" we all like to throw around. The modern discus can be made of many materials, but it does have to meet the correct weight and specified minimum and maximum diameters and thickness. The rim has to be very smooth because it is held in the hand, and could cut your hand or fingers.

We will cover discus throwing in this book, and how it relates to you younger kids. The discus you use in the actual event has a metal rim, weighs 1 kg (2.20 lbs) for USATF midget division and high school girls, and 1.6 kg (3.53 lbs) for high school boys. The technique of throwing envolves two full rotations. When you put together the weight and how you grip it with your hand, it can be very dangerous if it slips out and accidentially hits someone. So for safety reasons lots of precautions have to be taken. Training is a progression of steps to properly teach the technique. And with those steps, good safety habits should be developed. *NEVER* let spectators stand in front, on the sides, or in back of you during meets or practice. Especially if there is no safety cage around the throwing circle. We will first go over the "rotary with spin" technique of throwing. Last we will cover the lead-ups and lead-ins you will need to help you build up and improve your skills.

For General Practicing

For all your training and practicing it's best to go down to your local high school or college track to work on your technique. The reason is they will have the ring and throwing sector lines. You could set it up in your back yard if it is big enough (probably not likely), by marking a circular ring and throwing sector lines. But sooner or later you need to get the feel of the real field markings and where the cage abd throwing sector is located. With the sector lines and a circular ring you will know if your throw is a foul or not. We will ues a *right handed* thrower for our instructions unless otherwise stated. For left handed discus throwers everything will be flip flopped, or just the opposite. For circular instructions around the ring we will use the *hour positions* on a clock.

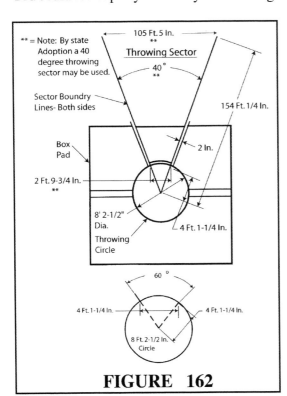

FIGURE 162

Drill No. 78- The Traditional Rotary Technique

The Basics are

This is a drill for you to learn the basic "rotary with spin" technique that young kids will be using. The discus can be thrown with either the left or right hand. Some young beginning kids may be using a "wrap" and then a shot put type

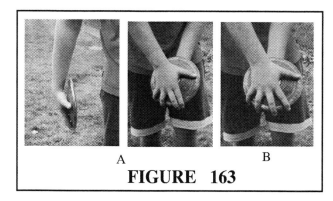

FIGURE   163

FIGURE   164

glide up to the front to make their throw. Either way, to start you stand at the very rear of the throwing circle, and face the rear with your back to the direction of the throw. The throwing circle is a circular area with an inside diameter of 8 feet 2-1/2 inches *(SEE FIGURE 162)*. Since most youth track teams or clubs use their high school facility, we will use the dimensional size of the throwing circle that conforms to the high school rules book. The throwing circle should have a protective cage, made of heavy nylon netting around two sides and the rear of the throwing circle. It is located approximately 10 feet 11 inches out from the center of the throwing circle, in all directions *(SEE FIGURE 167)*.

How to Hold the Discus

The discus is held in your right hand, and gripped with your fingers and your thumb. It is held on the pads of your fingers, with your thumb resting on the side *(SEE FIGURE 163)*. There are two variations of the finger grip. In one type of grip the fingers are all spread apart *(SEE FIGURE 163-B)*. In the other type of grip the index finger and the second finger are placed together rather than spread apart *(SEE FIGURE 163-A)*. The hand is flexed slightly inward at the wrist, with the finger pads curled around the rim of the discus.

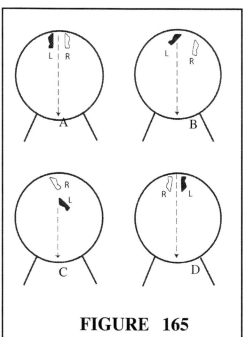

FIGURE   165

Your Footwork

The "rotary spinning" footwork is the same as the shot put rotary technique footwork in *DRILL 61 & 62*, except the arm is swung way back behind the body to start *(SEE FIGURE 164)*. Go back and check the shot put section out first so that you can see how the spin footwork technique works. There are four different starting positions for your feet.

In the first position both feet are pointing to the rear *(SEE FIGURE 165-A)* at the 6 o'clock position. In the second position the body and feet are turned more to the right *(SEE FIGURE 165-B)* at the 7 o'clock position . In the third position the body and feet are facing your left side *(SEE FIGURE 165-C)* at the 5 o'clock position . And in the last position the body and feet are facing the front *(SEE*

FIGURE 165-D).

You start your drive and spin to the front by driving to the left off your left leg while simultaneously pulling your right leg across your body as your right knee is pulled up to make a 90 degree angle between your right thigh and body torso. This combined action of both legs will cause you to drive across the ring and start your spin while you begin to gain rotational momentum to complete your first turn to the center of the ring. Try to keep your chest facing as close as possible to the 6 o'clock position until your left foot comes in contact with the ground. This helps keep the discus extended as far as possible behind your right hip for maximum leverage. Most discus throwers will make about 1-1/2 turns and steps to get to the front of the ring. As your feet touch the ground make sure you keep up with only the ball of your foot touching the ground, for better control.

The Delivery and Throw

On the throw and release the arm flexes and swings way around. The path the discus takes as it is thrown is called it's *orbit*. It's almost like the shot put throw, except the arm comes around in a big swinging arc from around the 6 o'clock

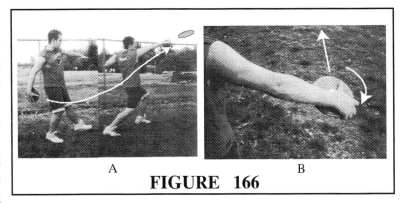

FIGURE 166

position. It starts at about waist level, dips down a little, arcs upward at about the 2 o'clock position, and ends about shoulder level at a 90 degree angle to your body torso *(SEE FIGURE 166-A)*. As the discus comes around for delivery it takes a high-low-high pattern. Your hips are "thrust" hard around to the left and forward, then the arms and the shoulder follow. Then you put a clockwise "spin" on the discus as you release it *(SEE FIGURE 166-B)*.

The Reverse

At the end just after your release you do a "reverse" the same way as in the shot put *(SEE DRILL NO. 60)*. Before the reverse you need to learn the technique of "blocking." This is a technique where the left foot on the last step points straight ahead and stops, or blocks, the left side of the body from spinning any farther while your right side hips and arms come around. To get effective blocking, bring your left arm elbow forcefully down the side of the body by your hips and rib cage. Imagine someone grabbing you from behind and you want to get away from them. You would probably try to elbow them as hard as you could right in their stomach. This is the type of move you make with your elbow.

Practice

Find a very large area to practice in. For safety reasons make sure the area to the front, sides, and rear, are all clear of people or animals. If you can find a high school with a throwing circle and a cage *(SEE FIGURE 167)* around it, this is ideal. To practice the traditional discus throw you start out by trying all four starting positions. Except you use the rings *(SEE FIGURE 139)* just like in the shot put, or a "frisbie," but not a discus. Usually one position will feel more comfortable to you. This technique is very difficult to learn. So it is very important for you to start out feeling comfortable. Have mom or dad come out and help you walk through the whole technique,

151

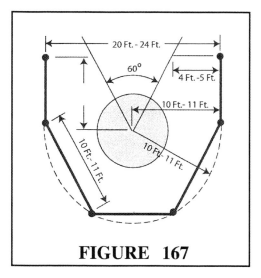

FIGURE 167

footwork and movements, first just until you get the feel of the rotary spinning movements. Then speed it up little by little as you get better and faster going through the movements. Eventually you will need to use the discus, to get the proper feel of throwing it. Learn to cup their hand with only their fingers on the disk. Make sure you learn to get good spin, torque, hip thrust, and blocking while you go through your training.

To practice "blocking" stand with your left foot pointing straight ahead, up against a stopboard or on a line. Then holding you left leg still, rotate your torso (body) to the right. Then have mom or dad say, "GO," and you swing your right arm and hips around to the front at 12 o'clock as if to throw the disk while pretending to elbow someone right behind you with your left arm. If you are having trouble, break the technique down into the five steps. The starting position including the grip, the rotary run-up, the throw, blocking, and the reverse at the end. Then go over whichever step it is that you are having trouble with. Walk through it slowly until you learn that phase, or step in the process. Do at least ten of these rotations at a training session.

Now we will get into the lead-ins and lead-ups to will help you improve on your basic core training skills, which are needed to help you perform the discus throw. These are preparatory in nature.

Drill No. 79- Throwing for Accuracy

FIGURE 168

The Basics are

This is a drill for you to learn how to make accurate throws. You will need to get a "hula hoop" or "ring" for this drill. And you will need to find a high jump standard that holds the bar, or a teather ball post maybe, for a target to aim at. What you try to do is throw the hoop or ring so it falls over the post *(SEE FIGURE 168)*. "Spin" on the discus is very important. To learn the technique you need to throw the hoop so it spins flat and goes up and over the post. It teaches you to lift your body upwards at the moment of release.

Practice

It might be more fun for you if you bring a friend over to work with on this. It won't be so boring because you will have a little competition. You can do this out in the back yard. Start at about ten yards away from the post. Then make adjustments from there, depending on how easy or hard it is for you. Have mom or dad come out and keep track of how many you get over the post, and how many you miss. Then after a session have mom or dad ask you how many you made and how many you missed. This is good mind training, and it tends to develop your competiveness. Make at least ten throws at a training session.

152

Drill No. 80- Slinging a Ball for Distance

The Basics are

This is a drill for you to build up your shoulders and arms. You will need a volleyball, basketball, and a light weight medicine ball for this drill. Start out using one hand for the throws, then go to two handed throws after four or five training sessions. Get into a sitting position, with your legs spread apart. Next you take the ball in either hand, then see how far you can sling it with your arm extended *(SEE FIGURE 169-A)*. As an alternative, do a standing throw some of the time *(SEE FIGURE 169-B)*. It will break up the monotony of always sitting for the drill.

FIGURE 169

Practice

Start out with a volleyball, then go progressively to the basketball, and last the light weight medicine ball. This is slowly building up your strength. Keep track of your distances, so you can see if you are improving. Try to remember how far your best throw went at each session. Start out with the sitting throw. For the standing throw concentrate on throwing your chest forward ahead of your arm. Also step way out and hard in the direction of the throw when you make your release. Make at least ten of either throw at a training session.

Drill No. 81- Discus Swinging

The Basics are

This is a drill for you to develop a better grip on the discus. From the standing position you grip the discus, then swing it backwards and forwards without letting go of it *(SEE FIGURE 170)*. Your arm swing should go about 20 degrees to either side of vertical, with your arm acting like a pendulum. This motion lets you get a better feel of the pressure against the fingers.

FIGURE 170

Practice

You will need to get a discus for this training. If you are serious about throwing the discus, you should have one at home to work with. For this practice training you curl, and spread, your fingers around the discus *(SEE FIGURE 163-B)*. DO NOT let the centrifugal pull force straighten out your fingers. At the end of the forward swing use your free hand to to squeeze it with both hands. This helps to keep it from slipping, or flying, out of your hand.

Your swings should be nice and easy, not too hard. The arm should be flexed, and move from front to back without bending. Keep the swings low. They do not have to go way up high in the air. Make at least ten of these swings at a training session.

153

Drill No. 82- Bowling the Discus

The Basics are

    This is a drill for you to develop your release of the discus off of your fingers. Also you are learning to control the spin and direction it goes when it comes off of your fingers. What you do is grip the discus, bring your arm backward, then let your arm swing down and bowl it on the ground

FIGURE 171

(SEE FIGURE 171). Just as you release the discus, you bend forward so that your hand almost touches the ground as it comes down for the roll.

Practice

    You will need to get a discus for this training. You could use a "frisby", but the weight of the real discus will work better. The instructions are for a right handed discus thrower. For a left handed thrower everything is just flip flopped or opposite. Stand with your left foot slightly forward, discus in hand. Then step out with your left foot, and bend at the knees as your right hand starts to come forward. The swing should be nice and easy.

    Now roll the discus out of your hand by squeezing it out, and making a fist as you let go. As the discus starts to come out of your hand, you pull your finger tips toward your palm, and in sequence. Starting with your little finger all the way through to your index finger. This is going to be hard for you younger kids to do. Don't give up though you can learn how to do this with lots of practice. Your wrist has to give a little snap, to get the discus to spin out correctly. If the ground surface is flat, the discus should roll straight ahead. It does not have to go too far because you are just working on perfecting your release, and not going for distance. Make at least ten of these bowling rolls at a training session.

Drill No. 83- Standing Throw

The Basics are

    This is a drill for you to develop the arc of the release. It is also a drill to teach you the flat release with the hand on top. The arc starts at your waist and swings up to shoulder heigth *(SEE FIGURE 166-A)*. As your hand comes around to the direction of the throw, your thumb is leading.

Practice

    Stand with your left side facing the front. If you are left handed, your right side should face the front. Before you start have mom or dad check your grip *(SEE FIGURE 163-B)* and make sure you are holding the discus correctly. Next you swing the discus back and forth around the body nice and easy a few times (wrapping) before you make the actual throw. This is going to be a standing throw right from the front of the ring, with no windup and no rotations. As you start to make your throw, you pivot on the balls of your feet, then bring the hips, followed by the chest, around facing the front ahead of your arm. The arc of the throwing hand should start at about waist high, and as it comes around it moves up to shoulder heigth *(SEE FIGURE 166-A)*. Then you release it off of your fingers nice and easy. Have mom or dad watch you carefully to see that your hand stays on top of the discus. The rotation off of your fingers should be clockwise (*SEE FIGURE 166-B*). Remember this is not for distance, but for form and technique only. It only needs to travel 15 - 20 feet out. Make at least ten of these throws at a training session.

Check *TABLE 10* to see some comparison distances for you to achieve in order to be competitive. The main records are "*American outdoor*" youth track & field records, but we have also added the local "*CYC*" and national "*CYO*" records for a comparison.

COMPARISON PERFORMANCE DISTANCES - DISCUS

BOYS		DISTANCE		
Age Division		Weight (Lbs.)	Meters (Feet - Inches)	Record - (Feet - Inches)
6 - 8 (Primary)	Satisfactory		12.80m (42 Ft.- 0 In.)	
	Good		15.24m (50 Ft.- 0 In.)	☐ 15.12m (49 Ft.- 7 In.)
	Excellent	1 Kg. (2.2)	17.68m (58 Ft.- 0 In.)	☐ 18.39m (60 Ft.- 4 In.)
9 -10 (Bantam) (Roadrunner)	Satisfactory		21.34m (70 Ft.- 0 In.)	
	Good		28.04m (92 Ft.- 0 In.)	☐ 29.44m (96 Ft.- 7 In.)
	Excellent	1 Kg. (2.2)	32.0m (105 Ft.- 0 In.)	32.39m (106 Ft.- 3 In.)
11 -12 (Midget) (Cub)	Satisfactory		28.96m (95 Ft.- 0 In.)	
	Good		38.10m (125 Ft.- 0 In.)	# 30.15m (98 Ft.- 11 In.)
	Excellent	1 Kg. (2.2)	45.72m (150 Ft.- 0 In.)	48.65m (159 Ft.- 7 In.)
13 - 14 (Youth) (Cadet)	Satisfactory		39.62m (130 Ft.- 0 In.)	
	Good		48.77m (160 Ft.- 0 In.)	# 41.68m (136 Ft.- 9 In.)
	Excellent	1 Kg. (2.2)	57.91m (190 Ft.- 0 In.)	61.52m (201 Ft.- 10 In.)
GIRLS		DISTANCE		
Age Division		Weight (Lbs.)	Meters (Feet - Inches)	Record - (Feet - Inches)
6 - 8 (Primary)	Satisfactory		6.10m (20 Ft.- 0 In.)	
	Good		10.67m (35 Ft.- 0 In.)	☐ 8.75m (28 Ft.- 8 In.)
	Excellent	1 Kg. (2.2)	15.24m (50 Ft.- 0 In.)	
9 -10 (Bantam) (Roadrunner)	Satisfactory		21.34m (70 Ft.- 0 In.)	
	Good		25.91m (85 Ft.- 0 In.)	☐ 28.58m (93 Ft.- 9 In.)
	Excellent	1 Kg. (2.2)	28.96m (95 Ft.- 0 In.)	30.58m (100 Ft.- 4 In.)
11 -12 (Midget) (Cub)	Satisfactory		19.81m (65 Ft.- 0 In.)	# 20.52m (67 Ft.- 4 In.)
	Good		27.74m (91 Ft.- 0 In.)	△25.53m (83 Ft.- 9 In.)
	Excellent	1 Kg. (2.2)	35.97m (118 Ft.- 0 In.)	37.46m (122 Ft.- 10 In.)
13 - 14 (Youth) (Cadet)	Satisfactory		27.43m (90 Ft.- 0 In.)	
	Good		35.05m (115 Ft.- 0 In.)	# 27.43m (90 Ft.- 0 In.)
	Excellent	1 Kg. (2.2)	42.67m (140 Ft.- 0 In.)	46.32m (151 Ft.- 11 In.)

N/A = Records not applicable or available in this age group.
All distances are measured in meters or feet and inches.
Unless otherwise noted all records are "American AAU/ USATF National Outdoor" youth (2002-2007).
△ = AAU/ USATF Private track club record.
☐ = Miscellaneous youth track club championship meet records.
= A "CYO" (Catholic Youth Organization) national record performance distance (2007).

TABLE 10

Hurdling

Explanation

Hurdling is a modern day Olympic sport. It is only one of two events in track & field that combines two of the single event skills found in a race. The skills are running and jumping. The jumping is really a low jumping technique called "hurdling" because of the special jumping technique skill required. Great Britain is credited with being the first country to have a hurdle race. When it started it was just running between the hurdles, awkwardly jumping over the hurdle, then proceding to the next hurdle. Now it is a sprint between hurdles, then jumping over the hurdle without hardly even breaking stride.

We will cover hurdling, and how it relates to you younger kids. It can be dangerous if you hit the hurdle, trip and fall. So precautions have to be taken. With the invention of the curved rocker hurdle, some of the danger has been removed. What it does is roll over forward and go right down out of the way if the foot hits it. And the hurdler, while slowed down a bit, keeps on running to the next hurdle. There are low hurdles and high hurdles. For the age group this book covers (6-14 yrs.), we will talk about low hurdles. High school hurdlers (15-18 yrs) use the higher hurdles for the 100m, 110m, and 400m races. We will not cover those in this book. Starting age group youth hurdles are in the 30 inch to 33 inch range. Also the youth hurdle event is down in the 80 meter distance range. The keys in hurdling are speed, tempo, timing, and technique. There are a certain amout of steps between each hurdle, which have to be adjusted for the size of the boys or girls in the race. If you are out of step for your age and stride, then you will hit the hurdle.

To keep especially you younger kids (6 yrs. old) from being scared about hitting a hurdle, you need to use a height of about12 inches to start training with. What you will have to learn how to do is spend as much time as you can on the ground sprinting, and the least amount of time in the air going over the hurdle. After you learn how to go over hurdles in a straight line, and you have been practicing awhile, you will need to learn how go over hurdles set up on a curve (200m and up). Being tall with long legs is helpful. The other factor is you need to have a lot of flexibility in your hips and be able to stretch your legs way out in front. We will first go over the technique of hurdling. Last we will cover the lead-ups and lead-ins you will need to improve your skills for this event.

For General Practicing

For all your training and practicing it's best to go down to your local high school or college track to work on your technique. The reason is they will have the hurdles and lane lines you will need. You could set it up in your back yard if it is big enough (probably not likely), by marking several lane lines, then buying several of your own hurdles. It will be expensive though. But sooner or later you need to get the feel of the real hurdles on a track with lane lines. We will ues a *right* lead foot hurdler for our instructions unless otherwise stated. For left lead foot hurdler everything will be flip flopped, or just the opposite.

Drill No. 84- The Hurdling Technique

The Basics are

This is a drill to help you to develop the basic skills for the hurdle event. First you run and accelerate toward the hurdle, then you takeoff with your lead foot going over first. As you takeoff, your lead foot is stretched out straight, your body leans forward with your head almost touching the knee on your lead leg. Your arm on the opposite side of the lead foot starts to stretch out in front, with the other arm stretching out to the rear. As you get up in the air, your trailing leg is bent at the knee, flattened out and pulled up close to your body. As your leading leg goes over the hurdle, the trailing leg stays up close to the body, so it clears and does not hit the hurdle. Once you have cleared the hurdle, your lead leg comes down quickly to the ground, and forces the body forward. The trailing leg unbends, comes upward and forward, and reaches out forward.

Your hips and shoulders stay parallel to the ground, keeping as straight a line as possible without moving up or down very much. Basically the hurdles are set apart so that you run about 3 strides between each hurdle. Your head should also stay in as straight a line as possible *(SEE FIGURE 172)*.

FIGURE 172

Practice

To practice the hurdling technique beginners will need to set up some obstacles to go over. You can probably set up a mini course in your back yard if it's large enough. Some cones with a rubber tube, PVC pipe, or a bamboo cane about 3 or 4 feet long stretched across them will work fine. For you younger kids to practice, use 4 or 5 obstacles on a scaled down short course. For the regular event race see the courses spaced out for your age and size *(SEE TABLE 11)*. They may need to be adjusted a little because of the differences in stride lengths of you younger kids. Then before you start, make sure you are properly warmed up and stretched out.

HURDLE EVENT SPECIFICATIONS						
BOYS						
Age	Distance	Hurdles	Height	To First	Between	To Finish
8 & Under	*60m	7	20"	29'-6"	21'-4"	39'-4"
9 -10	*70m	8	27"	29'-6"	22'-11"	39'-4"
11 - 12	80m	8	30"	39'-4"	24'-8"	50'-10"
13 - 14	100m	10	33"	42'-8"	27'-10"	34'-5"
	200m	5	30"	65'-8"	114'-10"	131'-3"
GIRLS						
Age	Distance	Hurdles	Height	To First	Between	To Finish
8 & Under	*60m	7	20"	29'-6"	21'-4"	39'-4"
9 - 10	*70m	8	27"	29'-6"	22'-11"	39'-4"
11 - 12	80m	8	30"	39'-4"	24'-8"	50'-10"
13 - 14	100m	10	30"	42'-8"	26'-3"	49'-2"
	200m	5	30"	65'-8"	114'-10"	131'-3"

All specifications are per USATF (2007), AAU (2008) Track & Field rules.
All heights and distances are in feet and inches unless otherwise stated.
* = Suggested set up for training the younger boys and girls.

TABLE 11

Especially the front and the back of the thigh muscles. Quadricep muscles also need to be stretched *(SEE EXERCISES 12, 15, 16, 17, 20)*. Several other things also need to be done before you start:

Leading Leg Selection

Your leading leg needs to be selected. Here is how to accomplish this. Stand with your feet together, then you slowly lean forward without moving your feet. When you lean so far forward that you are overbalanced, one of your legs will naturally step out first to keep you from falling. That leg should be your lead leg. You want to start out with this leg going over the hurdle first, then as you move along in your training, see if you are comfortable with this leg going over the hurdle first. A test will be after a period of time you switch, try with your other leg several times over a hurdle and see how it feels to you. If you need to, then switch legs.

Developing a Stride Pattern

Next you need to develop a stride pattern. To do this, set up a little 3 lane courses in the back yard *(SEE FIGURE 173)*. The easiest way to mark it is, use heavy brown twine that you can find almost anywhere. All you need is an area of about 45 feet long by 20 feet wide. Get some

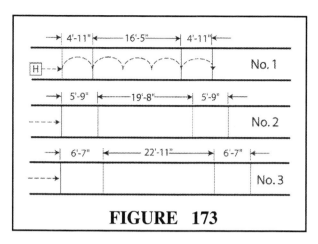

FIGURE   173

"U" shaped nails or wire to hold the twine down. Then if you want to have a really neat little course, get a can of bright orange spray paint and paint the twine. This way you can see the lines better. Now go to the start of course No.1 and start running towards it. Then jump over the first set of lines, leading with the lead leg you just picked. When you jump over you need to try and "clear" the lines as you go over.

In between the lines you make 3 strides. After the 3 strides, you jump over the next set of lines. To make it easier for you, count out loud, "Over - 1-2-3- over- 1-2-3" as you stride and run through the course. It will train your mind to think while you are hurdling. Have mom or dad watch you, and see if you are stepping into the second set of lines after the 3 strides. This means course No. 1 is too small for you. Then move over to course No. 2 where the line sets are farther apart. One of these three courses will more than likely fit your stride pattern. If not, then you may have to adjust the line set distances to fit your stride.

Clearing Low Obstacles

Your next step is place obstacles (hurdles) in each of the line sets in the course you choose. Now you have something to actually jump over when you run through the course. You can set up cones with rubber tubes, PVC pipe, or bamboo canes across them, or you could have two people hold a string across the line sets. The problem with the string idea is you may have trouble finding four people to hold the two sets of strings, so the cones will probably work better. Whatever you use for hurdles should be in the six to twelve inch high range. Place the obstacle 2/3 of the way in from the front of the line *(SEE FIGURE 174)*. Now you run through the course at about 3/4 speed to start. Make sure you jump over each obstacle with the lead foot first. Make sure you are taking the

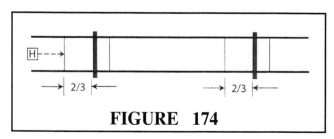

FIGURE   174

three strides in between. Until you get the feel of your stride pattern, say out loud, "Over - 1-2-3 - Over 1-2-3." This drill is for you to get the feel of the takeoff, pacing, rhythm between the hurdles.

As you get better at this, and run faster, you may notice you need to slow down to go over the obstacles just right with your three strides. So move to the next course *(SEE FIGURE 173)* where there is more space between obstacles. Or maybe you need to stretch out farther in your three strides to get to the next obstacle. You should then move down to the course where there is less space between obstacles. When you have picked the right course, run through it at least ten times at a training session.

Sprint Start and First Hurdle Approach

If you are using eight strides to get to the first hurdle (obstacle), then you should place your trailing leg forward in the starting blocks, and the lead leg in the back. If you have have long legs, and you are using only seven strides to get to the first hurdle, your lead leg should be forward in the starting blocks. In the case of you younger kids and beginners, nine strides is ok. If it does take you nine strides to get to the first hurdle, you put your lead leg forward in the blocks *(SEE FIGURE 175)*. This is one method.

There is another method where some coaches say always put your lead foot forward in the blocks, no matter the number of steps. What it is going to come down to is getting your lead leg to go over the hurdle first, and without slowing down or

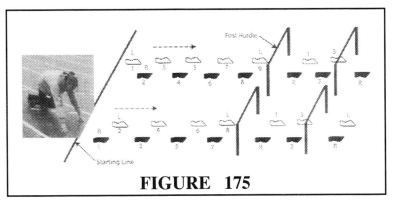

FIGURE 175

ending up with your trailing leg going over the hurdle first. The illustration is for a "left" leg forward hurdler. With a "right" leg forward hurdler, your feet are just the opposite.

Hurdles are spaced for the different age groups to have three strides in between hurdles. Hurdles are a "sprint" event. For you to practice your sprinting, then go back to the *"Sprinting"* section. Practice the same way you would as if you were a sprinter. Learn to have consistency to the first hurdle, then between each hurdle after that. To get your footwork straightened out you need to run through your starts, and the first two hurdles, at least five times at every training session.

The Finish

The finish of a hurdle race is the same as a sprint race. To practice your finish *SEE DRILL NO. 24* in the "sprinting" section. Run through your finish at least five times at a training session to get your lean perfected. Eventually after you have mastered the technique of hurdling, you will need to go out to your local high school and set up some obstacles at the distances in *Table 11*. Then have mom or dad come with you and say, "GO," or use a "clapper," and run full speed through to the finish line. Some of the time set up hurdles on the curve so that you can get the feel of hurdling as you run on the curves. Have mom or dad time you occasionally and check with the times in *Table 12* to see how you are progressing in your training.

Now we will get into the lead-ins and lead-ups that will help you improve on your basic *muscle memory* and *core training* skills, which are needed for you to perform successfully in the hurdle events. These are all preparatory in nature.

Drill No. 85- Jumping Low Obstacles

The Basics are

This is a drill for you six to eight year olds and beginners, just to help you get acustomed to jumping obstacles. Several obstacles are set up at knee heigth, or approximately 12 inches *(SEE FIGURE 176)*. Set up four or five obstacles with enough space bertween them so that you have room to get ready for the next jump. All you do at first is just concentrate and focus on jumping over each obstacle.

FIGURE 176

As an alternative get three to five of your friends to come over, then you can run a shuttle relay GAME with them using the same course. Make it fun and see which team has the best time stepping through the course during the training session. Have mom or dad come out and keep time for you.

Practice

To practice jumping low obstacles go down to one end of the course. Next run through the course, jumping over each obstacle with a lead leg going first. If it's too easy for you at 12 inches, then raise it several inches so that it's a little more chalenging for you. Run through the course at least ten times at a training session.

If you decide to run the shuttle relay GAME, choose two teams so it will be more interesting for you. Mom or dad will need a stopwatch to time you. Split each team in half, and put half of the team on one end and half on the team on the other end. Have mom or dad say, "GO," start the stopwatch. The first player on one end goes through the course jumping over each obstacle, then they tag their team mate at the other end as they finish. The team mate then runs through the course, and tags the next team mate, and so on until the last team mate finishes. Then mom or dad hits the stopwatch and times that team to see how they did. You could run this game several times at a training session, but keep the game to no more than 40 minutes. Then move on to some other type of training.

Drill No. 86- High Knee Marching and Skipping

The Basics are

This is a drill for sprinters. The basics are the same as in *Drill No. 23* in the "sprinting" section.

Practice

Practice this drill the same as if you are a sprinter.

Drill No. 87- Leading Leg Action with Lower Leg Extension

The Basics are

This is a drill to work on the action of your leading leg. First you walk along the side of the hurdles, then your leading leg goes over the hurdle. At the same time your trailing leg comes up, bends, then goes back down outside of the hurdle *(SEE FIGURE 177)*. After walking through

160

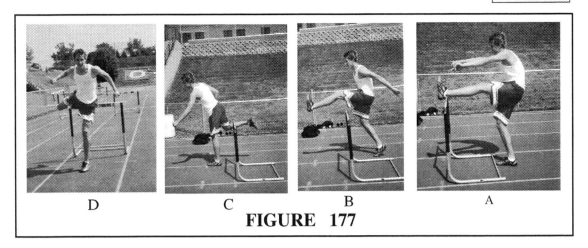

D   C   B   A

FIGURE   177

the drill several times to get the feel of your leg movements, go through the drill at a slow jog. This is a drill for your lead leg, so DO NOT worry about what your trailing leg is doing in this drill.

Practice

Set up three or four hurdles at the heigth your age group might use *(SEE TABLE 11, PG. 157)*. Except for you eight and under kids, the height drops down to about 18 inches, Use the indicated height size hurdles for you bigger kids. If you are really serious about staying in "hurdling" you might get mom or dad to help you make some adjustable standards (holders) to hold the the bamboo cane or PVC pipe. As an example, you might take a one inch square wood post, then put some nails in it to set the bamboo cane on. Some caution here if you do this then place the posts at least six feet apart. Then make the top of the post rounded and smooth so that if your leg comes down on it, or hits it, you won't get hurt. A couple of old broom sticks might even work better. If nobody in your family is handy at making things, then you can get the adjustable cones with holes in them, and a bar, all on the "InterNet." They are very inexpensive, and more transportable. However, you may need some kind of post to fit inside of them to rase them up to the height you need.

Start at one end of the row of hurdles, and along the outside edge. Position the hurdles apart far enough so that you can swing your leg through as you step without hitting the next hurdle. If your leading leg is your right leg, go to the left side of the row. If it's your left leg, go to the right side of the row. For these instructions we are showing a left lead leg hurdler. If the right leg is the leading leg, everything is just the opposite or flip flopped. Start out walking. Raise your left leg up, bringing your knee up to your chest, lean forward a little bit, and extend your leg on over the end of the hurdle *(SEE FIGURE 177-A)*. Next bring your trailing leg up, bend it, then step out with it along the outside of the hurdle end *(SEE FIGURE 177-C)*. Keep doing this all the way down the row of hurdles while walking. Then as you get a little better at this, and more fluid with your movements, speed it up to a slow jog. You may need to spread out the hurdles a little bit for the jog through so that your leg clears and does not hit the next hurdle. Practice this at least five times at a training session.

Drill No. 88- Trailing Leg Action with Partner Assistance

The Basics are

This is a drill to work on the action of your trailing leg. First make sure you are standing on the correct side of the row of hurdles. If the trailing leg is the left leg you stand on the right side of the row of hurdles. If it's the right leg, you stand on the left side of the row of hurdles. The trailing leg is the only leg that will go over the hurdles. You will be walking through at first, then slowly increasing the speed to a slow jog. Your partner will be assisting by holding your hands to keep you in balance while moving over the hurdle. Bring your trailing leg up, bend it, then tuck it in next to your body as it goes over the hurdle. Next you step down on the ground with your trailing leg, then step up with the other leg, then get ready to lift your trailing leg up again over the next hurdle *(SEE FIGURE 178)*. The other leg is always on the outside of the row of hurdles.

Practice

To practice this drill you will need to set the hurdles up the same way as in *DRILL 87*, except get mom or dad to come out and help. Start at one end of the row of hurdles, and along the

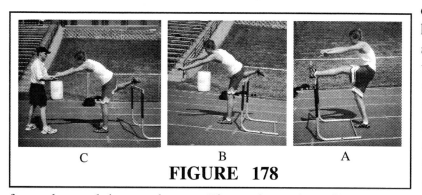

C   B   A

FIGURE   178

outside edge. Position the hurdles apart far enough so that you can lift your trailing leg through as you step, and without hitting the hurdle as you go over. Have mom, dad, or a coach hold your outstretched hands and make sure you lean

forward as you bring your leg over. They assist you by pulling you very slowly forward as you step out and extend the lead leg. Then you lift up your trailing leg, tuck it in, bring it over the hurdle, and then back down to the ground *(SEE FIGURE 178)*.

Make sure you turn your foot on the trailing leg outward so that it is moving horizontally over the top of the hurdle. Also flex your toes and don't let them drop down where they may hit the top of the hurdle as you go over. When your trailing leg hits the ground, you step up with your other foot. Keep doing this all the way down the row of hurdles. As you get better at moving your legs correctly you can speed it up to a slow jog. Go through the course at least five times at every training session. First with your lead leg, then switch if you can and go through five times with your other leg. This makes you more versitile, being able to use either leg as your lead leg.

FIGURE   179

Drill No. 89- Wall/Fence Trail leg Action
The Basics are

This is a trailing leg drill you can do at home all by yourself. Find a fence or wall, then put a low hurdle or obstacle out a few feet away from the wall. Stand behind the hurdle, then lean forward over the top of the hurdle and brace yourself with both hands against a wall or fence *(SEE FIGURE 179)*. Next stay in place, balance with both hands against the wall or fence, bend your trailing leg and tuck it in like going over the hurdle, then continually circle your trailing leg round and round over the outside edge of the hurdle.

Practice

Do as many of these circles as you can without touching your leg to the ground before your leg gets tired. The switch hurdle sides and work your other leg for as long as you can.

Drill No. 90- Running Approach Hurdle Clearance
The Basics are

This is a drill for mostly you older kids to work on. This is where you really sharpen up your skill for getting over the hurdle quickly. You need to get the feel of your takeoff point, your stride length going over, and your basic leg and feet positions and movements. Find a low hurdle you can easily clear, then use that one for this drill. The faster you approach the hurdle, the farther back you will need to be for your takeoff. Your upper body has to lean in towards the hurdle at takeoff. Your trailing leg has to be tucked in and up close to your chest. The whole movement over the hurdle needs to be very quick, going from a running position to a full low body stretchout, then almost snapping back to a running position, without losing a stride *(SEE FIGURE 172)*.

Practice

To practice this drill you should pick a hurdle heigth a few inches under the sanctioned heigth for your age group if possible *(SEE TABLE 11)*. To begin, get down on the ground in a "hurdlers stretch" exercise position *(SEE FIGURE 180)*. The hurdler on the left is way too stiff in the legs and spine. The hurdler on the right is little too stiff in the spine also. The hurdler in the center is loose and stretched out properly. While you are down on the ground in the position, observe that except for your head not looking up, this is

FIGURE   180

basically how you should look and feel going over the hurdle. Start by jogging up to the hurdle at a moderate speed, and concentrate on your form as you go over the hurdle. Here are three things you should try to do as you go over the hurdle during training *(SEE FIGURE 181)*.

- ■ Attempt to touch your leading leg toes with your opposite side hand.
- ■ Attempt to touch your leading leg with your chin.
- ■ Attempt to lay your chest down on your leading leg thigh.

Use only one hurdle, and after you have cleared the hurdle, then run past the hurdle about another 20 or 30 feet before you stop and come back. Concentrate and focus on just skimming over the top of the hurdle. You can speed it up a little each day as you get your form and technique worked out. Go over the hurdle at full speed at least three times at every training session.

FIGURE   181

Drill No. 91- 200m Hurdle Event Training

The Basics are

This is a drill for the longer 200m hurdle event. 11 and 12 year olds run the 80m hurdles. 13 and 14 year olds run the 100m and the 200m hurdles. The 200m hurdles is a longer race and takes a lot out of you young teen agers. You need to build up more endurance (aerobics) for this event.

Practice

To practice you need to do some distance training *(SEE DRILLS 30, 35, 36)*. Then work on some training such as the run-walk, "fartlek" training, and running up hills. These are all good. Also here is a tailored workout you can use:

1. Run a flat 50m, followed by 200m with 5 hurdles.
2. Run a 200m with 5 hurdles, then a flat 50m.
3. Run a flat 100m, followed by 200m with 5 hurdles.
4. Run a flat 150m, followed by 200m with 5 hurdles.
5. Run a 200m with 5 hurdles, then a flat 150m.

Summation

Here are several end of section, last pieces of advice for you. It is usually more comfortable to use a left leg lead when going over hurdles on a curve. Especially if you are running on on an inside lane. This is because the inward lean to the left as you run around the curve will make it easier to clear the trailing leg. This is another reason why we suggested you learn to use either leg as your lead leg if possible. As you come up to the last hurdle on the curve, and you are tired, switch to a right leg lead and aim at the outer right half of the hurdle with your lead leg, focusing on the black square on the hurdle bar to bring your trailing leg through. This is so that your trailing leg will be sure to go over the bar on the hurdle. Also if you use a left lead leg and go over too far to the right side of the hurdle, your trailing leg may be out in space *(SEE FIGURE 182)*. This is illegal and can disqualify you.

FIGURE   182

Check *TABLE 12* to see some comparison times for you to achieve in order to be competitive. The main records are "*American outdoor*" youth track & field records, but we have also added some local "*CYC*" and national "*CYO*" records for a comparison.

COMPARISON PERFORMANCE TIMES - HURDLES

BOYS		DISTANCE							
Age Division		# 60m	# 70m	80m	Record	100m	Record	200m	Record
6 - 8 (Primary)	Satisfactory	18.0	17.0						
6 - 8 (Primary)	Good	16.0	15.0						
6 - 8 (Primary)	Excellent	15.0	14.0		N/A		N/A		N/A
9 -10 (Bantam)	Satisfactory			16.0					
9 -10 (Bantam)	Good			14.0	△13.53				
9 -10 (Bantam)	Excellent	N/A	N/A	13.0	12.48		N/A		N/A
11 -12 (Midget)	Satisfactory			15.5		18.0		30.0	
11 -12 (Midget)	Good			13.5	△12.45	16.0	△15.25	28.0	△27.09
11 -12 (Midget)	Excellent	N/A	N/A	12.5	11.74	15.0	14.27	27.0	26.37
13 - 14 (Youth)	Satisfactory					16.5		27.5	
13 - 14 (Youth)	Good					14.5	△13.79	25.5	△26.22
13 - 14 (Youth)	Excellent	N/A	N/A		N/A	13.5	12.94	24.5	23.99
GIRLS		DISTANCE							
Age Division		# 60m	# 70m	80m	Record	100m	Record	200m	Record
6 - 8 (Primary)	Satisfactory	18.5	17.5						
6 - 8 (Primary)	Good	16.5	15.5						
6 - 8 (Primary)	Excellent	15.5	14.5		N/A		N/A		N/A
9 -10 (Bantam)	Satisfactory			16.5					
9 -10 (Bantam)	Good			14.5	△13.40				
9 -10 (Bantam)	Excellent	N/A	N/A	13.5	12.79		N/A		N/A
11 -12 (Midget)	Satisfactory			16.0		18.5		31.0	
11 -12 (Midget)	Good			14.0	△13.53	16.5	△15.74	29.0	△30.62
11 -12 (Midget)	Excellent	N/A	N/A	13.0	11.85	15.5	14.78	28.0	27.24
13 - 14 (Youth)	Satisfactory					17.5		30.5	
13 - 14 (Youth)	Good					15.5	△14.62	28.5	△28.11
13 - 14 (Youth)	Excellent	N/A	N/A		N/A	14.5	13.88	27.5	26.63

N/A = Not applicable or available in this age group.

All times are measured in seconds.

Unless otherwise noted all records are "American AAU/ USATF National Outdoor" youth (2002-2007).

△ = AAU/ USATF Private Track Club Record.

= Some approximated times and distances, as a check.

TABLE 12

Triple Jumping

Explanation

The triple jump has been around in the Olympics for a long time. It is very similar to the long jump. The difference is the triple jump has three phases or jumps. First a "hop," then a "step," then a "jump." Triple jumpers need to have great strength in their legs to rebound for each jump. They need to be excellent sprinters to get up the necessary speed and momentum to make a good jumps. Because triple jumpers heels, joints of the foot, knees, and hips, take such a pounding during the event you need to take precautions in training. The intensity of the training has to be slow, careful, and progressive in nature. Remember constant repetitive triple jumping has to be kept to a minimum. To lessen the shock of rebounding and jumping, try to work on surfaces that have some cushioning effect. Such as spongy grass (St. Augustine), or mats of some kind. For indoor training, gymnastic floor exercise mats work well.

This event is especially very hard on your heels and joints in your feet. Use "heel pads" in your shoes if you can find them because they will give a little added protection. Power training for "triple jumpers" is called *plyometrics*. It covers all the different types of rebound jumping, and depth jumping. Triple jumping for young kids starts at the 13 to 14 year old (youth division) ages, in USATF youth track and field. There has been some changes in triple jumping "technique" in recent years. But basically it is the same. The changes have come in the use of the arms, to gain lift in each jump. We will break the jump down into the techniques for the three phases (hop-step-jump). Then we will go ito the lead-ins and lead-ups to help you with your *core training* and *muscle memory*.

For General Practicing

For all your training and practicing it's best to go down to your local high school or college track to work on your technique. The reason is they will have the runway and sand pit you will need. You could set it up in your back yard if it is big enough (probably not likely). But it would be very expensive. But sooner or later you would need to go to your local high school anyway, just to get the feel of the real runway and sand pit. We will ues a *right* lead foot jump for our instructions unless otherwise stated. For left lead foot jumper everything will be flip flopped, or just the opposite.

Drill No. 92- The Hop Part of the Technique

The Basics are

This is a drill for learning to do the "hop" technique. Speed is the most important part of the triple jumping technique. So along with learning to hop, work on getting faster. After making a fast run-up you take off with a strong forward push from the jumping (power or favored) leg. Your body needs to stay upright, and in a flat horizontal trajectory, to conserve speed for the next part of the jump. To start the hop, the thigh of your non jumping (lead leg) drives upward to the horizontal position, and is then swung back to the rear. At the same time you push off with your jumping leg by lifting your thigh on that leg upward, making a wide stride stance at the mid point of your hop. As the jumping leg hits the ground, it is flexed so that it is ready to drive the jumper forward for the next part of the triple jump which is the "step." There is is a tremendous amount of stress put on your hop leg. That's why you hop with your favored leg *(SEE FIGURE 183)*.

166

Practice

To practice the hop, there are several different drills that will help you build up your hopping foot strength. They are *core training* your legs to hop.

FIGURE 183

Hopping for Distance

Perform five hops for distance using only your right leg (usually your power leg), and five hops using only your left leg. You can use a standing start, or for you younger kids you can use a short two step run-up *(SEE FIGURE 184)*. Lift your hopping leg, and both arms, forward and upward to help get more distance on the hops. Push off as hard as you can on all hops. Along with your arms, swing your free leg to assist in your hops.

FIGURE 184

Rabbit Hops

Perform three consecutive two legged jumps *(SEE FIGURE 185)*. Just for fun, and so it won't get to monotenous, get several of your friends to come over and train with you. Then say to them, "Lets see who can cover the longest distance with three consecutive hops." Then get a tape measure and measure your distances. To help in training, get a little book and keep track of your jumps. Try to remember what your best jump was at each training session.

You should learn to lean forward, and swing both arms forward and upward. This is to help you get more distance for your hops. Both of your legs need to extend together in one big powerfull push off. Do at least five sets of these jumps at a training session.

FIGURE 185

Repetitive Bounding

Repeitive bounding is another helpfull drill *(SEE DRILL 38, FIGURE 90)*.

Training Hops

After all the practice drills you need to go out and practice an actual competition type hop. Go out to the back yard in the grass, and mark a takeoff line. For this drill use a three to five stride run-up. Start out with a moderate speed run-up, then when you get to the takeoff line make a one hop, on one leg jump. After you come down from the hop, run out about another 30 feet before stopping. Have mom or dad come out and watch you carefully, and have them look at your form and distance. They can observe and help you improve your technique. A full all out speed run-up will come later. Measure your hop jump, and keep track in a notebook. These drills are very streuous, so take a days rest or more between sessions. Do at least three of these hops at a session if you can. Have mom or dad watch you closely, then if this is too strenuous on you, back off and only do one or two reps, or just quit for the day.

Drill No. 93- The Step Part of the Technique

The Basics are

This is a drill for learning to do the "step" technique. This will be the hardest part of the triple jump for you to learn. After making your "hop" you hit the ground, then push off for your "step," using your lead leg. By the way the step is usually shorter than the hop. In your takeoff for the "step," make sure your body stays upright. Your lead leg is flexed, and swung forward

FIGURE 186

hard. It becomes your cushioning leg as it lands after the step. It also needs to immediately push off hard after cushioning, to propel you forward for the last part of the triple jump, which is the "long jump." Your legs should be in a wide stride position, at the mid point between the hop and the step (*SEE FIGURE 186*).

Practice

To practice this drill there are several different drills that will help you build up your stepping strength for the middle part of the triple jump. Since this is the hardest part of the triple jump, you really need to concentrate and focus on the following drills. Don't slack off on them.

Combination of Hops and Steps

The "step" part is really just a long bounding stride. So the repetitive bounding training, for the "hops" part of the triple jump will take care of that core training for you. The combination is where you will do two hops, then two steps (*SEE FIGURE 187*). You can do this drill out in the

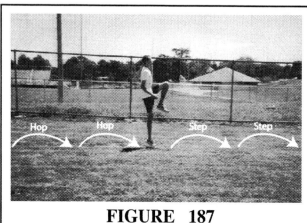

FIGURE 187

back yard. Mark off a starting line first. Start out with a standing start, then move to a short three stride approach. At the end of the steps, keep going and run out another 30 feet before stopping. Do at least three sets of these jumps at a training session.

For a variation of this drill so that it won't get too monotenous, bring several of your friends over. Then compete with them, to see who can get the longet distance for the set of hops and steps, during a session. Measure your combination of hops and steps, then keep track in a notebook. Try to remember what your best combination of jumps was. It's good mind training.

Repetitive Jumping and Bounding over Low Obstacles

This is a drill to condition you to get higher up in the air for your "hops" and 'steps." To do this drill you will need some cones, bamboo canes, or PVC pipes to use as the obstacles. You will also need some mats to land on. Maybe your local high school will let you use their indoor facility, with gymnastic floor exercise mats, and you bring the obstacles. Otherwise you will have to go out on the grass.   Place the obstacles in front of the mats, and place the mats where you will land on the them when you come down from a hop or a step *(SEE FIGURE 188)*. You can use a short two or three step

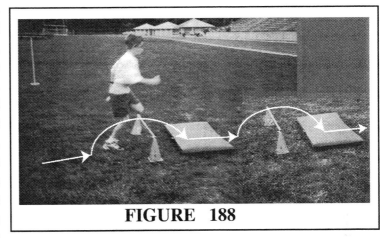

FIGURE   188

run-up. Go slow at first, then place the mats and obstacles a lttle farther apart as you get better and pick up your speed on this drill. This is to get you to stretch out more with each jump. Do at least three sets of these jumps at a training session.

Drill No. 94- The Jump Part of the Technique

The Basics are

This is a drill for learning to do the "jump" part of the technique. Your leading leg is swung from the step to the jump. Both your feet then come together to make the "jump" into the pit. The jump is just like the takeoff to make the "long jump." The "hang" technique from the long jump is most comonly used in this phase *(SEE DRILL NO. 44,45,46 & FIGURE 106, 107,108)*.

Practice

To practice this drill there are several different drills that will help you build up your strength to make the "jump" part of the triple jump.

The Standing Long Jump

Take some chalk with you and mark a line on the runway as your takeoff line. From a standing start, takeoff with your non favored leg. If

FIGURE   189

your leading (favored) leg is your right leg you would takeoff from you left leg. Step out hard with your leading leg, and lift your knee up high. Swing your arms forward and upward as hard and high as possible at takeoff, to get your momentum going. Once you start up in the air, then bring your arms forward, bend at your waist, and reach out forward with both legs. Next lean forward, bring your chest down to your knees, and land in the sand pit *(SEE FIGURE 189)*. Do at least five reps of these jumps at a training session.

FIGURE   190

2 Legged Jumps over a series of Low Hurdles

This is a drill to help you to get more springing power with your legs. Line up 2 or 3 hurdles in a row, with enough space in between to land and jump over the next hurdle with both feet. For you younger kids, the hurdles (obstacles) only need to be 12 inches high. Repeat the series of jumps at least 5 times at a session. Make sure you rest a little in between each series of jumps because this is very strenuous on your feet, legs, and hips *(SEE FIGURE 190)*.

Drill No. 95- The Run-Up
The Basics are

This is a drill for you to learn how to make the run-up for the first hop. The runway and the jumping pit for the triple jump is the same as for the long jump *(SEE FIGURE 103)*. The takeoff

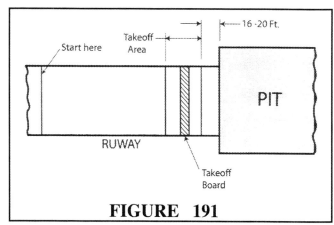

FIGURE   191

area is located about 16 to 20 feet back from the edge of the pit *(SEE FIGURE 191)*. The foul line for the takeoff is adjusted to fit the age group of the triple jumpers. USATF rules state the runway must be a minimum of 40m (131'-3") in length.

The suggested run-up can be from 9 to 11 strides for you younger kids *(SEE DRILL 42, FIGURE 103)*. Determine your run-up starting point line, and where your markers need to be, using the same method as in the "long Jump" *(SEE DRILL 42, FIGURE 103)*. Take these measurements and write them down so that you will always know exactly where you need to start.

Practice

To practice this drill go out to your starting point and take a few run-ups, just to see if your markers need adjusting. You don't need to make the whole triple jump sequence for practice run-ups, but you do need to run at full speed and make a hop. This is just to see where your foot will actually hit at takeoff. Whether you use a 9 or an 11 stride run-up is going to depend on which one you are more comfortable with. However as you get better the 11 stride run-up is going to give you more speed and momentum for your triple jump. That's what the run-up is about, going as fast as you can all the way through to the takeoff for your jump into the pit.

Drill No. 96- Full Triple Jump One Leg Bench Drill

This is a drill to work on your whole triple jump sequence using stands for a mini jump series. This drill is for *core training* and *muscle memory*. Stand in front of the first bench. You hop or bounce up using only one leg then drive off the bench on one leg, land in between on one leg, then hop up again on one leg. On the last bench you push off on one leg, then jump way out landing on both feet. Pre-calculate how far to space out the benches so that you don't trip and fall.

Practice

First you will need three low benches about 12 inches wide and 18 inches high, or three jump stands about the same size. The sequence is hop-step-hop-step hop-jump

Right   Right   Left   Left   Right   Right   Both

FIGURE 192

(SEE FIGURE 192). "Right" and "Left" refer to the landing foot. Do about three sets of this foot sequence at a practice session, resting a litlle between sets. The next time you practice switch starting legs so that both of your legs will develop equally. Then alternate legs at every practice.

Drill No. 97- Triple Jump Rules to Remember

This is information you need to remember if you are really serious about becoming a "triple jumper." There is a recommended ratio for each of the jumps that you should follow *(SEE FIGURE 193)*. The reason is if your "hop," or your "step" are too big in length and out of porportion, you may not have enough energy and strength left to make a good jump at the end.

When making your "hop," you CAN NOT land on the opposite foot you made the "hop" takeoff with. When making your "step," you CAN NOT land on the same foot that made the "hop". Your

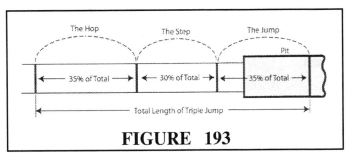

The Hop   The Step   The Jump

Pit

35% of Total   30% of Total   35% of Total

Total Length of Triple Jump

FIGURE 193

foot CAN NOT extend over the foul line when you make your "step" takeoff for the jump.

Check *TABLE 13* to see some comparison distances for you to achieve in order to be competitive. The main records are "*American outdoor*" youth track & field records, but we have also added some local "*CYC*" and national "*CYO*" records for a comparison.

COMPARISON PERFORMANCE DISTANCES -TRIPLE JUMP

BOYS		DISTANCE	
Age Division		Meters (Feet - Inches)	Record - Meters (Feet - Inches)
6 - 8 (Primary)	Satisfactory		
	Good		
	Excellent	N/A	N/A
9 -10 (Bantam) (Roadrunner)	Satisfactory	5.79m (19 Ft. - 0 In.)	
	Good	7.61m (22 Ft. - 0 In.)	Sub = 7.30m (23 Ft. - 11.41In.)
	Excellent	7.62m (25 Ft. - 0 In.)	
11 -12 (Midget) (Cub)	Satisfactory		
	Good		
	Excellent	N/A	N/A
13 - 14 (Youth) (Cadet)	Satisfactory	10.97m (36 Ft. - 0 In.)	△ 11.65m (38 Ft. - 2.5 In.)
	Good	11.89m (39 Ft. - 0 In.)	Sub = 12.12m (39 Ft. - 9 In.)
	Excellent	12.80m (42 Ft. - 0 In.)	13.73m (45 Ft. - .75 In.)
GIRLS		DISTANCE	
Age Division		Meters (Feet - Inches)	Record - Meters (Feet - Inches)
6 - 8 (Primary)	Satisfactory		
	Good		
	Excellent	N/A	N/A
9 -10 (Bantam) (Roadrunner)	Satisfactory	4.57m (15 Ft. - 0 In.)	
	Good	5.49m (18 Ft. - 0 In.)	Sub = 6.0m (19 Ft. - 8.23 In.)
	Excellent	6.40m (21 Ft. - 0 In.)	
11 -12 (Midget) (Cub)	Satisfactory		
	Good		
	Excellent	N/A	N/A
13 - 14 (Youth) (Cadet)	Satisfactory	9.45m (31 Ft. - 0 In.)	△ 10.29m (33 Ft. - 9 In.)
	Good	10.36m (34 Ft. - 0 In.)	Sub = 11.23m (36 Ft. - 11.25 In.)
	Excellent	11.28m (37 Ft. - 0 In.)	12.24m (40 Ft. - 2 In.)

N/A = Records not applicable or available in this age group.
All distances are measured in meters or feet and inches.
Unless otherwise noted all records are "American AAU/ USATF National Outdoor " youth (2002-2007).
△ = AAU/ USATF Private track club record.

TABLE 13

Pole Vaulting

Explanation

   Pole vaulting has been around since the beginning of modern day Olympics. In the early years poles were made of wood, bamboo, and aluminum. And the vaulters landed on grass, sand, or wood chips. As a kid I vaulted over a bambo bar with a bambo pole. With modern technology, poles are now made of a fiberglass and graphite composite material. They have special poles for young kids now. Their length and diameter are based on the vaulters body weight. Because of the greater heights, now there are thick landing pads to land on. High jump landing pads are *NOT* to be used for pole vaulting. There are special designed landing pads now just for pole vaulting that surround the pole vault box. The minimum size of a pole vault pit is 5m (16 Ft. -5 In.) square. That does not include the protective pads that go around the vaulting box. You can also get a crossbar now that is rubber tubing with a diameter of 5/16 inches. They are semi ridgid. For younger, inexperienced, vaulters you can use the high jump standards which are down in the heigth range of you smaller vaulters to use. Just don't use the high jump landing pads. If the run-up is grass, then vaulters should be using special vaulting spike shoes to keep from slipping. Some vaulters attach things on the crossbar, like brightly colored cloth strips so that they can see the bar much better. When they find the spot on the pole where their handholds are, they tape those spots so they can grip the pole at the correct place every time. The tape also helps them maintain their grip.

For General Practicing

   For all your training and practicing it's best to go down to your local high school or college track to work on your technique. The reason is they will have the runway, bar holders, bar and specialized landing pads you will need. You could set it up in your back yard if it is big enough and you had the right landing area (probably not likely). But it would be very expensive. But sooner or later you would need to go to your local high school anyway, just to get the feel of the real runway, bar, and landing pads. We will ues a *right* side pole holder for our instructions unless otherwise stated. For left side pole holder everything will be flip flopped, or just the opposite.

Drill No. 98- The Pole Vaulting Technique

The Basics are

   This is a drill for you to learn how to make a pole vault. USATF starts youth pole vaulting with 13 and 14 year old boys and girls in the youth divivsion.. The poles you use are based on your weight. At this writing, I have not seen any poles listed for under 70 pounds and ten feet long. So if you are just under the age of 13, you could theoretically practice with them as a beginner. However, the 70 pound kids I have seen are basically six, seven, or eight years old. And I am not sure they are strong enough, coordinated enough, or have the gymnastic abilities needed to pole vault. You younger kids will just have to try it out and see. Pole vaulting is broken down into six phases, sequentially. First the "*the lowering and planting the pole*," the "*the takeoff*," the "*drive swing*," the "*extension*," the "*clearance*" and last the "*landing*." We will start with how to hold the pole and go from there to the lead-ins and lead-ups to help you with your *core training* and *muscle memory*.

Lowering and Planting the Pole

How to Hold the Pole

Before you can make a run-up and plant, you need to learn how to "grip and carry" the

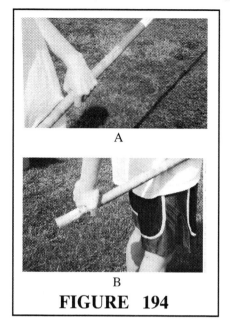

A

B

FIGURE 194

pole. First get a pole to use that is rated at or slightly above your body weight. I would NOT buy a pole until you have tried vaulting for at least one entire season, and preferably two or three seasons. And you are really serious about pole vaulting. The good poles are quite expensive, just to try them out. Instead see your nearest high school vault coach and see if you can train with them, and maybe use or borrow one of their poles.

Most vaulters are right handed, so we will use that for our illustrations. For a left handed carry and grip, everything would be flip flopped or just the opposite. The pole is carried on the right side of your body. The upper part of the pole is gripped with your left hand, in an over the top position *(SEE FIGURE 194-A)*. The lower part of the pole is gripped with your right hand. The thumb going over the top of the pole, making a "V" with your fingers, and your palm is facing forward *(SEE FIGURE 194-B)*.

As you hold the pole facing forward, your left hand is positioned slightly above waist high and about one foot in front of your hip *(SEE FIGURE 195)*. Your right hand is positioned at about hip heigth and about 1-1/4 feet behind your hip.

Your right hand pushes down and holds the front of the pole off of the ground, which also counterbalances the weight of the pole *(SEE FIGURE 195)*. The angle the pole is held, with respect to the ground, is usually whatever the vaulter is comfortable with. Remember the higher the front of the pole is up in the air, the more wind drag you will get. And this will slow down your run-

FIGURE 195

up slightly. Since speed is an important part of the vaulting process, usually you don't want to do anything that will slow you down.

The more speed you can get, the higher up on the pole you will be able to hold. Feet are about shoulder width apart. The body and the pole are facing forward. There is several more things that have to be determined before you get into your run-up, the "bend direction" of the pole, and the "vertical reach" point.

The Bend Direction of the Pole

If the "inside" and "outside" of the pole must be identified because for a right side pole holder, the outside of the pole must face down, and be and turned just slightly to the right. For a left

174

side pole holder the outside of the pole must face down and be turned just slightly to the left. Basically in either case the "soft" side (inside) has to be facing the vaulters stomach as they go up in the air. If the inside and outside of the pole are not identified on the pole there are several ways to identify those edges. The easiest way is to take a chair and the pole, and go out to a flat driveway or flat back yard.

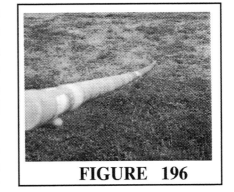

FIGURE 196

Put one end of the pole on the ground or driveway, and the other end on the top of the chair back, or even your finger. Roll it across the top edge of the chair back or finger, and see which way it bends the most *(SEE FIGURE 196)*. When it is sitting on the chair or finger correctly with the most bend, the "strong" side (outside) will face down, and the "soft" side (inside) of the curve will face up.

The Vertical Reach position

Young and beginning vaulters also need to find their vertical reach position on the pole. This is so that you are holding the pole at the right heigth for your takeoff. Stand with pole right in front of you. Then you slide your right hand all the way up the pole as high as you can reach. The left hand should be right at about your throat area *(SEE FIGURE 197)*. Next move your top hold point up about 2 -4 inches above this position. The new position will let you young vaulters starting out hang on the pole, and only be lifted a minimum heigth off the ground. This where you want to hold the pole when starting to vault the first time. It might also help if you mark these two places on the pole with tape so that you hold it in the same place each time. Now you are ready for the run-up.

FIGURE 197

The Run-Up

You need to learn to make a fast, but relaxed, run-up. Near the end of your run-up, and before the plant, you need to really hit your top speed. And remember again, the higher up the front end of the pole is held, the greater the air resistance is on the pole. Also with the front end way up high, it is farther away from the plant box, which then requires more accuracy to make a good plant. Run-ups should start out with a three stride run-up for beginners, then progressively work up to five strides, then seven strides, then nine strides, and later on all the way up to 11 to 13 strides.

For illustration purposes we will show the nine stride run-up, and show the feet positions *(SEE FIGURE 198)*. The check marks are used to see exactly where you are in your run-up. The more speed there is on the run-up, the higher the vault. To measure the starting line for the run-up, take the

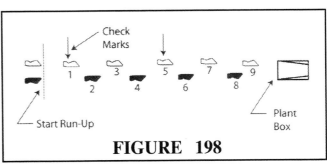

FIGURE 198

pole and stand it straight up against the bottom end of the plant box. Next you reach up as high as you can on the pole with your right hand *(SEE FIGURE 197)*. Now with your hand holding the pole at that point, slowly walk backward until the pole is about at a 45 degree angle. At this point you will need mom or dad to assist you with this part of the procedure. They hold the pole to make sure the end stays against the end of the plant box.

FIGURE   199

Then you take another step backward as you slide your right hand up another two to four inches towards the top of the pole, then lift your right leg *(SEE FIGURE 199)*. As you are standing directly under the pole, have mom or dad come over and mark the spot of where your left leg is located. This is your take off point. Next get a tape measure, and *mark down* this distance from the plant box for future reference. Now turn and face away from the plant box, and put your left foot on this mark. Next have mom or dad take the tape measure and fix it to this spot. Then have them stretch it out way down near the end of the run way.

Now sprint as fast as you can down the runway holding the pole, towards where mom or dad has the tape stretched out. Start out with your right foot taking the first step. As you take the first step shout out, "One," then "Two, Three," and so on with each step until you get to the stride number you will be using. You younger kids start out with a three stride run-up. Older beginners can start out with 5 strides. When they hear "three," or whatever the number is, have mom or dad mark that spot and it's measurement. Write this distance and the takeoff distance down in a small notebook. You will need to know these distances when you are competing in a meet. You are allowed to put markers down in a meet. When you are better at vaulting, then you can progressively move the count up to five, seven, nine strides and on up.

The Plant

The "plant" of the pole needs to have the front end of the pole going into and against the end of the plant box *(SEE FIGURE 200)*. The pole plant usually

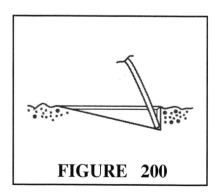

FIGURE   200

begins on the third to last stride, with the pole dropping down into the plant box. It depends on what you are most comfortable with, and how old you are. You then push the pole forward with your right arm extended, and then upward. Your left arm pushes forward, and against the pole. When you combine the downward pull from your right arm as you start to go up, with the forward push of the left arm, the pole bends and flexes. This is where you are going to need some strength. So work on those arm strengthening exercises.

The Takeoff

For your takeoff you push forward, then get directly behind the pole. As you start to go up your weight is hanging from your right arm, which is extended above your head. This is where you need to be strong in the hands and arms, just to hang onto the pole without letting go and falling. This is why you need to practice where there are special pads surrounding the plant box, in case you fall backwards. Your leading right leg has to kick out and drive hard upwards. And the trailing left leg hangs down in an extended position *(SEE FIGURE 201)*.

FIGURE 201

The Drive Swing

Your "drive swing" phase starts shortly after you leave the ground on your takeoff. You move forward and upward in a stretched position. As your stretched takeoff leg catches up with your lead leg, then both legs start a fast upward swing. You rock back, and pull yourself into an upside down position *(SEE FIGURE 202)*. Imagine you are hanging motionless on a set of gymnastic rings, then you are asked to pull your hips up as high as possible over your head. This is basically what you will be doing. The only difference is you are hanging on a moving pole. You continue to move the pole to a vertical position during the swing. A "**TIP.**" *DO NOT* throw your head back while trying to raise your hips way up.

FIGURE 202

The Extension

Your extension is next as the pole straightens you begin to push yourself up and straighten out your whole body which includes your torso, hips, knees and feet. You shoud be moving parallel to the pole and as close to it as possible as it unbends. As you continue to extend upwards along the pole, you start a body turn around the pole. This turn starts when your right shoulder reaches the height of your right hand. Learn to use your legs and arms to assist you in this turn. Keep your legs together and your body trunk ridgid to avoid a loss of vertical velocity *(SEE FIGURE 203)*. A "**TIP.**" Try to turn your left hip into your top hand as your body turns and extends. At this point your stomach should be facing the crossbar.

The Clearance

Once your body gets turned and you continue to extend, then you release the pole with your right hand when it reaches full extension. Next your arms are quickly moved

FIGURE 203

away from the crossbar, and you rotate your thumbs down and inward. This causes your elbows to rotate away from the crossbar. All the way through the clearance phase you need to keep your chin tucked in close to your chest until it crosses over the crossbar. If you lift your head up too soon, your chest will be thrown into the crossbar possibly knocking it off. As you do get clear of the crossbar, swing both arms up and arch your back *(SEE FIGURE 204)*. This move keeps your body and arms away from the crossbar, and prepares you to land on your back on the landing pad. Remember to relax as you are falling. *DO NOT* tense up.

FIGURE 204

Your Landing

Your landing is also very important. NEVER land on your feet. This is a good way to sprain an ankle. If that happens you will not be able to make a good run-up. Stay in good shape, both mentally and physically because you need to understand and learn to control your body while in mid air. The whole vault only lasts a second or two, so you need to know from *core training* exactly and automatically what to do. One or two seconds is not enough time to do much analyzing on your situation at any point of the vault. Just relax and land on your back.

Practice

Make sure you go through all the lead-up and lead-in practice techniques before you ever go out and attempt a full technique pole vault. Then you can make two or three practice vaults at a session, then rest. If you borrow a pole, make sure it is rated at or near you weight or don't use it. For the whole pole vault sequence *SEE FIGURE 205)*.

Now we will start the lead-ups and lead-ins.

Drill No. 99- Beginners Vaulting Technique Practice
The Basics are

These are a series of drills that are designed to help you young kids and beginners get initiated to pole

FIGURE 205

vaulting. Follow these drills sequencially to get the feel of what pole vaulting is all about. It starts with the step and drive part of the technique.

The Step and Drive

Go to the end of your high school or college long jump pit runway next to where the sand pit starts, or go along one edge of the sand pit. Take the pole and get your grip set up *(SEE FIGURE 197)*. Stand back 1-1/2 steps from the end of the sand. Put the tip of your pole down on the ground. Then leaving the tip where it is, take two steps back, and put both feet together. Next take one very short quick step forward with your left foot. Next raise your right foot up, and forward with your knee parallel to the ground, just like you are

FIGURE 206

about to make a vault. Don't jump yet though. Just raise the knee and stop *(SEE FIGURE 206)*. This is for simulating the takeoff. Do this five or six times until you are comfortable with it.

One Step Vault Without a Turn

This part of the drill is to simulate the takeoff jump. This is the next step in the sequence from the "step and drive." To practice this, go to same place you started the previous drill. Now do the "step and drive," but this time you jump into the long jump sand pit, and land with both feet side by side, and with the pole next to your body *(SEE FIGURE 207)*. Make your jump a very "springy" type of takeoff. Do this five or six times until you are comfortable with it.

FIGURE 207

One Step With a Turn

This part of the drill is to simulate the rotating turn before going over the bar. Go back to the same starting point and perform the "one step without a turn," except this time you make a 1/2 turn to your left while in the air so that you land facing back towards

FIGURE 208

the starting point *(SEE FIGURE 208)*. Make sure you turn just before your landing, but *not too early*. This is so that you get the proper timing with your turn. Do this five or six times until you are comfortable with it.

The Vault for Distance

By now you should be jumping far out into the sand using good technique. Start by placing a length of rubber tubing, or a crossbar, out on the sand at about the farthest point reached by you

FIGURE 209

so far in your jumping. Now go back to the starting point and vault for distance, going over the bar lying on the ground *(SEE FIGURE 209)*. Make sure you remember to do the 1/2 turn every time so that you are facing back towards the starting

point. Do this five or six times until they are comfortable with it.

Now to make it more interesting and competetive, put some "cones" under the bar and raise it to about 12 inches high. Next place it 12 inches closer to where you start your the vaults. This time you need to go over it without touching it *(SEE FIGURE 210)*. Do this five or six times or until they are making it over the bar without touching it.

FIGURE 210

Now raise it again 12 inches higher, and 12 inches closer. At this point you will probably need to find some adjustable high jump standards to put the bar on because the cones won't work. Do this five or six times or until you are making it over without

touching the bar .

Keep moving the bar in closer to you until it gets to a point three feet away from you as you stand at the starting point. Then keep moving it higher and higher as long as you can keep clearing it without touching it. Do this until you miss or touch the bar. Now say to yourself, "Guess what- I'm vaulting." Pretty easy wasn't it. However, eventually though you are will need to go over to the high school or college vaulting area, with a landing pad, and practice using a full 9 stride run-up. Also when you start getting up to heights of six feet or more you will need to work on the gymnastic body control drills. For the full pole vault technique *SEE FIGURE 205*.

Now we will get into the specific *core training* lead-ins and lead-ups that will help you improve on your basic skills and *muscle memory*, which are needed to successfully perform in the pole vault. These are preparatory in nature.

Drill No. 100- The Rope Swing

The Basics are

This is a drill for working on the "drive swing" (ride) pull up. To work on this you will need to go down to your local high school, YMCA, or playground where they will have a climbing rope. Grab the rope with both hands, take a step forward, and pull your legs up to almost a vertical position *(SEE FIGURE 211)*.

Practice

To practice this drill you grab the rope with the right hand up as high as you can reach.

FIGURE 211

Make sure before you start that there are gymnastic landing pads underneath, in case you fall. This drill will develop your abdominal muscles and upper body strength. Take a step, swing forward, then lift your knees upward and over your head. Attempt to touch the rope with both your knees and your feet. Then come back down. Do at least five of these at each practice session. Just climbing up the rope using only your arms and hands, will build up your arm strength for the pull-up. But remember, you only need to climb up eight to ten feet. Do at least three or four of each of these techniques at a practice session.

Drill No. 101- Back Extension to a Handstand

The Basics are

This is a drill for building the coordination and strength to do your push away from the pole and then the extension to get you over the crossbar. From a squatting position, you put both of your hands behind your head, rock backwards, roll over, and push up into a handstand *(SEE FIGURE 212)*. At the full handstand position, you push up and back, bring your knees back down towards your chest, and try to end up in a standing position if possible.

FIGURE 212

Practice

To practice this drill you will need to find a gym or a high school where they have gymnastic landing pads. This is for your safety. For you younger kids your mom or dad should come out and work as a "spotter" for you. What you do is get mom or dad to stand right beside you, and with their hand around behind your knees they help you flip over and keep your body straight while going through the movements. After you get stronger and better at this, then mom or dad won't need to help you. Do at least four or five of these handstands at a practice session.

Drill No. 102- Underswing and 1/2 Turn Dismount

The Basics are

This is a drill for improving your skill at making the 1/2 turn just before you go over the crossbar. From the upright position on a horizontal bar you swing way out around under the bar, then thrust your legs upward. As your head is starting to pass under the bar, you start your 1/2 rotation by scissoring your legs up and down. Next as your head has passed under the bar, and your arms come up into the extended position, you let go of the bar and make a 1/2 rotation release and

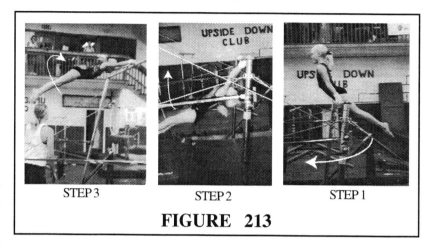

STEP 3   STEP 2   STEP 1

FIGURE   213

catch to your right so that you are facing the floor. At that point you are almost horizontal, so the next thing you need to do is fold at the waist, and bring your legs under you for a landing on your feet *(SEE FIGURE 213)*.

Practice

To practice this drill you need to find a gym or a high school where they have a horizontal bar with gymnastic landing pads underneath. This is for your safety. You will need to get mom or dad or someone at the gym to act as a "spotter" for you younger kids. This is where the spotter stands just out of your way, then when you come around from the underswing the spotter puts both of their hands by your waist and legs and assists you in rotating and landing.

Mom or dad or someone will need to help you younger kids up to the upright position on the top of the bar *(SEE STEP 1)*. Then when you are ready you push back away from the bar, drop down, and swing under the bar. Make sure you swing hard enough so that your legs can come around and lift up toward the sky *(SEE STEP 2)*. As your head gets almost under the bar you need to scissor your legs, your right foot down and your left foot up. Then just as you start to come around to the horizontal position and your arms are extended from the bar, you let go of the bar and make a 1/2 rotation release and catch to your right. This is where mom or dad may have to spot you, help you make the release, rotation, and catch on the bar. When you have made the rotation and catch correctly, then you should be facing down *(SEE STEP 3)*. Next you can swing back down and dismount from the bar where mom or dad can catch you. This will be hard for you younger kids to learn, so you need to be patient while you attempt to learn how to do this move. Do at least five or six of these 1/2 rotations at a practice session.

As an alternative for you younger kids, have mom or dad get you a weight lifting bar and a home made landing pad to work out with in the back yard. Then both mom and dad can hold the bar up at shoulder heigth, then let you do your swings and release with this set up.

Check **TABLE 14** to see some comparison vaulting heights for you to achieve in order to be competitive. The main records are "***American outdoor***" youth track & field records, but we have also added some local "***CYC***" and national "***CYO***" records for a comparison.

COMPARISON PERFORMANCE DISTANCES -POLE VAULT

BOYS		DISTANCE	
Age Division		Meters (Feet - Inches)	Record - Meters (Feet - Inches)
6 - 8 (Primary)	Satisfactory		
	Good		
	Excellent	N/A	N/A
9 -10 (Bantam) (Roadrunner)	Satisfactory		
	Good		
	Excellent	N/A	N/A
11 -12 (Midget) (Cub)	Satisfactory	1.83m (6 Ft.- 0 In.)	△ 2.70m (8 Ft.- 10.3 In.)
	Good	2.44m (8 Ft.- 0 In.)	
	Excellent	3.05m (10 Ft.- 0 In.)	
13 - 14 (Youth) (Cadet)	Satisfactory	2.29m (7 Ft.- 6 In.)	△ 3.99m (13 Ft.- 1 In.)
	Good	3.20m (10 Ft.- 6 In.)	Sub = 3.38m (11 Ft.- 1 In.)
	Excellent	4.11m (13 Ft.- 6 In.)	4.28m (14 Ft.- 0.5 In.)
GIRLS		DISTANCE	
Age Division		Meters (Feet - Inches)	Record - Meters (Feet - Inches)
6 - 8 (Primary)	Satisfactory		
	Good		
	Excellent	N/A	N/A
9 -10 (Bantam) (Roadrunner)	Satisfactory		
	Good		
	Excellent	N/A	N/A
11 -12 (Midget) (Cub)	Satisfactory	1.52m (5 Ft.- 0 In.)	△ 1.70m (5 Ft.- 6.9 In.)
	Good	2.13m (7 Ft.- 0 In.)	
	Excellent	2.74m (9 Ft.- 0 In.)	
13 - 14 (Youth) (Cadet)	Satisfactory	1.98m (6 Ft.- 6 In.)	△ 3.20m (10 Ft.- 6 In.)
	Good	2.59m (8 Ft.- 6 In.)	Sub = 2.90m (9 Ft.- 6 In.)
	Excellent	3.20m (10 Ft.- 6 In.)	3.45m (11 Ft.- 4 In.)

N/A = Records not applicable or available in this age group.
All distances are measured in meters or feet and inches.
Unless otherwise noted all records are "American AAU/ USATF National Outdoor " youth (2002-2007).
△ = AAU/ USATF Private track club record.

TABLE 14

Steeplechase

Explanation

The steeplechase is derived from a combination of cross country running, distance running, and hurdling. It is a modern day Olympic event. Basically you run lap after lap around the track, then on every lap you cut over and jump over the water barrier once. The hurdles and the water jump barrier are heavy sturdy barriers made to support the weight of several runners at the same time. The rules let runners jump up on and off the water barrier if they chose to, which is what most runners do. Some elite world class steeplechase runners have so much power in their legs that they hurdle the barrier, and almost clear the water behind it.

This is the exception though, and not the rule. But is is legal. I *DO NOT* advise any of you younger kids to try this until you become a teen ager. This event is usually not available until young kids get to be 15 to 16 years old in USATFs intermediate division. Since this book is basically written for 6 (primary division) through 14 year olds (youth division), we will only briefly cover the "steeplechase" so that you will at least have some idea if you might like to try it later on? The USATF youth athletics division steeplechase starts at 2000m for 15 and 16 year olds. That's roughly five times around a 1/4 mile oval track.

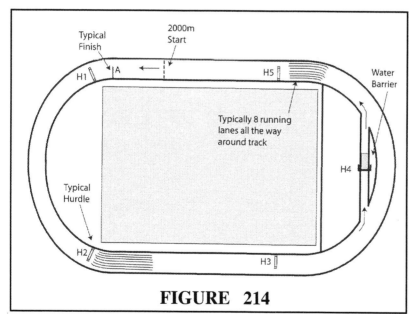

FIGURE 214

It has 18 hurdles to go over and five water jumps that you need to go over in the 2000 meter race distance. From the water jump hurdle to an on track hurdle is approximately 1/5 of a steeplechase lap. Then from an on track hurdle to the next hurdle will be 1/5 of a steeplechase lap.

Runners in a 2000m steeplechase race do not have to jump hurdle H1 and H2 during the first half lap. From there on they jump five hurdles per lap for the remaining four laps. For a track layout of a typical steeplechase race event *SEE FIGURE 214*. High schools do not even offer a "steeplechase" event, only colleges.

Drill No. 103- The Hurdle and Water Jump Technique

The Basics are

This is a drill for improving your skill at making it over the on track hurdles and water jump. First of all before you even try this technique, you need to have some experience in "cross country," "distance racing," and "hurdling." Go to those sections of this book, read through them, and practice them, using the techniques used in each of those events. To clear the water jump barrier

FIGURE 215

most runners make a single leg takeoff which lands on the top edge of the barrier. Then they make a strong push off, to land in the shallow end of the water jump *(SEE FIGURE 215)*.

Practice

To practice this technique you will probably need to find a college track where a steeplechase course is available. Also you should have shoes that are made for this event. Because if there is not enough spikes up near the toes you could slip on the top of the barrier. They do make shoes especially for this event that do not deteriate from getting wet. Start out at about 100 feet in front of a hurdle barrier, then jog toward it. When your approach is about 32 to 50 feet away from the water jump, you need to accelerate in order to get up enough momentum to jump up on the barrier. The takeoff is usually about five to six feet in front of the barrier. First you lean forward and push off with your strong (power) leg. Next you flex your other free leg so that the instep part of your foot can be placed on the top edge of the barrier. When your free leg is firmly on the barrier, you bend it to about a 90 degree angle in a crouch position *(SEE FIGURE 215)*.

When you have your balance, your body leans forward so that it can pass very low over the barrier. As your body starts to pass over the barrier, you roll your support leg foot over the forward edge of the barrier so that your spikes dig in and help you to push off forward without slipping. Your strong leg clears the barrier, then is driven out forward. Aim it to land way out near the shallow end of the water. Also you need to extend your arms upon landing in order to keep your balance and move on. Run past the barrier about 40 to 50 feet, then stop and come back to the starting point. Do at least five or six of these water jumps at a practice session.

Drill No. 104- Aerobic and Anaerobic Training

The Basics are

Steeplechase runners need both aerobic and anaerobic endurance. See the section on *"Distance Running, page 71"* for drills and practice on "distance running" and "cross country." This builds up your endurance. Without endurance you will not make it as a steeplechase runner. So if you are not sucessfull at some of the other events, but normally have a lot of energy, like to run, and can jump, then you could become good at this event. And there is not that much competetion to have to go against. Think about it.

Drill No. 105- Hurdling Training

The Basics are

Steeplechase runners also need to learn how to clear an on track steeplechase hurdle. They are sturdy hurdles, not like regular hurdles. They are sturdy so that more than one runner can step up on them at the same time. They are 30 inches high. If you hit them trying to hurdle them you could get seriously hurt because they don't give any or fall over. So you younger kids and beginners step up on the hurdles and on over until you develop the necessary technique and strength to hurdle and clear them when you get older. This training will also help you develop the technique of getting over the water jump barrier which is similar. See the section on "*hurdling*" for *core training* drills and practice, to help you learn the "hurdling" techniques.

Drill No. 106- Water Jump Landing

The Basics are

Steeplechase runners have to learn how to land in the water after clearing the water barrier. To simulate this, put a steeplechase barrier along the edge of the long jump sand pit. Then get a running start to jump up on the steeplechase hurdle, then push off and jump into the sand. The drag of the sand on your feet simulates and has the same effect as when you land in the water. And you don't have to get wet practicing.

Practice

To practice this technique go over to the local college, that has a long jump pit and a steeeplechase course. You need to have a steeplechse course, or you won't be able to find a steeplechase type hurdle sturdy enough to hold your weight for practicing. *DO NOT* use the thin edge roll over hurdles that you see there. They won't hold your weight and they will fall over, which will get you hurt. Set the steeplechase hurdle up at the edge of the long jump pit. Then get back far enough (at least 30 feet) away to make a run-up to the hurdle. Next you run up to the hurdle, and when you are about four or five feet away you push off with your strong (power) leg, then bring your other (free) leg up and onto the top edge of the hurdle. When your free leg is balanced on the hurdle you squat, then bring your trailing leg (strong leg) on over, push off with your free leg, and jump way out in the sand with your strong leg landing first. Do at least five or six of these sand jumps at a practice session.

Check *TABLE 15* to see some comparison times for you to achieve in order to be competitive. The main records are "*American outdoor*" youth track & field records, but we have also added some local "*CYC*" and national "*CYO*" records for a comparison.

COMPARISON PERFORMANCE DISTANCES -STEEPLECHASE

BOYS		DISTANCE	
Age Division		2000m (Minutes - Seconds)	Record - (Minutes - Seconds)
9 -10 (Bantam) (Roadrunner)	Satisfactory		
	Good		
	Excellent	N/A	N/A
11 -12 (Midget) (Cub)	Satisfactory		
	Good		
	Excellent	N/A	N/A
13 - 14 (Youth) (Cadet)	Satisfactory		
	Good		
	Excellent	N/A	N/A
15 - 16 (Intermed.)	Satisfactory	9:30.0	
	Good	7:30.0	△ 6:13.44
	Excellent	6:30.0	6:02.84
GIRLS		DISTANCE	
Age Division		2000m (Minutes - Seconds)	Record - (Minutes - Seconds)
9 -10 (Bantam) (Roadrunner)	Satisfactory		
	Good		
	Excellent	N/A	N/A
11 -12 (Midget) (Cub)	Satisfactory		
	Good		
	Excellent	N/A	N/A
13 - 14 (Youth) (Cadet)	Satisfactory		
	Good		
	Excellent	N/A	N/A
15 - 16 (Intermed.)	Satisfactory	10:30.0	
	Good	8:30.0	△ 7:06.29
	Excellent	7:30.0	6:57.46

N/A = Records not applicable or available in this age group.
All times are measured in minutes and seconds.
Unless otherwise noted all records are "American AAU/ USATF National Outdoor " youth (2002-2007).
△ = AAU/ USATF Private track club record.

TABLE 15

Hammer Throwing

Explanation

The hammer throw is a modern day Olympic event. At first it was just for male competitors, now it is for male and female athletes. It is the most complex of all the throwing events. USATF only introduces this event starting with 15 and 16 year olds (intermediate division). Many high schools do not even offer this event for their track team. This can be a dangerous event. We will only briefly go over the fundamentals. What makes this event dangerous is the hammer flying a long distance in the air, could hit a bystander and very seriously injure or even kill them. Also as you whirl around with this weight, the centrifugal force is very high. Now, for that reason they reduce the weight of the hammer appropriately for 15 and 16 year olds.

However, all that being said there are ways now that young kids could begin to train for this event sometime in their future. One of these ways is to use a three to four foot long "broom handle," the other is a "ball in a net" with a handle attached. If you do attempt to work on training for this event, then make sure you observe all the safety precautions. And they are, find a very large area, keep all spectators way far away in all directions, and have mom or dad stay way back out of the way while you are throwing. Even "broom handles," and "balls" in nets, can slip out of your hands, and fly off in any direction to accidentally hit someone. We will only briefly go over the basic hammer throw techniques because this book is basically for five through fourteen year olds,.

For General Practicing

For all your training and practicing it's best to go down to your local college track to work on your technique. The reason is they will have the ring, throwing sector lines and a protective cage. Don't even think about practicing in your back yard or the park using a real hammer. It's way too dangerous. With the sector lines and a circular ring at the college you will know if your throw is a foul or not. We will ues a *right handed* thrower for our instructions unless otherwise stated. For left handed hammer throwers everything will be flip flopped, or just the opposite. For circular instructions around the ring we will use the *hour positions* on a clock.

Drill No. 107- The Hammer Throw Technique
The Basics are

This is a drill for improving your skills for making a hammer throw. Make sure you are strong enough and mature enough to even try this technique. It is especially important you have a strong upper body and lots of shoulder strength. So before you start, go to the appropriate sections in this book, and work on strengthening those parts of your body. First thing you need to understand is, how do you grip the hammer handle. A right handed thrower grips the handle with their left hand, then wraps their right hand over the top of their left hand *(SEE FIGURE 216)*. Left handed throwers are just the opposite, you grip the handle with your right hand and wrap your left over the top.

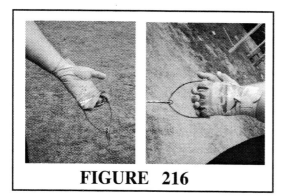

FIGURE   216

The hammer is thrown inside of a ring which is seven feet in diameter. The thrower stands at the rear of the ring, with their back towards the front (direction of throw) of the ring. The throw goes out into a throwing sector similar to the shot put *(SEE PAGE 111)*. The feet are about shoulder width apart. The hammer is placed on the ground to the right rear of a right handed thrower, with their shoulders turned to the right. They start a throw by pulling the hammer upwards and to their left. After the hammer comes around to the left as far as possible, the thrower ducks under it, and keeps rotating around to their left as it keeps coming up and then down.

As it goes around it makes a pathway going from a high point to the throwers left rear, to a low point at the throwers right front. Typically in the technique they will make three or four turns to the left until they release the hammer while facing the front *(SEE FIGURE 217)*. Some coaches say, have beginners make only one or two turns until they master the technique. Then they can progessively move to three or four turns.

FIGURE 217

As the thrower goes around, the movements are called "preliminary swings." As each swing goes around the hammer is progressively accelerated. Also as you start your rotations the left foot is pivoted 180 degrees on the heel, and the right foot is pivoted 180 degrees on the toes. Next you rotate on around another 180 degrees on the ball of your left foot. Following that you pick up your right foot, bring it fully around , and place it on the ground parallel to your left foot.

Step 6   Step 5   Step 4   Step 3   Step 2   Step 1

FIGURE 218

This gets you through the footwork for one turn *(SEE FIGURE 218)*. Then you keep making a sequence of these turns until you face the front on the last turn *(SEE FIGURE 219)*. As the hammer picks up speed there is increasingly more centrifugal pull. To counter act this pull, the thrower has to squat, sit back a little and flex their legs. At the end of the last turn when the right foot comes down the thrower makes a powerfull pulling, then lifting upwards makes their delivery or release.

Following the release, the thrower executes a "reverse" so that they don't step out of the ring and foul *(SEE DRILL NO. 60)*. Another technique to keep from fouling is just after releasing you lower your body back and away from the front of the ring, then flex both of your legs.

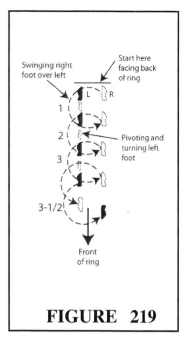

Swinging right
foot over left

Start here
facing back
of ring

L   R

1

2 — Pivoting and
turning left
foot

3

3-1/2

Front
of ring

FIGURE 219

Practice

If you are really serious about training to become a hammer thrower, get some special hammer thrower shoes for safety reasons. If you can't afford them, then get some of the thinnest sole sneakers you can find. Thick soles sneakers won't work. And last get some special hammer thrower gloves to protect your hands. Go through the sequence slowly at first by walking, then speeding it up littlte by little. It's may be hard to find a college with a ring and cage. So here are several other ways you can practice the technique. You will still need to take all the necessary safety precautions though. The first way to practice is using a three to four foot long "broom handle." The second one is using a "basketball in a net."

Hammer Swings using a Broom Handle

This is an introductory technique just to help you get the feel of the arm action. You can use an old broom handle, cut it off to about three to four feet in length. Make sure it is smooth without any splinters. You are allowed to use gloves in the hammer throw. I suggest you get some. They have special gloves you can buy just for this event, which will protect your hands. Grip the end of the broom handle with your left hand, and the right hand right on top of it. Your arms are extended.

Start with the handle near the ground to your right rear. Then you look forward and flex their legs slightly. Next you start to swing the broom handle upwards toward your left side. At the same time you twist your hips to the right before the swing. Now keeping your feet basically in the same place, you swing the handle on around so that it's low point is to the right front of your body. When the handle gets as far as possible to the upper left each time, you duck underneath as it passes over your head, and then on down to your right side again. While still keeping your feet in the same place, continuously rotate the handle around several times *(SEE FIGURE 220)*.

FIGURE 220

Going slow at first by walking through in slow motion, then speeding it up as you get better at making the moves. Remember to shift your hips to the right when the handle swings to your left, then shift your hips to the left when the handle swings on around to your right. Another way to practice the swing is use a baseball bat. Do about five reps of this at a session, with a short rest in between.

Hammer Swings using a Basketball in a Net

This is an another introductory technique to help you get the feel of the arm action. To do this you use a long piece of net with a handle, then you place a basketball or a beach ball in the net.

190

The biggest problem with this technique is going to be finding a net with a handle. You will probably need to make your own. You swing the "ball in the net" the same way as with the broom handle *(SEE FIGURE 220)*, except you are using the "ball in the net."

Next we will go into a lead-up that will help build up your *core training* strength for performing the hammer throw technique.

Drill No.108- Throws with a Medicine Ball

The Basics are

This is a drill for improving your throwing strength. By throwing the medicine ball from several different stances you can develop the muscles needed to throw the hammer. The first is the two handed throw up in the air *(SEE FIGURE 221-A)*. This throw simulates the upward thrust as the hammer is released. The second is a two handed overhead throw *(SEE FIGURE 221-B)*. This throw simulates the backward lean required when you release the hammer. The third is a two handed sling of the medicine ball around and over your shoulder *(SEE FIGURE 221-C)*. This throw simulates the upward rotary lift of the hammer during your release. The fourth is a two handed overhead throw against a wall, then turn, and catch *(SEE FIGURE 221-D)*. This throw simulates the extension of your body while rotating.

A   B   C   D

FIGURE 221

Practice:

Go through each of the four types of throws about five or six times each at a practice session.

Check *TABLE 16* to see some comparison throwing distances for you to achieve in order to be competitive. The main records are "*American outdoor*" youth track & field records, but we have also added the local "*CYC*" and national "*CYO*" records for a comparison.

COMPARISON PERFORMANCE DISTANCES - HAMMER THROW

BOYS		DISTANCE		
Age Division		Weight	Meters (Ft. - In.)	Record - (Ft. - In.)
9 -10 (Bantam) (Roadrunner)	Satisfactory			
	Good			
	Excellent		N/A	N/A
11 -12 (Midget) (Cub)	Satisfactory			
	Good			
	Excellent		N/A	N/A
13 - 14 (Youth) (Cadet)	Satisfactory			
	Good			
	Excellent		N/A	N/A
15 - 16 (Intermed.)	Satisfactory		54.86m (180 Ft.- 0 In.)	
	Good		64.0m (210 Ft.- 0 In.)	△ 65.66m (215 Ft.- 5 In.)
	Excellent	12 Lb.	70.10m (230 Ft.- 0 In.)	72.53m (237 Ft.- 11 In.)
GIRLS		DISTANCE		
Age Division		Weight	Meters (Ft. - In.)	Record - (Ft. - In.)
9 -10 (Bantam) (Roadrunner)	Satisfactory			
	Good			
	Excellent		N/A	N/A
11 -12 (Midget) (Cub)	Satisfactory			
	Good			
	Excellent		N/A	N/A
13 - 14 (Youth) (Cadet)	Satisfactory			
	Good			
	Excellent		N/A	N/A
15 - 16 (Intermed.)	Satisfactory		39.93m (131 Ft.- 0 In.)	
	Good		42.06m (138 Ft.- 0 In.)	△ 44.67m (146 Ft.- 7.82 In.)
	Excellent	4 Kg.	44.20m (145 Ft.- 0 In.)	46.84m (153 Ft.- 8 In.)

N/A = Records not applicable or available in this age group.
All distances are measured in meters or feet and inches.
Unless otherwise noted all records are "American AAU/ USATF National Outdoor " youth (2002-2007).
△ = AAU/ USATF Private track club record.

TABLE 16

Combined Events

Explanation

Combined events are when one competitor is competing in more than one event, and they score points based on their times, heights, or distances. Then these points are are combined, or added up into one score. The highest total score wins the event. These type of events go all the way back to ancient greece and their games. Modern day Olympics had only men participating in combined events, then in 1964 women had their first event. Now days there are a number of combined events, even for you younger boys and girls. They are scaled down appropriately for you to be able to participate. USATF offers a "Triathlon" for 9 to 10 year olds, and a "Pentathlon" for 11, 12, 13, and 14 year olds. Private track clubs even have these events for 6, 7 and 8 year old competitors. Some of these events are completed in one day. Other combined events last for 2 days, depending on the number of athletes competing. Here are these events as they relate to you younger kids.

Triathlon (3 events in one day- 9 & 10 Yr. olds- Bantam Division)
Shot Put - 6 Lb.
High Jump
200m (for girls only)
400m (for boys only)

Pentathlon (5 events in one day- 11 & 12 Yr. olds- Midget Division)
Shot Put - 6 Lb.
High Jump
Long Jump
80m Hurdles
800m (for girls only)
1500m (for boys only)

Pentathlon (5 events in one day- 13 & 14 Yr. olds- Youth Division)
Shot Put - 6 Lb. (for girls only)
Shot Put - 4 Kg. (for boys only)
High Jump
Long Jump
100m Hurdles
800m (for girls only)
1500m (for boys only)

We will not put the scoring tables in this book. If you really want to see how all of these points are scored for each event, then go to *WWW.IAAF.Org/Downloads/IAAF Scoring Tables* on the InterNet.

For some suggested point totals, to gage where you are in your combined events training, then *SEE TABLE 17.*

COMPARISON PERFORMANCE DISTANCES -COMBINED EVENTS

BOYS		TRIATHLON		PENTATHLON	
Age Division		Total Points	Record (Points)	Total Points	Record (Points)
6 - 8 (Primary)	Satisfactory				
	Good				
	Excellent		N/A		N/A
9 -10 (Bantam) (Roadrunner)	Satisfactory	500	△ = 883		
	Good	700	Sub = 677		
	Excellent	900	1032		N/A
11 -12 (Midget) (Cub)	Satisfactory			2800	△ = 3120
	Good			3000	Sub = 2836
	Excellent		N/A	3200	3674
13 - 14 (Youth) (Cadet)	Satisfactory			2500	△ = 3485
	Good			3000	Sub = 2599
	Excellent		N/A	4000	4418
GIRLS		TRIATHLON		PENTATHLON	
Age Division		Total Points	Record (Points)	Total Points	Record (Points)
6 - 8 (Primary)	Satisfactory	200			
	Good	300	△* = 466		
	Excellent	400			N/A
9 -10 (Bantam) (Roadrunner)	Satisfactory	600	△ = 1402		
	Good	800	Sub = 1063		
	Excellent	1000	1450		N/A
11 -12 (Midget) (Cub)	Satisfactory			2800	△ = 3329
	Good			3000	Sub = 2719
	Excellent		N/A	3200	3459
13 - 14 (Youth) (Cadet)	Satisfactory			2900	△ = 3459
	Good			3100	Sub = 3235
	Excellent		N/A	3300	3521

N/A = Records not applicable or available in this age group.

Points are the total for all the combined events.

Unless otherwise noted all records are "American AAU/ USATF National Outdoor " youth (2002-2007).

△ = AAU/ USATF Private track club record.

* = Special record which included long jump, shot put and 200m dash.

TABLE 17

194

New Parent Orientation
(Track & Field 101)

The Sport of Track & Field with Cross Country

The Sport

The sport of track and field goes way back to anceint times. It is known by most people all over the world now as "Track & Field." But it is closely related to "The Olympics" as part of the summer games. Most of the modern track and field events evolved from the anceint greek Olympic games. Basically track and field is running, jumping, and throwing. Then you also have "cross country", which is basically out running in the counrty side. It's uphill, downhill, over rough ground, and away from the outdoor track stadium. It has almost become like a separate sport in itself now in the USA. It is gaining popularity now with you younger kids. Originally the olympics were just between the greek people. Now many countries are included. The international "Olympics" are directly controlled by the "IOC" (International Olympic Committee). Basically in the "Olympics" all events are contested by the top (world class) athletes from each of these different countries. When the athlete from each country wins or places in an event, they are given points for their country. At the end of the Olympics each countries points are added up for a total. The country with the most points is considered the winner. This is all unofficial though, and kept track of by newspaper sports reporters day by day. A lot of honor and prestege goes to the winning countries.

The Organizations

In the "USA" (Unitied States of America), there are many levels of track and field competition. Basically the "Youth Athletic Divisions" are controlled by the USATF (USA Track & Field) or the AAU (Amateur Athletics Union), which work with each other. For kids they have "The Junior Olympics" program. Then beyond that each city has it's own private track clubs. And they will follow the USATF or the AAU rules, or both. Then there are other organizations. One is the "CYC" (Catholic Youth Council) in St. Louis, Mo. The "CYO" (Catholic Youth Organization) is similar to the "CYC," except they are a nation wide catholic youth organization. They have their own rules which are similar, but with some variations from the other organizations. Also you have NFHS (National Federation of State High School Associations) which control track & field at the high school level. I know all of this must be very confusing to you by now, but that's just the way it is. It seems like they should all be following a single set of rules for a common goal, our children, but for some reason they don't.

The Olympics

In the Olympics when a competitor wins in a *championship* event, they are awarded a gold medal. If they finish second in an event, they get a silver medal. If they finish third in an event, they get a bronze medal. If a team of competitors wins a *championship* event, then each member of the team gets a medal. There are team *championships* also. Team points are given when a member of the team wins or places in an event. If the team member finishes first they are given 1 point. If they finish second they are given 2 points, and so on. The team with the lowest total of points wins. In some events team scoring is by time. The team with the lowest overall total time is the winner. Then at the end of the meet each teams total points and times are all added up together for a team total. The winning team get a trophy instead of a medal. This is one method.

Youth Sports

In "CYC" track & field the team with the most points is the team winner. The first 6 places overall get team points. First place gets 10 points, second place 8 points, third place 6 points, fourth place 4 points, fifth place 2 points, and sixth place 1 point. Winners usually get ribbons. CYC breaks down into age groups. The 6 year old group, the 7-8 year old group, the 9-10 year old group, the 11-12 year old group, the 13 year old group and the 14-15 year old group. Each group has their own championships and records.

The AAU is now more associated with the Junior Olympics and the lower age groups. 6 year olds are in the "Primary" Division, and 7-8 year olds are in the "Sub-Bantam" Division. The USATF picks up at the "Bantam" Division which is 9-10 year olds, the "Midget" Division which is 11-12 year olds and the "Youth" Division which is 13-14 year olds. Then they go up from there with other divisions. In USATF the team can win with the lowest point score, or by the lowest times total. Between the two organizations, they take care of USA National Championships and records.

In "CYO" track & field they break down into their own special divisions by names and grade levels. They are the "Roadrunner" Division which is 3rd-4th grade, the "Cub" Division which is the 5th-6th grade and the "Cadet" Division which is the 7th-8th grade. They have their own championships and records also.

Then you have private track clubs which usually participate in AAU or USATF sanctioned meets and championships. They keep their own club records.

This book covers basically up to 14-15 years old (8th graders). We keep comparison times, heights, distances and records at the end of each event section. However, since these "stats" change quite often we can not keep up with them every year in a new book. We put out a new edition track & field book now about every 2 -3 years. So we are adding dates to the records in our tables now. This way you can tell if the information is fairly new or way out of date.

Considerations

When considering everything that is going on out there in youth track and field as a sport (growing all the time), it's best if you are a parent to just go out, sit in the stands, cheer, and enjoy watching some good performances by young kids, maybe yours. I know I do every chance I get.

Track Meets

Track meets are just what the name implies, a meeting. This is where all the clubs or teams come together in one big gathering (meeting) to see who is the best at each event. Not all track meets are championship meets though. Some track meets are preliminary meets. They may be a month, or several weeks, in advance of a championship meet. Preliminary trial meets eliminate the weaker competitors so that the championship meet has only the best at each event competing. This way it turns into a situation where you have the best pushing the best. And this is when champions are determined, and records are sometimes set in each event. The AAU "Junior Olympic Games" championship track meet will last as long as eight days. Where a smaller organization championship track meet will only last maybe One day, and be scheduled on a weekend. In championship track meets, the contestants have to meet a qualifying time, height, or distance, to even get into the meet. Track meets are held at regional locations all over the USA. For smaller organizations or clubs the

196

track meets are usually held at a local high school track. You can go on the InterNet and probably find out where there is a track meet going on near you. Or you can type in "Track & Field Clubs (put your city name here)," then when a name comes up look on their web site for meet dates.

Getting Ready for Meets

This is very important for you kids and your parents to understand. When you get to your first team or club you will get training to help you get into a track meet. First if you want any chance to get a metal or a ribbon, and be the best you can be, you have to be in top shape and ready for the meet. To accomplish this you may need mom or dad to help you out. This is because in some cases it may be the only meet you will be in for the whole season. It's not like other sports where there will be a next game. On private track clubs they might have up to 15 meets during the summer. There are several *key* things you need to do. First make sure you know the "time", and the "place", where the meet is going to be held. Then make sure you get there ahead of time. If at all possible *DO NOT* get there late, or at the last minute. Second make sure you come with the right uniform and the appropriate clothing, liquids, and equipment, needed for the projected weather at the time of the meet. Third make sure they *DO NOT* do anything too strenuous or tiring the day before the meet. That day is a rest and recuperation day.

As a head coach, I lost a chance to get my team into a championship because on the same day of an evening playoff game, one of my kids had half of the team over to his house for a swim party. Halfway through the game they got tired and basically "ran out of gas" so to speak. We lost the game. What really hurt was not that we lost the game, but we had a very good team and we had won a previous game without too much trouble against the team we were playing. We should have won the playoff game. I know winning isn't everything, but I felt really bad for the kids because they missed a very good chance for a championship. The kids and I will never know what might have happened because of the swim party, . It was an unintensional mistake by the parent to have let this happen. This was in the summer and they could have went swimming on many other days during the summer. Why am I mentioning this. The reason is hopefully it won't happen to you because you remember this little story.

Track and field is a sport where skill, speed, strength, and thought focus, are all very important because it takes an extra individual effort by you to perform. When you get to the meet, check in right away with your coach. They will give you last minute individual instructions and strategies to follow. Hopefully you have learned the basic fundamentals I have indicated for each event in this book. Above all though have "fun," "be a good sport," "be a good teammate," "listen to your coaches" who are there to help you, and "be polite" to the officials. After all they have a really tough job to do at track meets, just to make sure everything works smoothly as it should.

Officiating

There are many things that have to be done to get the track and field ready for a meet. There are also many things to go over and check, just to make sure all the rules are followed. This is why a track meet needs many officials. There are as many officials at a USATF or AAU meet as is necessary for the meet to run smoothly. There is however a minimum number of personnel required, just to have a track meet. The following list will just give you some idea under USATF, Rule 110, of who these people are, and how many there are. In the case of "CYC" (in St. Louis, Mo) there will be less total officials because they do not have all of the regular events in their track meets. In a regular USATF youth division track meet, all the events in this book may be held. In an regular AAU junior olympics track meet all the events in this book are held except the "steeplechase and the "hammer" throw. Here are some typical numbers for officials at a meet. They are for outdoor meets and not necessarily for indoor meets.

Event Management Personnel

Meet Director
Games Committee
Competition Director
Assisant Competition Directors, as needed

Management Officials	*Minimum Outdoor*
Technical Manager	1
Jury of Appeal	3
Referee - Track	1
Referee - Field	1
Referee - Combined	1
Referee - Outside Stadium	1
National Technical Officials	3
Photo Finish Operator	1
Competition Secretary	1

Competition Officials	*Minimum Outdoor*
Clerks of Course	6
*# Finish Line Judges	12
Finish Line Coordinator	1
Field Judges	
#Pole Vault, High Jump	4
#Long Jump, Triple Jump	4
#Shot Put, Weight	6
#Discus, Javelin, Hammer	6
#Umpires	12

Competition Officials	*Minimum Outdoor*
*#Timers	12
Photo Finish Judges	2
Starter	1
Recall Starter	2
Lap Scorers	2
#Marshals	5
Wind Gauge Operator	2

Inspector of Implements	2
#Walk Judges	5
#Race Walking Officials	2
Recorder of Records	1

* = Where adequate automatic photo finish devices are available, this number should be reduced substantially.

\# = Reduced number, or not required for CYC (in St. Louis, Mo).

Support Personnel (as needed)

Announcer	Doctor
Surveyor	Performance Board Operators
Press Steward	Awards Custodian

The following officials and support personnel are recommended for the conduct of cross country and road events.

Referee	Course Umpires
Starter	Course Recorders
Clerk of Course	Chute Umpires
Cheif Finish Judge	Chute Controller
Finish Judges	Competition Secretaries
Judges Recorder	Marshals
Timers	Doctors
Timers Recorder	Press Steward
Jury of Appeal	Lap Counters

Some of the Rules

Judges will usually have a distinctive arm band or badge to identify them. Coaches should not act as an official at an event where someone they coach is competing. Way too much conflict of interest. We will not go over all of the rules for a meet, there are just too many. We will discuss a few of the more controversial rules that come up during a meet.

One of them is false starts. USATF rule 302 says, "No penalty shall be imposed for the first false start, but the starter shall disqualify the offender, or offenders, on the second false start." False starts are called on individuals, not on the "field." The "field" means all the runners lined up on the starting line for a particular race. If more than one competitor false starts, each one making a false start may be charged with a false start. The starter (official) determines if they think the other competitors false started also.

If a competitor does not cause the false start in the opinion of the starter, they may not be charged with a false start. If a false start is *NOT* due to any of the competitors (say, some other noise or something), then no competitor will be charged. What you need to learn is "focus" very hard straight ahead, and listen only for the sound of the starters gun, or other device. *DO NOT* under any circumstances look right at the starter. Also make sure you *DO NOT* do what the competitor next to you does by waching them, like jump way out or move in some manner before the gun goes off.

199

Starting blocks are usually optional in the youth divisions. Their use or a runners stance is left up to each individual competitor. My feeling is starting from "starting blocks" or the down position is a definite advantage if properly used for the shorter sprints, relays, and hurdles.

If you are participating in the field events such as the long jump, high jump, and shot put, then make sure you read the section in this book for that particular event. Then be sure you learn how to keep from fouling. This is so that you will be less likely to be disqualified. Officials are trained to watch for fouling. Don't wait for your coach to teach you, learn about it yourself and make sure you are well informed ahead of time. You younger kids will probably need to go over and over on these rules, with mom and dads help, just to make sure you understand them.

These are just some rules that keep coming up. Your coach will also help you understand these rules and some of the other rules when you get to your first team or club.

Glossary
Track & Field/ Cross Country Terminology

Aerobic Running: This is running at low intensity speeds so that oxygen intake and consumption are the same, therefore this type of running can be sustained for a long priod of time.

Anaerobic Running: This running is done at great intensity speeds so that oxygen intake is less than oxygen output, therefore this type of running can only be sustained for a short period of time.

Anchor Leg: This is the last leg for a runner on a relay team.

Baton: This is a stick that is passed from one relay runner to another.

Blind Pass: This is a nonvisual (no look back) baton exchange used in sprint relays.

Blocking: This is a term referring to a competitor using their front leg to stop their spin at the release point as they are whirling around and preparing to release the shot or a discus.

Check Mark: This is a mark on a field event runway, or the track, to aid the competitor in either beginning at the same distance from the takeoff board each time, or where to start a run-up for a relay excahange zone.

Clapper: This is a devise made from two pieces of wood hinged together on one end so that when the two pieces of wood are smacked together hard they make a sound similar to a starters gun firing.

Combined Events: These are events like the "Triathlon" and "Pentathlon" where the competitor is competing in more than one event.They get points for each event. The points are totaled, and the competitor with the most points wins the event.

Cross Country: This is a form of distance racing where the runners may run up or downhill out in the countryside as opposed to on a flat oval track.

Crossbar: This is the bar which a high jumper or pole vaulter must clear.

Curb: This is found on the inside corner or edge of the track.

Dash: This is an older term uded to describe shorter races such as the 50m, 100m, and 200m.

Discus: This is one of the field events in track and field in which a cylinder-like object (disk) is thrown. It is also the disk itself. The weight and size of the discus varies according to the age of the participants.

Down Start: This is a position for sprinters to get into for a faster start where they get down with both hands on the starting line as opposed to standing up and leaning. One foot is way back and the other staggered just a little back from the line. This gives them a better push off for a faster start.

Downsweep: This is a relay handoff technique where the carrier hands off the baton using a downward arm and hand motion.

False Start: This is moving or jumping over the starting line for a race before the gun is fired.

Fartlek: This is a Swedish term meaning "speed play". It is a type of training in which a runner varies running speeds over a long distance.

Flight: This is a term used to describe the in-air techniques used in long jumping and triple jumping.

Flop: This is a style of high jumping in which the jumpers back passes over the bar before the feet.

Foul Line Arc: This is a arc shaped line at the end of the javelin throw runway, from which the javelin thrower must not go over when they release their throw.

Glide Technique: This is a technique used by shot putters where they push off from the back of the ring and kind of shuffle glide forward up to the stopboard to release the shot.

Grip and Carry: This is a term that describes the way pole vaulters hold the pole when getting ready to make their run-up.

Hammer Throw: This is an event where the competitors whirl around several times within a ring then sling a ball attached to a wire with a handle on it. The throw is out in front of them between sector lines for distance.

Hang Technique: This is a technique used by long jumpers where they push up off the takoff board and kind of hang in the air during their flight while the legs and arms are bent backwards then thrust forward and extended to make the landing.

Hitch Kick Technique: This is a technique used by long jumpers where they push up off the takoff board and make a cycling scissor kick with their legs during the flight to get more forward thrust momentum for longer distances in their landing.

Hop Technique: This is a technique used in triple jumping where the competitor jumps or hops up on one leg, making a big hop and landing on the same leg, which is then flexed to get ready for the "step" which comes next.

Hurdle: This is a movable frame devise with a crossbar between it's supports, used in the "hurdle" events. They come in different heights, depending on the age group size of the competitor.

Hurdling: This is a term to describe a competitor that sprints out then stretches their legs out almost in a "splits" position, to jump over a hurdle bar while at a nearly full sprint.

Interval Training: This is a type of running training which contains four variables. The number of repetitions, the distance, the tempo of run, and the rest time interval.

Javelin: This is a long speer type of implement, which has sharp pointed ends, that the thrower thows out in front of them for distance. For kids they now have a shorter length "mini javelin" or "turbojav" as is sometimes referred to where both ends are rounded for safety reasons.

Kick Sprinting: This is a form of running or sprinting, usually near the finish of a race, where the runner sprints by striding out farther and pushing off with their toes (kicking) as opposed to shorter strides where they pump their legs up and down harder and lift their knees up higher.

Lactic Acid: This is a by-product of exercise that will result in the fatigue of muscles.

Lanes: These are lines clearly marked all the way around the track that runners have to stay within, to keep them from running into each other when they are sprinting around the oval track. Since the distance around each lane for one lap is longer, going from the inside to the outside of the oval, they have stagger marks so that each runner runs the same distance.

Lean: This is a technique runners use at the finish line where they throw their arms back, lean forward, and thrust their chest forward as they pass the finish line or tape. In a close race this can make the difference of winning and losing because the first runners chest crossing the line wins.

Marching, High Knee: This is a training drill or exercise to help competitors build up their push off leg drive for sprinting, hurdling and other events. The competitor walks or marches straight ahead while lifting each knee way up as high as they can.

Medicine Ball: This is a special heavy ball used in strength training for different parts of the body. They are usually about the size of a volleyball.

Overload: This is building strength by gradually increasing the weight load of the exercise, or number of repetitions.

Passing Zone: This is a 20 meter zone in which the baton in a relay race must be exchanged. The actual hand to hand exchange must take place though within a 10 meter part of the forward end of the zone. The receiver of the baton can start their run for 10 meters before the exchange part of the zone. Sort of getting a head start. These are now being marked on the track with large different colored triangles and lines.

Pit: This is a long strip of sand into which a long jumper and a triple jumper make their jumps.

Plant Box: This is a box in the ground at the end of the pole vault runway where the end of the pole slides into when the vaulter begins their vault takeoff. This box keeps the the end of the pole from slipping on the ground and causing the vaulter to fall.

Pole Vaulting: This is an event where the competitors run down a runway and use a long pole to vault themselves over a crossbar way up in the air.

Pop-Ups: This is a form of training for high jumpers before a jump where they make a run-up to the crossbar, then just push straight up off their strong foot and come back down. They don't make the jump over the bar. This programs them to make the correct push off, arm action, and body position for the actual jump.

201

PR (PR'd): This is an abbreviation or term for "Personal Record". It is also being used to describe when a comprtitor has made their own personal best effort in an event.

Race Walking: This is a race where the competitors all walk around the track as fast as they can go. The rules say though that some part of each foot must touch the ground at all times. It's almost like waddling down the track.

Relay Leg: This is the distance each runner travels in a relay race.

Reverse: This is a move used by shot putters, discus throwers, and javelin throwers where they swing the right leg around to the left up against the stopboard or a foul line to keep their momentum from causing them to foul and move outside of the ring, throwing circle, or foul line arc.

Ride-Up: This is when a pole vaulter leaves the ground and starts to extend their legs upward for the ride up in the air towards the crossbar.

Ring: This is the circular area that shot putters and hammer throwers need to stay within to make their throws. The front edge has a stopboard or toeboard.

Rock-Back: This is when the pole vaulter pulls up towards the top hand on the pole, then leans (rocks) back with their feet pointing straight up in the air, and prepares to push up over the crossbar.

Rotary Technique: This is a technique used by shot putters, discus throwers, and hammer throwers where they spin around in circles while making their run-up forward to release the implement (shot, discus, or hammer). The spins are to build up speed and momentun for the release.

Run-Ups: This usually referrs to a high jumpers, long jumpers, triple jumpers, and pole vaulters approach to the takeoff point for a jump. For high jumpers these runs may be straight or they may be curved.

Shot: This is the round metal ball used in "shot putting."

Shot Put: This is a event where the competitor pushes, or puts, a round metal ball way out in front of them for distance, from within a circle called a "ring."

Standing Long Jump: This is an event in some track meets for the real little kids where they stand with both feet on the takoff board then jump forward for as far as they can out straight ahead. No run-up is made.

Starting Blocks: These are two separate strips with adjustable blocks on them that are used for sprinters to push off from when they start a race in the down position. They temporarially attach to the track and give runners a faster start.

Steeplchase: This is a long distance race where the runners have to jump up on, or over several barriers. One has a water pool on the other side. Similar to "hurdles", except the barrier is much sturdier, higher, and is fixed in place.

Step Technique: This is a technique used in triple jumping where the jumper pushes off with the hop leg, making a big step and landing on the opposite leg, which cushions and is then immediately flexed after landing to get ready to push off for the long jump which comes next.

Stopboard: This is a curb type board in the front of the ring, in the form of an arc, on which or over a shot putter must not step. Sometimes referred to as a "toeboard."

Stopwatch: This is a special devise or watch used to time the competitors for a race. It basically has a button to push when the race starts (gun is fired), and is pushed again when they cross the finish line.

Takeoff Board: This is the board across the runway from which a long jumper pushes or takes off from.

Tempo Training: This is a type of running training which runners use to estimate the duration or distance of a run. Or another way of pacing themselves at different times during a race.

Throwing Circle: This is a circular area, similar to the shot put ring, that discus throwers have to stay within to throw the discus.

Throwing Sector: This is a specified arc shaped area in front of throwing circles, rings, and runways, in which a thrown implement (shot, discus, or javelin) must land.

Track Meet: This is when all the competitors come together at a track, to compete with each other. Meets may last a day, several days, or weeks in some cases like the "Olympics".

Trailing Leg Action: This is a hurdling technique where the hurdler brings the trailing leg up, bends it with the bottom of the foot facing outward, then tucks the knee in close to their body. This lets them bring the leg back down quickly and smoothly to the ground so that they don't lose momentum or speed as they go over the hurdle.

Trial: This is an attempt in a field event.

Triple Jump: This is an event similar to the long jump, except the competitor hops first, then skips, then makes a long jump out into the sand pit. It is sometimes referred to as the "hop"- "skip"- and "jump."

Upsweep: This is a relay handoff technique where the carrier hands off the baton using a upward arm motion.

Vertical Reach: This is a dual meaning term. First it is used to describe how high up a jumper can reach with one hand extended. They stand flat footed on the ground, extend one hand straight up, and a mark is measured at the tip of their fingers. Then they crouch down and jump upwards as high as they can with the extended hand. That point is measured, and that is their vertical reach. <u>Second</u> is a pole vaulting term where the vaulter places their back (top) hand on the pole in a position so that they are holding the pole at just the right height for their vault.

Visual Pass: This is the pass used in distance relays in which the outgoing runner visually looks back and watches the incoming runner during the baton exchange.

Equipment

Each of you track and field competitors, boys or girls, will have a simple uniform. You will have a jersey or tee shirt, running shorts, and shoes *(SEE FIGURE 222)*. The material has to be non-transparent, especially when wet. Something to point out here. Track meets will usually take place in any kind of weather. This means rain, wind, heat, and maybe even light snow. So competitors are allowed to wear warm up jackets and pants when not competing in an event. Usually though a meet will be called off if there is thunder and lightening in the general vacinity.

Girls   Boys
Jerseys

Running Shorts

Track Shoe Socks

Warm Up Suit

Girls   Boys
Bodysuits

Track Shoes

Hammer Throw
Glove

FIGURE 222

Certain events allow gloves to be worn (hammer throw). You may compete with or without shoes, or with only one shoe. I have to say there are many different kinds of shoes. They have them for almost every event, for the weather, and for all kinds of track surfaces. Have mom or dad remind you to *MAKE SURE* you are ready for any weather related conditions or circumstances. However, before you go out and spend lots of money on shoes, *make sure you are serious* about track and field as your sport. Specialty spiked shoes can get very expensive, and mom or dad do not have a money tree out in the back yard. Think about a Christmas or birthday gift.

Remember you grow out of the shoes every year sometimes even sooner because your feet are still growing. If you are going to get some good track shoes, then get shoes that are specially made for your particular speciality event. As an example, there are high jumpers shoes with spikes in the right places, just to make sure you don't slip on your takeoff. There are removable spike shoes and permanent spike shoes. And by the way you can get special socks for the shoes if you need them for any foot or shoe related problems.

There is all kinds of miscellaneous equipment, and accessories, for track and field competitors. There are "body" and "speedsuits" for wind resistance that some sprinters use to gain an edge. If you are serious about javelin throwing, then you may want to get your own "mini javelin." You can get "markers," to mark where you start, and where your different steps are located for the long jump or other run-ups. If you are going to become a serious shot putter, you may want to get your own "medicine ball," and a shot. If you do decide to have mom or dad buy you your own shot, check the chart and tables in the section for that event, to *MAKE SURE* you get the right size for your age group. The "medicine ball" is also good for training youself in the other weight events (discus, and hammer throwing).

There is specialized training equipment *(SEE FIGURE 223)* to help build up your body for the different events. As an example there is a "strength chute" device. It fastens around the

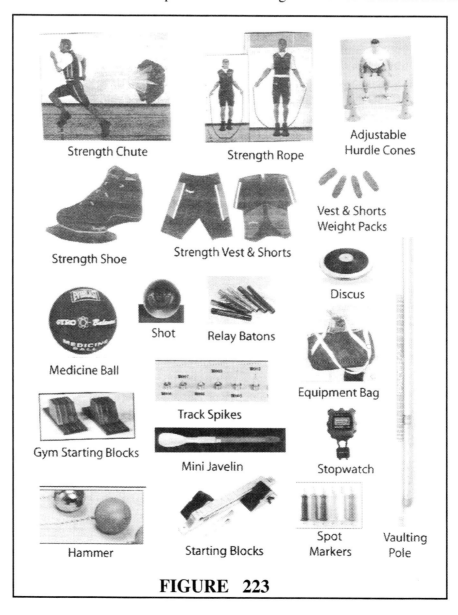

Strength Chute

Strength Rope

Adjustable Hurdle Cones

Strength Shoe

Strength Vest & Shorts

Vest & Shorts Weight Packs

Discus

Medicine Ball

Shot

Relay Batons

Equipment Bag

Gym Starting Blocks

Track Spikes

Mini Javelin

Stopwatch

Hammer

Starting Blocks

Spot Markers

Vaulting Pole

FIGURE 223

waist, and has a mini parachute attached that flows out behind. It drags in the air and makes you work harder, which builds up your legs and lower body muscles for faster running. There is a jump rope called "Heavyrope." It builds up and strengthens your upper body and increases cardiovascular (aerobic) stamina. There is a special workout shoe now called "strength shoe." This shoe basically has no heel, and that causes the calf muscles to to carry all the body's weight, and makes you work harder. What it does is stretch the calf muscle and achille tendon, which gives jumpers and runners more explosive power. There are weighted training vests and shorts, which helps you build your acceleration and aerobic endurance. They have pockets in them for changing the weight, by using weight packs. All of these special weighted trainers were developed by coach Bob Hurley Sr. (basketball). He says, "By using them, you could add 5 to 10 inches to your vertical leap, and trim 2/10 of a second off of your 40 yard dash time."

There is "protective" equipment such as special gloves for "hammer" throwers *(SEE FIGURE 222)*. There is lots of "accessory" type of equipment, like carry cases and bags for your clothes, mini javelin, shot, discus, vaulting pole, and hammer. There are adjustable hurdle cones, to train hurdlers *(SEE FIGURE 223)*. There are stopwatches to get your times. There are many kinds of screw in spikes, for removable spike shoes. For sprinters and relay runners there are several kinds of starting blocks. There is the more common outdoor adjustable type block, and there is is an indoor type block that sticks to the floor where ever you put it. It lets you practice starts indoors, and you don't have to glue it or nail it down to the floor *(SEE FIGURE 223)*.

Then there is the rest of the "standard" equipment you need for each different event not mentioned so far, such as a pole for vaulting, a discus, a hammer, and batons for the relay runner *(SEE FIGURE 223)*. You can find most of the equipment at your local sporting goods, or athletic equipment store. However, if you have a computer you can find all of the different types of equipment on the *"INTERNET."*

Try these other excellent books for teaching or learning sports fundamentals

These Jacobob Press LLC books are available at our web site jacobobpress.com, your local Borders bookstore, amazon.com or by calling the publisher direct at (314) 843-4829

 Teach'n Football (2nd Edition) - Have mom or dad help you learn all the basic fundamentals you need to play the game of football, and all in one book. They will have fun helping to teach you. You will have more fun playing the game because you will feel like you know what you are doing. This book is complete with everything you need to know. It covers all the positions, new parent orientation to the game of football (Football 101), equipment required, field size, glossary and general game rules.
ISBN 0-9772817-5-2, soft cover paperback, perfect bound, 8 x 10-1/2, 192 pages.

 Teach'n Basketball (2nd Edition) - Have mom or dad help you learn all the basic fundamentals you need to play the game of basketball, and all in one book. They will have fun teaching you. You will have more fun playing the game because you will feel like you know what you are doing. This book is complete with everything you need to know. It covers all the positions, new parent orientation to the game of basketball (Basketball 101), equipment required, court size and general game rules.
ISBN 0-9705827-6-5, soft cover paperback, perfect bound, 8 x 10-1/2, 151 pages.

 Teach'n Baseball & Softball (2nd Edition) -Have mom or dad help you learn all the basic fundamentals you need, to play the game of baseball or softball, and all in one book. They will have fun teaching you. You will have more fun playing the game because you will feel like you know what you are doing. This book is complete with everything you need to know. It covers all the positions, new parent orientation to the games of baseball and softball (Baseball/Softball 101), equipment required, glossary, history, field size and rules.
ISBN 0-9772817-1-X, soft cover paper back, perfect bound, 8 x10-1/2, 204 pages.

 Teach'n Soccer - Have mom or dad help you learn all the basic fundamentals you need, to play the game of soccer, and all in one book. They will have fun teaching you. You will have more fun playing the game because you will feel like you know what you are doing. This book is complete with everything you need to know. It covers all the positions, new parent orientation to soccer (Soccer 101), equipment required, glossary, field size and general game rules.
ISBN 0-9705827-3-0, soft cover paperback, perfect bound, 8 x 10-1/2, 138 pages.

 Teach'n Volleyball - Have mom or dad help you learn all the basic fundamentals you need, to play the game of volleyball, and all in one book. They will have fun teaching you. You will have more fun playing the game because you will feel like you know what you are doing. This book is complete with everything you need to know. It covers all the positions, new parent orientation to volleyball (Volleyball 101), equipment required, court size, glossary and general game rules.
ISBN 0-9705827-7-3, soft cover paperback, perfect bound, 8 x 10-1/2, 144 pages

 Teach'n Rink Hockey - Have mom or dad help you learn all the basic fundamentals you need, to play the games of ice hockey and roller hockey, and all in one book. They will have fun teaching you. You will have more fun playing the game because you will feel like you know what you are doing. This book is complete with everything you need to know. It covers all the positions, new parent orientation to rink hockey (Rink Hockey 101), equipment required, rink size, glossary and general game rules.
ISBN 0-9705827-8-1, soft cover paperback, perfect bound, 8 x 10-1/2, 181 pages.

 Teach'n Field Hockey - Have mom or dad help you learn all the basic fundamentals you need, to play the game of field hockey, and all in one book. They will have fun teaching you. You will have more fun playing the game because you will feel like you know what you are doing. This book is complete with everything you need to know. It covers all the positions, new parent orientation to field hockey (Field Hockey 101), equipment required, field size, glossary and general game rules.
ISBN 0-9705827-9-X, soft cover paperback, perfect bound, 8 x 10-1/2, 195 pages

 Learn'n More About Skateboarding (2nd Edition) - You Young boys and girls can learn all the basic fundamentals you need to skateboard, and all in one book. And mom or dad can help you if needed. They will have fun teaching you. And you will have more fun learning because you will feel like you know more about what you are doing. This book is complete with everything you need to know. It covers many of the tricks, new parent orientation to skateboarding (Skateboarding 101), where you can skate, glossary, and staying safe.
ISBN 0-9772817-3-6, soft cover paperback, perfect bound, 8 x 10-1/2, 140 pages.

Learn'n More About Fencing - You young boys and girls can learn all the basic fundamental skills you need to fence, and all in one book. And mom and dad can help if needed. They will have fun teaching you. And you will have more fun learning because you will feel like you know more about what you are doing. This book is complete with everything you need to know. It covers foil, epee, saber, new parent orientation to fencing (Fencing 101), equipment required, strip size, glossary, history, reference information section, and general rules. *ISBN 0-9772817-4-4, soft cover paperback, perfect bound, 8 x 10-1/2, 196 pages.*

 Learn'n More About Boxing - You young boys and girls can learn all the basic fundamental skills you need to box, and all in one book. And mom and dad can help if needed. They will have fun teaching you. And you will have more fun learning because you will feel like you know more about what you are doing. This book is complete with everything you need to know. It covers punching, defending, counterpunching, new parent orientation to boxing (Boxing 101), equipment required, ring size, glossary, history, reference section and general rules. *ISBN 0-9820960-0-3, soft cover paperback, perfect bound, 8 x 10-1/2, 200 pages.*

 Basketball Drills & Plays Handbook - You young coaches and assistant coaches will have all the drills and plays you need to get started, and all numbered for easy reference. All your players will have more fun learning and playing because they will feel like they know more about what they are doing out on the court. This book is complete with 154 basic fundamental drills and plays covering both the offensive and defensive phases of the game of basketball. *ISBN 0-9772817-6-0, soft cover paperback, perfect bound, 5-1/4 x 8-1/4, 100 pages.*

 Baseball & Softball Drills, Plays, and Situations Handbook - You young coaches and assistant coaches will have all the drills and plays you need to get started, and all numbered for easy reference. All your players will have more fun learning and playing because they will feel like they know more about what they are doing out in the field and at bat. This book is complete with 147 basic fundamental drills, plays and situations,covering all the offensive and defensive phases of the games of baseball and softball. *ISBN 0-9772817-8-7, soft cover paperback, perfect bound, 5-1/4 x 8-1/4, 108 pages.*

 Football Drills & Plays Handbook - You young coaches and assistant coaches will have all the drills and plays you need to get started, and all numbered for easy reference. All your players will have more fun learning and playing because they will feel like they know more about what they are doing out on the field. This book is complete with 156 basic fundamental drills and plays, covering all the offensive and defensive phases of the game of football *ISBN 0-9772817-9-5, soft cover paperback, perfect bound, 5-1/4 x 8-1/4, 116 pages.*

 Soccer Drills & Plays Handbook - You young coaches and assistant coaches will have all the drills and plays you need to get started, and all numbered for easy reference. All your players will have more fun learning and playing because they will feel like they know more about what they are doing out on the field. This book is complete with 134 basic fundamental drills, plays,and alignments, covering all the offensive and defensive phases of the game of soccer *ISBN 0-9772817-7-9, soft cover paperback, perfect bound, 5-1/4 x 8-1/4, 112 pages.*

Index

Z